STUDIES IN RUSSIA AND EAST EUROPE
formerly Studies in Russian and East European History

Chairman of the Editorial Board: M. A. Branch, Director, School of Slavonic and East European Studies

This series includes books on general, political, historical, economic, social and cultural themes relating to Russia and East Europe written or edited by members of the School of Slavonic and East European Studies in the University of London, or by authors working in association with the School. Titles already published are listed below. Further titles are in preparation.

Phyllis Auty and Richard Clogg (*editors*)
BRITISH POLICY TOWARDS WARTIME RESISTANCE IN YUGOSLAVIA AND GREECE

Elisabeth Barker
BRITISH POLICY IN SOUTH-EAST EUROPE IN THE SECOND WORLD WAR

Richard Clogg (*editor*)
THE MOVEMENT FOR GREEK INDEPENDENCE, 1770–1821: A COLLECTION OF DOCUMENTS

Olga Crisp
STUDIES IN THE RUSSIAN ECONOMY BEFORE 1914

D. G. Kirby (*editor*)
FINLAND AND RUSSIA, 1808–1920: DOCUMENTS

Martin McCauley
THE RUSSIAN REVOLUTION AND THE SOVIET STATE, 1917–1921: DOCUMENTS (*editor*)

KHRUSHCHEV AND THE DEVELOPMENT OF SOVIET AGRICULTURE

COMMUNIST POWER IN EUROPE 1944–1949 (*editor*)

MARXISM–LENINISM IN THE GERMAN DEMOCRATIC
REPUBLIC: THE SOCIALIST UNITY PARTY (SED)

THE GERMAN DEMOCRATIC REPUBLIC SINCE 1945

Martin McCauley and Stephen Carter (*editors*)
LEADERSHIP AND SUCCESSION IN THE SOVIET
UNION, EASTERN EUROPE AND CHIN

Martin McCauley and Peter Waldron
THE EMERGENCE OF THE MODERN RUSSIAN STATE
1856–81

Evan Mawdsley
THE RUSSIAN REVOLUTION AND THE BALTIC FLEET

J. J. Tomiak (*editor*)
WESTERN PERSPECTIVES ON SOVIET EDUCATION IN
THE 1980s

Series Standing Order

If you would like to receive future titles in this series as they
are published, you can make use of our standing order
facility. To place a standing order please contact your
bookseller or, in case of difficulty, write to us at the address
below with your name and address and the name of the
series. Please state with which title you wish to begin your
standing order. (If you live outside the UK we may not have
the rights for your area, in which case we will forward your
order to the publisher concerned.)

Standing Order Service, Macmillan Distribution Ltd,
Houndmills, Basingstoke, Hampshire, RG21 2XS, England.

The German Democratic Republic since 1945

Martin McCauley

MACMILLAN
PRESS

In association with
School of Slavonic and East European Studies
Univeristy of London

First edition 1983
Reprinted 1986

Published by
THE MACMILLAN PRESS LTD
Houndmills, Basingstoke, Hampshire RG21 2XS
and London
Companies and representatives
throughout the world

Printed in Hong Kong

ISBN 0-333-26219-0 (hardcover)
ISBN 0-333-43359-9 (paperback)

For Luise Kring

Contents

List of Tables and Maps		ix
Glossary and List of Abbreviations		x
Maps		xii
Introduction		1

1 GERMANY: THE VICTORS AND THE VANQUISHED   6

Introduction — The Potsdam Agreement — New State Organs — Economy and Society — The Fusion of the KPD and the SPD — The First Elections — The Cold War and the Division of Germany — Towards a People's Democracy — The SED becomes a Party of a New Type — Culture

2 THE IMPACT OF STALINISM, 1949–53   42

The Founding of the GDR — The SED and the Non-socialist Parties — The Construction of Socialism — The Soviet Union and the German Question — The Uprising of 17 June 1953

3 COMPLETING THE BUILDING OF SOCIALISM, 1953–61   67

The New Course — The GDR and Sovereignty — Social Change — The Impact of the Twentieth Party Congress on the GDR — Ulbricht Defeats his Critics — Education — Culture — The Decision to Build the Wall

4 STATE, SOCIETY AND DEVELOPED SOCIALISM   103
The New Economic System of Planning and Manage-
ment of the Economy — Changes in State and Society
— Second Thoughts About Reform — The Economic
System of Socialism (ESS) — The Scientific—Techni-
cal Revolution — Changes in the SED — Foreign
Policy — Developed Socialism — The First Secretary
Goes — Culture

5 REAL, EXISTING SOCIALISM   149
Honecker Becomes First Secretary — The Eighth
Party Congress — Changes in the Ideology — The
Chief Task — The Party and the State — The Ninth
Party Congress — The New Programme and Statute —
— The Tenth Party Congress — The Economy —
Social Policy — Cultural Policy — Foreign Policy —
The Third World — The Contemporary Situation

Chronology   195
Bibliography   265
Index   274

List of Tables and Maps

TABLES

1.1 Kreis and Landtag election results, 20 October
1946 31
4.1 Social composition of the SED 128
5.1 Number of items per 100 households 177

MAPS

1 Germany xii
2 The Länder of the SBZ/GDR (May 1945–July
1952) with their capital cities xiii
3 The Bezirks of the GDR with their capital cities
(formed 23 July 1952) xiv

Glossary and List of Abbreviations

Bezirk	County
Bezirkstag, -e	County parliament
Bundesrat	Upper house in West German parliament
Bundestag	Lower house in West German parliament
CC	Central Committee (of communist party)
CDU	Christian Democratic Union of Germany
CMEA	Council for Mutual Economic Aid (also Comecon)
Comecon	Council for Mutual Economic Aid (also CMEA)
CP	Communist party
CPSU	Communist Party of the Soviet Union
CSU	Christian Social Union
DBD	Democratic Peasants Party of Germany
DDR	German Democratic Republic (also GDR)
DFD	Democratic Women's Association of Germany
DM	Deutsche Mark; West German and West Berlin currency
DTSB	German Gymnastics and Sports Association
DWK	German Economic Commission
EAC	European Advisory Commission
ESS	Economic System of Socialism
FDGB	Free German Trades Union Association
FDJ	Free German Youth Movement
FRG	Federal Republic of Germany (also West Germany)
GDR	German Democratic Republic (also DDR)
Gemeinde	Parish, community
KPD	Communist Party of Germany
Kreis	District
Kreistag, -e	District parliament

Kulturbund	Cultural Association
KVP	People's Police in Barracks (see also NVA)
Land	Province
Landtag, -e	Provincial parliament
LDPD	Liberal Democratic Party of Germany
LPG	Collective farm (also kolkhoz)
MTS	Machine Tractor Station
MVD	Soviet Ministry of Internal Affairs (from March 1952; see also NKVD)
NDPD	National Democratic Party of Germany
NF	National Front
NES	New Economic System
NKFD	National Committee for a New Germany
NKVD	Soviet People's Commissariat of Internal Affairs (until 1952, then renamed MVD)
NSDAP	National Socialist German Workers Party (also Nazi Party)
NVA	National People's Army
Politburo	Political Bureau; elected by CC at each congress; most important party organisation
SAG	Sowjetische Aktiengesellschaft = Soviet Limited Company
SBZ	Soviet Zone of Occupation
SED	Socialist Unity Party of Germany
SMAD	Soviet Military Administration in Germany
SPD	Social Democratic Party of Germany
SPK	State Planning Commission
UN	United Nations
USSR	Union of Soviet Socialist Republics (also Soviet Union)
VdgB	Association for Mutual Peasant Aid
VEB	Nationalised enterprise
Volkskammer	People's Chamber; GDR parliament; unicameral
VVB	Administration of Nationalised Enterprises 1952–8
VVB	Association of Nationalised Enterprises 1948–52, 1958–

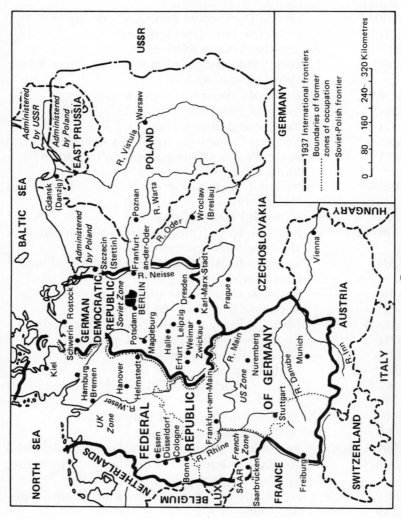

Germany

0   50   100   150
Kilometres

MECKLENBURG
● Schwerin

BRANDENBURG
Potsdam ●
● Berlin

SAXONY-
ANHALT

Halle ●

SAXONY

Erfurt ●

THURINGIA

● Dresden

———— Länder Boundaries
- - - - Future Bezirk Boundaries

The Länder of the SBZ/GDR (May 1945–July 1952)
with their capital cities

The Bezirks of the GDR with their capital cities
(formed 23 July 1952)

Introduction

Germany paid a heavy price for defeat in the Second World War. Besides the human losses much territory had to be surrendered. The Elbe became the dividing line between East and West just as it had been the frontier between Germans and Slavs many centuries ago. East Prussia was lost to the Soviet Union and Poland and Silesia and Pomerania also went to Poland. Had these territories remained part of Germany they would have formed part of the Soviet zone of occupation. Together with what later became the GDR they would have formed the nucleus of a potentially powerful state with its own raw materials base in Silesia and fertile land in Pomerania. Given the refusal of the Polish nation to accept a communist government bound to the Soviet Union in eternal marriage and the willingness of the GDR population to accept such a state of affairs as a *fait accompli*, the Soviet Union may be having second thoughts about the wisdom of the settlement arrived at in 1945. Poles and Germans shared some common beginnings in 1945. Neither people had liberated itself from fascism and this permitted the occupying power to impose a political system of its liking. Poland had lost her sovereignty in 1939 as a result of German and Soviet aggression and longed for independence once again in 1945. However it was the Red Army which liberated Poland and this compounded a tense situation. Since 1945 the Poles have been trying to break the Soviet connection and the emergence of a free trade union, Solidarity, between August 1980 and December 1981 revealed how thin the ice of the legitimacy of the communist party was. Only the instruments of coercion, the army and police, both closely supervised from Moscow, saved the power of the party. Such a state of affairs is almost inconceivable in the GDR. Most of Prussia became part of the GDR in 1945 and Prussian traditions, far from being derided, are being cultivated by the present leadership. The main tradition

1

is respect for the state. This, in turn, has led to respect for the law. In no other socialist state does the citizen possess such an inbred concern for lawful behaviour.

The German state was smashed in 1945. The KPD/SED, under the guidance of the Soviets, set about reestablishing a powerful state. To do this it had to set up the instruments of control, central and local government, trade unions, youth movement and so on and mould them in its own image. As the SED became stronger so concern for law grew. The uprising of June 1953 revealed how precarious the SED's hold on the population was. Most startling for the party was the lack of loyalty in the political and civil police. Building up reliable instruments of coercion, which eventually involved an army, became a top priority. This, by and large, had been achieved by the late 1950s.

Hence the possibility of a fresh start in 1945 was missed in the Soviet zone. Only the destruction of state power made it possible in 1945, since German history has so far revealed that the working class is not revolutionary; revolutionary in the sense of having the willpower and ability to overthrow the state and establish its own dictatorship. Left to herself Germany would have gone socialist in 1945. But what type of socialism would have emerged, the Leninist or the social democratic variant? Almost certainly the latter. However no occupying power wanted this to happen, each for its own peculiar reason. Hence the most important reason for Germany developing as she did after 1945 was the international situation. As tension between the great powers increased, so the room for manoeuvre for independent German political, economic and social initiatives diminished. Gradually state power was reestablished in both halves of Germany and it then became natural to adopt traditional methods and practices.

Strictly speaking there was a revolution in the east. Power passed from the Reich to the Soviet Union and was then handed gradually to the communist party. Power passed from one social class to another but without the working class actually capturing power for itself. It was presented with power by the occupying power. This meant that communists were beholden to the Soviets, psychologically and politically. The international situation was such that the Soviets felt they could not afford Germans any leeway and tried to force an alien system on them.

Many bridled at this, first and foremost, social democrats. Others, especially communists who wanted to develop socialism with a German face, were perceived as just as dangerous.

The most startling post-war event in communism was the denunciation of Stalin by Khrushchev at the twentieth CPSU congress in Moscow in February 1956. This legitimated the view that a communist party can be in error. As it turned out de-Stalinisation never really got off the ground in the GDR, mainly due to the skilful use of power by Walter Ulbricht, the SED leader.

Another turning point was the building of the Berlin Wall in August 1961. Until then those who did not agree with the direction the state was taking could leave. Emigration after 1961 was illegal so internal emigration became the norm for those, perhaps the majority of the population, whose first loyalty is not to the GDR state.

Today the GDR state is very powerful; the communist party dominates the instruments of control and coercion and at its back is the Soviet Army. It may appear ironic that a party which professes to be Marxist should have constructed a strong state, an entity which Marx and Lenin agreed had to be smashed. Soviet experience here is very relevant. After the October Revolution Lenin discovered that the Russian working class, in whose name the Bolsheviks had seized power, was quite unable and unwilling to construct the type of socialist society he envisaged for Soviet Russia. This led to the communist party usurping the role of the working class in constructing a new society. Power was concentrated in the party and a large party bureaucracy gradually emerged. Through the nomenklatura or system of appointments it came to control the state apparatus, the armed forces, the political police, indeed all institutions of significance. The state reappeared in a new guise. It was rehabilitated when it was discovered that it was a powerful weapon in the struggle to build a new society. The state as such was not evil, it only became evil when it fell into the wrong hands.

Hence in 1945 the Soviet authorities reopened Buchenwald, for instance, to incarcerate German political prisoners, implying that concentration camps are not in themselves evil, it all depends on who is being kept in them.

Germans found in and after 1945 that they were in no

position to express their true feelings and opinions. Any criticism of the occupying power could be construed as evidence of fascist sympathies. Everyone had to learn to speak two languages, one at work and when in contact with state organs, and the other at home or among friends. This, of course, had also been the situation between 1933 and 1945. This has continued to the present day and has produced a population which knows what the state wants it to say in given circumstances. However this need to disguise one's true feelings engenders cynicism and despair. The state is concerned with conformity, not with beliefs. If a citizen acts as if he believes then the state is satisfied.

This curtailing of frank, open debate has channelled the energies of the population in other directions. The material achievements of the GDR since 1945 are formidable and are the result of German efficiency and hard work. Not surprisingly, the GDR is one of the top dozen industrial nations in the world and has the highest living standard of any socialist country.

The state which has emerged in the GDR is the strongest in German history. Only the collapse of Soviet willpower to defend the GDR could undermine it. Paradoxically this very strong state feels insecure: witness the Wall and the increasing role being played by the military and political police. The SED is aware that the majority of its members are not believers. Probably about 10 per cent really believe in Marxist–Leninist ideology and are guided by it. The rest are in the party because they need to be in it to hold down their jobs or secure promotion. The intelligentsia needs to join the party and this has produced a situation where those with further education make up almost a quarter of its membership. The vast majority of the intelligentsia is not committed to the ideology but to its area of expertise. Politically the mind switches off; when coping with technical problems it switches on again. Leisure is taken seriously. The educated need some outlet for their enquiring minds and many find it in German music, art and literature. However German culture for them ends in 1945. Their passion for the German past is shared by the state, always in search of forbears which will add to its legitimacy. Frederick the Great, Goethe, Clausewitz, Luther and Scharnhorst, to name only a few, have seen their reputations refurbished.

While the power of the state is great, its authority or legitimacy is low. The Wall illustrates this. The best years were the 1970s when the economy performed very well. However the 1980s are proving a difficult decade since the terms of trade have turned against the GDR. This means that the country must export more to import the same amount. Increasing living standards boosted the self-confidence of the SED and increased the legitimacy of the regime in the 1970s. Now living standards are stagnating, with little prospect of real improvement due to the poor resource base of the country. This situation will produce discontent but not enough to threaten the stability of the state. East Germans will continue to seek out their niche in society and fit into it. They have become past masters at conforming. Only the Church, at present, offers an alternative system of values and a forum for discussion. Christians are mindful of the fact that the state will not tolerate direct criticism of its activities and this requires believers to observe self-discipline.

What has emerged in the GDR is state socialism, administered by an army of party and state bureaucrats. Individual initiative has been supressed in favour of group initiative. Hierarchy is of great importance. The leading functionaries in the party and state bureaucracies, the army and the police have coalesced into a new ruling class. They do not actually own the means of production but dispose over surplus product. They take a disproportionate share of the surplus product in relation to their contribution to society's well-being. These bureaucrats are not a transient but a permanent phenomenon.

This brief study outlines the development of the GDR from economic ruin to modest prosperity. On the economic and social plane the GDR has acheived great success; in all other respects her performance has been disappointing. Despite her achievements the GDR has not proved a magnet for other states. Very few of the two million unemployed in West Germany actually wish to move there to take up a job. The GDR is respected but not loved.

The title of this book implies that the German Democratic Republic came into being in 1945. Technically speaking the GDR came into existence in 1949 but the GDR practice of regarding the whole period since 1945 as part of GDR history is here adopted.

1 Germany: the Victors and the Vanquished

Introduction

Many Germans thought of killing Adolf Hitler but the eventual assassin turned out to be the Führer himself, on 30 April 1945 in Berlin. Symbolically he was executing himself for the crime of having embroiled the world in a bloody conflict – it cost 55 million lives of which over 6 million were German – and for having lost. If death absolved him of the responsibility of healing the material and human wounds, the survivors were faced with this mammoth task. Germany was truly united in 1945, united in hunger, desperation and despair. Over one third of the national product and about 15 per cent of all dwellings had been destroyed; 25 million Germans had lost hearth and home, as refugees, evacuees or as those in search of somewhere new to live. The area conquered by the Red Army had suffered grievously and the battles there had been fierce. Reconstruction and renewal were not a matter of choice, they were imperative.

The unconditional surrender of the German Wehrmacht on 8 May 1945 – the government came to an end on 23 May 1945 with the capture of Grand Admiral Dönitz, his ministers and the remnants of the Wehrmacht leadership – meant that there could be no repeat of the myth of November 1918, namely, that Germany had been stabbed in the back by the politicians. This time the Reich had been brought to its knees militarily and this was plain for everyone to see. Defeat had come after seven years of military violence which had seen neighbouring countries annexed and their governments made fascist. The consequences of defeat, however, were not clear. Germany's search for *Lebensraum*, or living space, had led to some client

6

states in Eastern and South-eastern Europe joining the Wehr-macht in its campaign against the Soviet Union in the hope of securing some of the spoils and of finally putting paid to the 'red threat'. After the Red Army had driven the Wehrmacht from its soil it could move into these regions as liberators or avengers. The Germans had curried support by claiming that they were protecting the region against the Bolshevik threat. Military defeat, however, opened the floodgates and moreover sapped the willpower and the self-confidence of the political classes, producing a vacuum which the USSR was only too willing to fill.

American and British leaders may have sensed that the Soviet Union could pose problems after the war but they agreed that the first priority was the military defeat of Germany. Politics could then take over. The USSR, on the other hand, made no such distinction and always consciously pursued military–political goals. The Western Allies had been taken aback at the German–Soviet Non-aggression Pact of 23 August 1939 which had made war in Europe inevitable. From Stalin's point of view he had been richly rewarded for this *démarche*; terri-tory from the Baltic to the Black Seas. After Great Britain had allied herself to the USSR when Germany attacked the latter and the United States had joined the grand coalition after Germany had declared war on her in December 1941, it did not take the Western Powers long to perceive that the Soviet Union had no intention of retreating from the terri-tories which she had annexed. By 1945 the USSR had acquired the status of a world power and despite the dissolution of the Communist International (Comintern) in 1943 she had not given up her goal of a world socialist revolution. In fact the Comintern's functions were taken over by the International Department of the Secretariat of the Central Committee of the communist party. The Soviet Union had arrived on the world stage and as such was determined to be involved in deciding the future of Europe and if possible the world. She would only concur to measures which permitted her to retain the sphere of influence she had gained by military conquest in Eastern and South-eastern Europe and in Germany. Security was of primary importance to Moscow and this reinforced her determination to stay put. As Stalin said to Milovan Djilas, Tito's personal envoy, in Moscow in April 1945: 'This war is not as in the past; whoever occupies a territory also imposes on it his own social system. Everyone imposes his own system as far as his army has power to do so. It cannot be otherwise' (Djilas 1969: 90).

The two powers which had contributed most to the defeat of Germany and Japan were the Soviet Union and the United States and this presented them with a golden opportunity to reshape the political configuration of the globe. Never before had such a chance presented itself; never before had two powers so dominated the world. The two powers, however, emerged from the war with different experiences: the USSR had come within a hair's breadth of military defeat on several occasions, the United States had always known that she would be the victor sooner or later and she had not experienced war on her own soil. Victory did not still the Soviet Union's need for security; if the pact with Germany had not saved the country from attack, could any future agreement with a capitalist power ever be relied upon to guarantee legitimate Soviet security needs? The Americans drew certain lessons from their war with Nazi Germany. One of them was that a totalitarian domestic policy leads to a totalitarian foreign policy and another was that if peace was to be preserved Germany and the whole region formerly under her control had to be won over to democracy, understood as American-style liberal capitalism. Yet another was the need to extend the benefits of the open American society — the best of all possible worlds, in American eyes — resting on a market economy in which protectionism, preference and tariffs had been eliminated. Along with this businessman's view of the world went a streak of idealism. Rooted in President Woodrow Wilson's ethics, it held that foreign policy had to be morally defensible. It was not enough for the United States to be right, she had to be seen to be right. It was an exhalted vision which denied the right to spheres of influence and the use of force to settle disputes, and proposed the creation of a world authority — the United Nations — to guarantee the security of all states and to mediate all international altercations. Wilson had failed to carry American public opinion with him but his ideals lay deep in the consciousness of many American policy-makers. President Franklin D. Roosevelt was also touched by this idealism but he was in addition a realist. He informed Cardinal Spellman in September 1943 that the

Americans and the British had been forced into a shotgun marriage with the Soviets during the war but that he hoped that a 'real and lasting partnership' would emerge. Europeans would just have to endure 'Russian domination, in the hope that in ten or twenty years' they would learn to live 'well with the Russians'. Hence it is clear that Roosevelt did not perceive the Soviet Union as a threat to US security. He set out to conclude an agreement with Stalin personally, even if parts of it ran counter to the interest of his British allies.

The Western Allies avoided committing themselves to any hard and fast agreement on how Germany was to be treated after the war. They were agreed, however, on the elimination of national socialism and militarism, that no war was ever again to be unleashed from German soil and that Poland was to move westwards — this involved acquiring some territory at the expense of Germany. It was unclear whether the refashioning of Germany could only be agreed at the highest level or whether the United States would need to retain a military presence in Europe.

The proposal to dismember post-war Germany into several states was floated by Roosevelt at the first meeting of the Big Three at Tehran from 28 November to 1 December 1943. It fitted well into the concept of unconditional surrender which had been agreed at the Conference of Casablanca in January 1943. Agreement on the occupation zones was reached at Yalta in February 1945; the details were to be worked out by the European Advisory Commission (EAC). Stalin engaged in a tactical volte-face on dismemberment on Victory in Europe Day when he made clear that Soviet policy was not to dismember or destroy Germany. Returning German communists made much of this tactical move and argued that the USSR was the only power concerned with keeping Germany as an entity. The Soviet Union had launched the first of many initiatives on Germany.

It was not until 5 June 1945 that the four Commanders-in-Chief (Eisenhower) (USA), Lattre de Tassigny (France), Montgomery (GB) and Zhukov (USSR)) issued a declaration stating that 'there was no longer a central German govenment . . . capable of meeting the demands of the victorious powers'. Germany was divided into four zones and Berlin into four sectors; the Allied Control Council was established to deal with all matters affecting the whole of Germany but each occupying power could promulgate laws and instructions and issue orders in its own zone. The document spoke of German authorities carrying out the instructions of the Control Council and this revealed that the control agreement worked out by the EAC on 14 November 1944 had not envisaged the complete break-down of German administration. Furthermore the Control Council did not immediately come into being since the Soviets demanded that British and American troops be withdrawn from Mecklenburg, Saxony and Thuringia — they had captured about one-third of the territory of the Soviet zone of occupation — as a precondition. The British Prime Minister, Winston Churchill, wanted the Americans to stay put so as to have a bargaining counter, irrespective of the fact that the area had already been assigned to the Soviet Union. Uppermost in his mind was the fear of communism penetrating the whole of Europe.

President Harry Truman, who had succeeded Roosevelt after the latter's death on 12 April 1945, did not concur and made it clear that his policy was to carry out to the letter all agreements reached with the allies of the United States. British and American troops withdrew to their zones and on 1 July 1945 Soviet troops took over; on 3 July British and American units occupied West Berlin with the French following on 12 August 1945. An inter-allied Kommandatura responsible for Berlin took office on 11 July 1945 but it was not until 30 July 1945 that the Control Council for Germany came together for its first meeting.

The Soviets were the best prepared for occupation. Three groups of German communists had been flown to Berlin, Saxony and Mecklenburg—Pomerania even before hostilities had ceased. The leaders of these groups were Walter Ulbricht, Anton Ackermann and Gustav Sobottka respectively. Their task was to help the Red Army reestablish civil administration. As Ulbricht remarked:

> We had worked out all the details, from the setting up of the administration to the organisation of culture. We also had a list of opponents of Hitler whom we assumed lived in Berlin. These included communist and social democratic members of the Reichstag as well as leaders of the bourgeois opposition to Hitler. Thus prepared, we arrived in Germany

on 30 April 1945 and on 1 May we reached Berlin and began work immediately. (*Neues Deutschland* 17 April 1965)

The Berlin which greeted Ulbricht and the other nine members of his group was almost unrecognisable. Only 370 000 of the 1.5 million dwellings were undamaged, the transport system was not functioning and the food and health situation was critical. Total power rested in the hands of the occupying power and communists took all their orders from the Soviets. Among the primary tasks were the drawing up of lists of Nazis; the checking of all civil servants; the listing of all empty buildings; the opening of small shops; the provision of food for hospitals; and the protection of available food stocks. One of the Ulbricht group, Wolfgang Leonhard, has sketched in the picture which guided the communists.

Germany would have to go through a long period of occupation. Permitting political parties to reemerge would be quite out of the question during the first year of occupation . . . As soon as political activity became possible, an anti-fascist mass organisation called Bloc of Militant Democracy was to come into being. A land reform was desirable but at the earliest could not be carried out until the summer of 1946. (*Die Zeit* 7 May 1965)

Special attention was to be paid to setting up local government in those Bezirks which were to be occupied by the Western Powers. Here not more than one-third of the posts were to be filled by communists to ensure that these communists stood a good chance of being confirmed in office by the Americans, British and French. This did happen initially. Ulbricht's guiding principle was simple: 'Everything must appear democratic but we must concentrate all power in our hands.' What was to happen to all the communist and people's committees which had spontaneously appeared and to the National Committee for a Free Germany (NKFD) groups which had hitherto functioned illegally? They were all liquidated on Ulbricht's orders and their members told to continue their work in the committees of the Bezirk administrations. Following Soviet practice, Ulbricht eliminated all independent initiative. The anti-fascist democratic revolution was not to come about spontaneously but was to be administered from above — just like socialism later. A Berlin city government was confirmed in office by the Soviet commandant Colonel General Bezarin on 14 May 1945 with Dr Arthur Werner as mayor. He did not belong to any party but seven of the sixteen members were communists and they controlled the departments of personnel, education, social welfare, finance, posts and communications and labour deployment. The city government began work on 19 May 1945 and similar scenes were enacted all over the Soviet zone. Communists had occupied local government posts before 1933 but never before had communists controlled local government. All this before the Communist Party of Germany (KPD) had been reestablished. The Soviets acted unilaterally in setting up local government; the other occupying powers were much slower in entrusting Germans with administrative functions.

The Soviet Military Administration in Germany (SMAD) was set up on 9 June 1945 to administer the Soviet Zone (SBZ) and Soviet military administrations were established in each Land and province on 9 July. SMAD's first head was Marshal Georgy Zhukov and he was succeeded by Marshal Vasily Sokolovsky in April 1946. General Vasily Chuikov took over in March 1949. SMAD was the key institution in the SBZ until its dissolution in 1949 and as such guided the evolution of the zone in the direction favoured by Stalin. It was the instrument of power and its task was to establish the instruments of control and coercion in the area. What shape this would take and, more important, how rapidly this could be put into effect depended on the international situation and especially on the Soviet Union's relations with the United States. As it turned out SMAD laid the foundations for the later integration of the GDR in the socialist bloc.

SMAD operated at two levels. Overtly it issued instructions and orders which regulated political, economic, social and cultural life, covertly it supervised all the key decision-makers in its zone. It worked most closely with communists and communist policy initiatives were always agreed with it beforehand. SMAD's master was in Moscow from whom it received instructions but it in turn could advise on what policy should be adopted. German communists, for their part, received their instructions, usually couched in the form of advice, from SMAD, but they could also influence policy formation by proferring their advice. Stalin's judgement was based on the information and counsel he received from his secret chancellery. The Soviet dictator made sure that he had access to several sources of information, first and foremost that of the political police. Besides the communist party and the political police, the Red Army also sent back intelligence reports to Moscow. The greatest influence on the evolution of the SBZ in the immediate post-war years was exerted, however, by the international situation.

SMAD's Order no. 1 was to set iself up but Order no. 2 on 10 June 1945 changed the political face of the Soviet zone. It permitted the creation of anti-fascist political parties which were dedicated to the eradication of fascism and the strengthening of democracy and civil freedom. Organisations such as trade unions were also to come into existence. However it was pointed out that all parties and organisations were to be under the supervision of and to follow the instructions of the Soviet military administration as long as it existed. This represented a volte-face in Soviet policy towards Germany. It took not only German communists by surprise but also the Western Allies who were not consulted and who then found themselves under pressure to legalise political activities in their zones as well — something which they did later but only at local level to start with. Order no. 2 permitted all-German parties functioning at national level. The new approach had been agreed at a conference of Soviet and German communists in Moscow in early June and the communists in the SBZ were then informed: there was not to be a united socialist party but the Communist Party of Germany (KPD) and the Social Democratic Party (SPD) were to be refounded; bourgeois parties similar to the old Democratic Party and the Zentrum Party were to come into existence and all the new parties were to form an anti-fascist democratic bloc. It would appear that A. I. Mikoyan, deputy chairman of the Council of People's Commissars, played an important role in the Soviet change of policy. He had been in Berlin as early as 9 May 1945 and presumably came to the conclusion that the remnants of fascism were not as strong as anticipated and that anti-fascist forces were willing to cooperate in the restoration of Germany. The reestablishment of the Weimar party system signalled the fact that the Soviet zone or indeed Germany for that matter was not expected to go socialist.

To use the analogy of Russia in 1917, Germany in 1945 was experiencing its February Revolution; the October Revolution which would usher in socialism would follow later.

The KPD was the first party to appear, on 11 June 1945. Its manifesto did not speak of a socialist transformation of Germany but of completing the revolution of 1848. It opposed the imposition of the Soviet system on Germany since this would not have corresponded to the 'conditions of development' at that time. Mention of the dictatorship of the proletariat was nowhere to be found. The KPD appealed for the creation of an 'anti-fascist democratic regime' in a 'democratic republic'. Private enterprise and trade were to flourish unhindered. Communists who had remained in Germany during the national socialist era did not draw up the manifesto: it had been composed in Moscow by émigré KPD functionaries. Thirteen of the sixteen signatories (of whom two were female) returned to Germany in the train of the Red Army. All of them had experienced the Stalinisation of the KPD during the Weimar Republic and had survived the dreadful purges of 1936–8 which had enveloped foreign communists as well as the Soviet population. The nominal head of the KPD was Wilhelm Pieck but the guiding spirit was Walter Ulbricht. The other key party functionaries were Anton Ackermann and Franz Dahlem. The Soviets appeared to have a malleable force in their hands, one which could be relied upon to put Soviet German policy into effect.

The skeleton of the KPD had already emerged before the official reappearance of the party. The members of the Ulbricht, Ackermann and Sobottka groups had been active in their respective areas and cadres had also reformed local organisations on their own initiative. Communists had been told to 'begin the reorganisation of cells so as to make it possible for a Bezirk organisation to come into being and to be ready to act on central directives' (Weber 1980: 19).

If the émigré leadership was content with the new line, many activists were not. They would have preferred a united party of the left; some adopted traditional communist tactics and began in 1945 where they had left off in 1933. Some clung to the old goals of the dictatorship of the proletariat or a republic of soviets. Others wanted the communist youth movement to reappear. The party line propagated by the leadership was

quickly enforced, the more so since the depredations of the
Nazis had left the party with few cadres. Those who had survived had been cut off from central directives and so had been
forced to evolve their own tactics. Some of these could be disciplined, since strict adherence to orders from the centre had
been instilled in them before 1933. Others had developed some
independence. The tactic used by the KPD was to swamp the
recalcitrant cadres by new entrants. The KPD was no longer to
be a narrow, sectarian party but to become a 'party of the
people', a national party (Leonhard 1972: 330). Ulbricht was
very frank in a letter to Wilhelm Pieck on 17 May 1945: 'We
must bear in mind that the majority of our comrades have
sectarian views and so the composition of the party must be
altered as soon as possible by drawing in active anti-fascists
who are now proving themselves in the work they are doing'
(Ulbricht 1953–71 II: 205). While the KPD had gained respect
among anti-fascists for its opposition to national socialism –
something that Ulbricht later admitted had not weakened
Nazism – it was still seen by the vast majority of the population
as the 'Russian' party. When there were complaints about the
behaviour of Soviet soldiers the KPD argued that its task
was the reconstruction of Germany and not the passing of
judgement on the behaviour of the occupying power. The
KPD leadership also sided with the Soviet Union when there
was a conflict between Soviet and German interests.

The SPD published its appeal on 15 June 1945 but its central
committee would have preferred that the party had not come
into existence. Otto Grotewohl, the leader, Max Fechner,
Gustav Dahrendorf and others had attempted to set up a
united socialist party with the communists but Ulbricht and the
KPD would not agree. Despite this the party's manifesto
declared that it was aiming at the 'organisational unity of the
German working class'. The SPD was not so reticent as the
KPD about its goals: a democratic state and a socialist economy
and society. This meant that agricultural development should
be centred on cooperatives; banks, insurance, mining, raw
materials and the energy sector should be nationalised. On
19 June five representatives of the KPD and five from the
SPD met to discuss relations but Ulbricht waved aside all
requests for a united party. He declared that the moment for
the fusion had not yet arrived. 'A premature fusion contains

within itself the seeds of a new split and thereby discredits the concept of unity.' Nevertheless the two parties agreed to coordinate their efforts and an action programme was drawn up.

The Christian Democratic Union of Germany (CDU) appeared as the third party on 26 June 1945. Thirty-five signatures were appended to the party's manifesto with Dr Andreas Hermes at the top. The founding group had 50 members: 20 Protestants, 20 Catholics from the old Zentrum Party and 10 members of the former Democratic Party. The CDU stood for private property but favoured a united trade union movement and the nationalisation of raw materials and mining. The CDU was Christian, democratic and socialist.

The fourth party to appear was the Liberal Democratic Party of Germany (LDPD) and it was the most bourgeois. It favoured private property, the rule of law, an independent civil service and judiciary and peaceful coexistence of peoples. The LDPD was founded in Berlin but successors to the Democratic Party appeared in Dresden, Halle, Weimar and elsewhere. However they all joined the LDPD so that there were four central parties in the SBZ in July 1945.

On 14 July 1945 all four came together to form the 'bloc of anti-fascist democratic parties', each party nominating five members to the committee. The bloc was to decide policy but all decisions were to be unanimous, a conscious rejection of the coalition politics of the Weimar Republic. In this way the KPD was able to ensure that no anti-communist coalition came into existence. The bloc decisively shaped SBZ politics since similar bodies were set up at the local level. Here communists could engage in power struggles with the other parties, always knowing that the occupying power was holding the ring. The first mass organisation also came into existence. A preparatory trade union committee for Berlin was set up on 15 June 1945 and its members came from the communist, social democratic, Christian and liberal trade unions. For the first time in German labour history a single trade union was to represent all workers and this permitted the KPD, also for the first time to join the mainstream of trade union politics. Communist influence in what became the Free German Trades Union Association (FDGB) when it was set up in February 1946 grew significantly from the outset.

Youth committees were established after Marshal Zhukov

had given the go-ahead on 20 June 1945 but Walter Ulbricht made it clear on 25 June that there was not going to be a communist youth movement but a 'unified, free youth movement'. Anti-fascist youth committees were founded at the local level. Communist influence was very strong from the very beginning. The Free German Youth Movement (FDJ) was set up on 7 March 1946 and its first chairman was Erich Honecker.

The political initiative in Germany was seized by SMAD and it licensed four parties. These parties were seen as all-German and exercised considerable influence over the evolution of parties in the western zones in the immediate post-war years. Whereas the parties in the western zones (representing all views except the right) followed in the tradition of Weimar party and coalition politics, those in the east found that the anti-fascist democratic bloc increasingly restricted their room for manoeuvre. While communists never succeeded in recapturing their pre-1933 strength and influence in the western zones, in the east they were on the march and quickly dominated political life.

The Potsdam Agreement

The Potsdam Conference which met between 17 July and 2 August 1945 took decisions crucial to Germany's future. Meeting in the Soviet zone, it symbolically acknowledged the increased power of the USSR. Marshal Stalin became the key personality; President Truman was meeting him for the first time and Winston Churchill for the last time as the latter was replaced by Clement Attlee on 28 July after Labour's victory in the general election. Truman, the conference chairman, was determined to reach agreement on all major issues and proposed that outstanding questions and the detailed working out of the decisions taken should be passed to a Council of Foreign Ministers. Here the Soviet minister, Molotov, was much more experienced than James Byrnes of the United States or Ernest Bevin of Great Britain. A communiqué published on 2 August made clear that the Allies looked forward to a long period of occupation. Truman and Attlee accepted the Soviet *fait accompli* as regard Germany's frontiers in the east but it was stated that the final decision on the frontiers would have to wait until the peace conference, which in fact was never convened. The territories east of the rivers Oder and Neisse were to be under Polish administration and not to be considered part of the SBZ. Königsberg and the adjoining region were acknowledged as part of the USSR. Germans living in Poland, Czechoslovakia and Hungary were to be expelled. Stalin gave Truman and Attlee to believe that practically all Germans had left Poland but this was quite inaccurate. It transpired that about five million Germans were to be forcibly removed from the countries named. This was one of the issues Churchill had intended to take up with Stalin after the election but the British voters ensured that Churchill never raised the matter. The three powers underlined the fact that they had no desire to annihilate or enslave the German people but rather to help them find the road to freedom and democracy. The four commanders-in-chief (France was nevertheless not admitted to the conference), however, held supreme power in Germany and were to act accordingly to their own judgement in their own zone but in unison in all-German affairs. State secretaries were to head 'central German administrations for finance, transport, commerce, foreign trade and industry' and be supervised by the Control Council. 'No central German government' was to be formed for the time being. Germany was to be completely disarmed and demilitarised and the National Socialist Party (NSDAP) banned. Nazi laws were repealed, national socialists sacked and war criminals handed over to the courts. (The Nuremberg Trials began on 20 November 1945.) A democratic educational and legal system, a democratic civil service, democratic parties and trade unions were all to come into being but the needs of 'military security' took precedence.

Germany was to be treated as an 'economic entity' but her war potential was to be eliminated as was the 'over-concentration of economic power', in the form of trusts and syndicates. The recovery of the German economy was to be based on agriculture and consumer goods industries. Regarding reparations, the Soviet Union and Poland were to take theirs from the Soviet zone, the Western Allies and other states from the western zones. The Soviets were also to get 25 per cent of the industrial equipment which was deemed superfluous to peacetime requirements; 15 per cent was to be compensated for by providing foodstuffs and raw materials and the other 10 per cent was a gift.

The Potsdam Agreement was very far ranging. Besides the fact that the Allies were to dictate the development of Germany, the latter also had to pay reparations and make restitution for the appalling suffering of the Nazi era. Fascism and militarism were to be extirpated and a new democratic state was to emerge. The slogan of demilitarisation, denazification and democratisation was easy to agree to but difficult to execute. Given the radically different socio-political systems in the Soviet Union and the West there was certain to be conflict over what democracy really meant.

No Great Power had evolved a detailed policy towards Germany in the summer of 1945. They were aware of what they did not want but were uncertain about how the transformation of Germany could be effected. France, for instance, feared a resurgent Germany and therefore set out to prevent a unified Germany. In a note to the other three powers on 7 August 1945 she opposed the emergence of political parties and all-German central administrations. This undermined the competence of the Control Council and made it unlikely that it could take far-reaching decisions on Germany. France had this power since she had acknowledged but did not feel bound by the Potsdam Agreement since she had been admitted to the Control Council without being obliged to accept the Agreement.

Soviet policy towards Germany was very flexible. On the one hand she wished to expand her sphere of influence to include East Germany and on the other she had long-term hopes of seeing the whole of Germany go socialist. Her policy sought to capitalise on all the opportunities offered and as such was determined to a considerable degree by her relations with the United States. Germany was the most important country in Europe as far as Moscow was concerned. If Germany fell into the camp of the adversary it would nullify all gains in Eastern and South-eastern Europe. In 1945 the USSR was stretched to the limit economically and militarily and hence had to pursue a policy which allowed her time to recover her strength. She needed reparations and, if possible, American credits. However, security took pride of place in Soviet thinking; if American help could only be obtained by making concessions in Eastern and South-eastern Europe then short-term economic gain had to be forgone. Communist parties were informed in 1945 that the immediate goal was not a socialist revolution but the strengthening of the communist position. No risky attempts at seizing power were to be made. In the interim, communist parties could evolve their own road to socialism and this meant that there was no immediate plan to sovietise Eastern and South-eastern Europe. This also applied to the SBZ and permitted the communists there to improve their position in the anti-fascist democratic movement. Once they had won the upper hand communists would then have various options open to them.

New State Organs

On 4 July 1945 Marshal Zhukov confirmed in office an administration in Land Saxony and Land Mecklenburg and in the province of Brandenburg and on 16 July in Land Thuringia and in the province of Saxony—Anhalt. (These two provinces became Länder in 1947.) Rudolf Friedrichs (SPD) became president in Saxony; he had become the first mayor in Dresden after the war. Karl Steinhoff (SPD) headed the administration in Brandenburg, Wilhelm Höcker (SPD) in Mecklenburg, Friedrich Hübener (LDPD) in Saxony—Anhalt and Rudolf Paul, non-party, in Thuringia. Of the eighteen vice-presidents, six were members of the KPD, four of the SPD, five of the CDU and LDPD and three were non-party (*DDR* 1975: 41—2). All parties were represented in the administration. For instance in Land Saxony in early 1946 there were 440 KPD members, 512 SPD members, 90 LDPD members, 87 CDU members and 901 non-party officials. At the end of 1945 in the city of Leipzig 2000 communists, 4000 social democrats, 600 Christian and liberal democrats and 12 000 non-party officials were employed (Weber 1980: 26). SMAD Order no. 17 on 27 July 1945 created eleven central German administrations. Although originally these administrations were only to be responsible for the Soviet zone, they were seen as embryonic all-German bodies. They were set up during the Potsdam Conference but their existence was not made known until later. There were administrations for transport, information, energy, trade, industry, agriculture, finance, labour and social security, health, education and justice. Five of the presidents were KPD members such as Edwin Hoernle (agriculture), Wilhelm Koenen (labour and social security) and Paul Wandel (education), three belonged to the SPD, there was one Christian democrat and one liberal democrat and one did not belong to any party. Hence the KPD was overrepresented. Later five more administrations, for statistics, refugees, internal affairs, interzonal and foreign trade, and sequestration were added. Hence central, Land, provincial, Kreis and Gemeinde organs (the last two were supervised by the local Soviet commander) rapidly came into being and set about the formidable task of rebuilding the shattered country. Weeding out former national socialists, agreed at Potsdam, permitted SMAD to carry through a thorough personnel reform and by 1948 about 520 000 persons had been sacked. Denazification afforded SMAD the opportunity of replacing those dismissed with communists or communist sympathisers so that as functions were gradually handed over to Germans the KPD acquired the key positions. Communists not only dominated administration but acquired control over the police and judiciary as well. Police functions, such as traffic control and the struggle against crime, were made the responsibility of a new force as early as June 1945 but the new policemen, recruited more for their political reliability than their skill at keeping law and order, were not issued with weapons until the end of October 1945. The new People's Police (*Volkspolizei*) were the responsibility of the first deputy president of internal affairs in the Land and provincial administrations and after the elections of 20 October 1946, when Land and provincial governments were established, of the Ministers of the Interior. The emergence of the German administration for internal affairs in July 1946 signalled the centralisation of police control. There was no power-sharing in the police. Communists held all the top posts and in Saxony at the end of 1945 59.1 per cent of the police force were members of the KPD (Norden 1963: 68). At the end of 1945 and the beginning of 1946 political sections were set up, the so-called K5, in Land, provincial and Kreis police administrations. Already by the middle of 1946 they were responsible for political offences which the Soviet administration did not regard as directed against them (Fricke 1979: 41). Needless to say the K5s were strictly supervised by the Soviet political police (NKVD — after March 1946 the MVD) but the nucleus of the East German political police was forming.

The 'anti-fascist democratic revolution' involved the 'reeducating' of former Nazis and other undesirables and this was the responsibility of the NKVD. They simply took over some of the old concentration camps, for example Buchenwald and Sachsenhausen, and continued using them until 1950. The number of political prisoners may have been as high as 200 000 over the period 1945–50, with one-third of them dying while in the camps. About 30 000 prisoners were deported to the Soviet Union (Fricke 1979: 73–9). Not only former NSDAP members were to be found in the camps: judges, lawyers, police officials, teachers, journalists, doctors, scientists, factory and landowners, often irrespective of their attitude to national socialism, rubbed shoulders there. The 'bourgeois elite' was a special target. The effect on the population was intended to be prophylactic.

The communists were particularly concerned not to allow the 'bourgeois' legal system with the rule of law and the privileged position of judges and lawyers to reemerge. The removal of about 85 per cent of judges because of their Nazi sympathies created a vacuum which was filled by giving 'honest antifascists and democrats, not younger than 25 or older than 45 years of age with a completed primary school education' a crash course in law which lasted six months. They then went to work: in Saxony in mid-1947 about 17 per cent of all judges and lawyers were 'people's judges and lawyers' (Benjamin *et al.* 1976: 106).

Economy and Society

Along with the restructuring of the political system went fundamental changes in society. The first major move was a land reform in the autumn of 1945. Striking at the large landowners was designed to eliminate their economic power and political and social influence which had always been great. A land reform was favoured by three of the four parties; only the liberal democrats had not advocated one in their founding manifesto. The initiative was seized by the Central Committee of the KPD on 8 September 1945, but, of course, this move had been agreed beforehand with SMAD. Otto Grotewohl, the chairman of the SPD, voiced the resentment of many in September 1945: 'The political aspect of the land reform is the elimination of the negative influence of the Junkers on the fate of Germany. Large landowners have been the backbone of reaction for hundreds of years . . . They were the enemies of all moves towards freedom in Germany' (Grotewohl 1952: 20). All the land belonging to those who had over 100 hectares was confiscated: this affected about 7000 landowners who lost about 2.5 million hectares. This was added to a central land fund which also included state-owned land and about 600 000 hectares previously owned by high-ranking Nazis. Hence by December 1945 the land fund included 3.3 million hectares (35 per cent of the agricultural land in the SBZ) and of this 2.2 million hectares had been distributed among about 560 000 applicants, mostly smallholders, landless peasants, refugees and industrial workers. The average size of a new farm was 7–9 hectares. The remaining 1.1 million hectares remained in the hands of the state and local authorities. About 500 collective farms were founded on this land, accounting for about 3 per cent of the agricultural land in the Soviet zone – the nucleus of the future socialist agricultural system (Trittel 1975: 15). The reform radically altered the structure of the zone's agriculture. The proportion of farm under 10 hectares in size rose from 19.6 per cent to 42 per cent, and those between 10 and 20 hectares from 21.2 per cent to 27.3 per cent. Farms over 100 hectares dropped from 28.4 per cent to 3.6 per cent of the agricultural land (Ulbricht in *Einheit* 10/ 1955: 849). Abolishing large farms and increasing the number of farms by a third contributed to a sharp fall in agricultural output; 35.5 per cent less in 1946 than in 1938. SMAD and the KPD were quite prepared to accept that these farms would be inefficient, indeed this was deliberate policy since it was believed that peasants would quickly perceive the advantage of setting up collective farms. The agrarian reform was the agreed policy of all four bloc parties but it produced the first real conflict in the bloc. The CDU opposed the seizure of the land without compensation and this led to the dismissal of the chairman Dr Andreas Hermes and his deputy Dr Walter Schreiber on 19 December 1945. Jakob Kaiser and Ernst Lemmer replaced them. The CDU, however, welcomed the coming into being of the Association for Mutual Peasant Aid (VdgB) in 1946. They emerged from the peasant committees set up during the agrarian reform and they collected all the equipment of the confiscated estates in Machine Lending Stations. These in turn hired out their implements and equipment to the peasants. The associations also provided seed and horses.

Education was another area of crucial importance. Besides the lack of buildings and books there was the fact that 72 per cent of the teachers in the Soviet zone had been members of the NSDAP. The KPD and SPD launched an appeal for a democratic educational reform on 4 November 1945 at a meeting in Berlin at which the chairman of the LDPD, Dr Wilhelm Külz, also spoke. The aim was to provide the same education for all children, irrespective of social origin. Church and state were to be separated and this meant the end of church schools against which the CDU protested. The law on the democratisation of the German schools was passed by Land and provincial administrations in May/June 1946; it had been elaborated by the central German administration for education and was essentially the KPD–SPD programme which was floated in October 1945. About 40 000 new teachers were needed: three-month courses were inaugurated in the autumn of 1945 and in early 1946 this was extended to eight months and in 1947 to one year. Sons and daughters of workers and peasants were the preferred students. In 1946–7 some universities began 3 to 4-year teacher training courses. Many universities had opened by the beginning of 1946; about 8000 students were enrolled. The German Academy of Sciences, the old Prussian Academy, began its activities on 1 August 1946. The proportion of children from worker and peasant families attending secondary education rose from 19 per cent in 1945–6 to 36.2 per cent in 1949 (*DDR* 1975: 73). In order to enable more of these students to enter university, special preparatory classes were begun in 1946.

The reform of industry was of special significance. SMAD's Order no. 124 of 30 October 1945 seized the property belonging to the German state, Nazis, war criminals and banned organisations and Order no. 126 the following day confiscated the property of the NSDAP and its organisations. Some of these enterprises were turned into Soviet limited companies (SAG) and others were passed over to the German administrations in March 1946. At the end of 1945 about 25 per cent of factories had restarted production and gross industrial output in the SBZ in June 1946 was about 43 per cent of the 1936 level and a year later about 54 per cent. About 4800 of the 7000 enterprises seized were in Saxony and in February 1946 the KPD there proposed a referendum on the nationalisation of those enterprises which belonged to 'war and Nazi criminals'. Walter Ulbricht took up this idea at the first Reich conference of the KPD on 2–3 March 1946 and SMAD also nodded approval. Eventually the bloc parties came out in favour but only after considerable oppositon by the CDU and LDPD. One point made was that such a radical change could only be carried through on an all-German level. The KPD (SED as of April 1946) had much to lose if the eventual referendum on 30 June 1946 had gone against it. However intense propaganda secured a 77.6 per cent vote in favour; 16.5 per cent were against and 5.8 per cent of the votes were spoilt. Interest was enormous: 93.7 per cent of those eligible did vote. Enterprises belonging to undesirables were nationalised in the other Länder and provinces without a referendum so that practically all major enterprises, especially in heavy industry, were soon in state hands. By early 1948, 9281 concerns, including 3841 industrial enterprises, had been nationalised. Although this represented only 3 per cent of all factories, it accounted for about 40 per cent of gross production (*DDR* 1975: 94).

Economic conditions after the war were particularly difficult (26 per cent of capital stock had been destroyed during the hostilities) and were compounded by the small raw materials base and the limited amount of heavy industry in the zone (86 per cent of Germany's heavy industry was in the British zone). On top of this came dismantling. Soviet reparation squads seized whatever they thought would be of value for the recovery of the Soviet economy. Especially hard hit were machine building, chemicals and optics. Most of the railway lines lost one of their tracks. Industrial capacity was sharply reduced: the iron industry by 80 per cent, the cement and paper industries by 45 per cent and energy production by 35 per cent (Lenz 1979: 31). Reparations were also taken from current production. Order no. 167 of 5 June 1946 transferred a further 213 firms, worth about 2500 million marks, into SAG.

(In 1953 the GDR government had to pay about 2550 million marks to repurchase them.) The SAG accounted for about 25 per cent of SBZ industrial output (Weber 1980: 31). Reparations cost the East German economy between 1945 and 1953 an estimated 66 400 million marks or US$15 800 million (*DDR-Handbuch* 1979: 907).

The Fusion of the KPD and the SPD

The fusion of the two socialist parties which gave rise to the Socialist Unity Party (SED) was a major turning point not only in the politics of the Soviet zone but also of Germany as a whole. The KPD was originally against a united workers' party. Evidently the leadership thought that with the help of SMAD, the policies of the anti-fascist democratic bloc, the land reform and the nationalisation of much of industry and the unity of action with the SPD, the KPD would rapidly dominate politics in the SBZ. The KPD thought it would have time to train an army of functionaries who would play leading roles when the SED did come into existence. Rank and file members had to learn to accept strict discipline and this involved unconditional support for the occupying power. Gradually the Communist Party of the Soviet Union (CPSU) – its new name in March 1946 – headed by Stalin had to be seen as the model to emulate. Since a separate SPD party had come into existence, the KPD had a useful guide to the drawing power of social democracy and the identity of those who were attracted to it.

On the other hand the central committee of the SPD regarded the organisational unity of the working class as the precondition for the socialist transformation they aspired to. The lessons drawn from the disastrous conflict between the KPD and the SPD which had smoothed the way for national socialism, the common suffering in prison and concentration camps and the acceptance by the KPD of the parliamentary road to socialism appeared to have overcome old antagonisms. Given the social democratic tradition in the SBZ, the SPD felt confident that it could dominate a united party. On these issues the SPD in the Soviet zone was much further to the left than the SPD in the western zones. There Kurt Schumacher, who had not linked up with communists during his time in prison, opposed all suggestions of a fusion with the KPD and remained very suspicious of communist motives. The coolness of the western SPD and the aggressive tactics of the KPD, however, gradually cooled the SPD ardour for fusion in the Soviet zone.

The KPD changed course in September 1945 when it proposed a united party. In November 1945 Wilhelm Pieck, the nominal leader, called for fusion 'as soon as possible'. Also in November 1945 communists had done badly in elections in Austria and Hungary. Evidently the KPD felt that the tide was turning in favour of the SPD. Nevertheless the KPD had been very successful in recruiting new members and with a view to fusion stepped up recruitment towards the end of 1945. Whereas on 20 November 1945 the party only had 270 000 members there were about 375 000 at the end of the year — about the same as the SPD (Weber 1980: 32). The KPD was strikingly sucessful in the countryside and here the land reform had a major impact. SMAD, too, favoured the KPD at every turn. The SPD had 679 000 members on 20 April 1946 when the parties fused (compared to 581 000 in the same territory in 1932) but the KPD claimed a membership of 619 000 (McCauley 1979: 17). As the KPD was gradually taking over positions in the state, administration, economy and education its resources were stretched to the limit. It needed social democrats to fill second rank and many lower positions until it had trained its own. Then there was the point that many careerists had joined the KPD just to get a post and as time passed their unsuitability became more and more apparent. The KPD had now become a party with a new membership, with the 'old' cadres being swamped by the new intake.

Once the KPD had decided on fusion, SMAD encouraged the formation of KPD–SPD local committees of action which in turn put pressure on the central SPD leadership which was dragging its feet. The conference of 60 (30 representatives from each party) convened in East Berlin on 20–21 December 1945 to prepare unification. The SPD leaders repeated the view of the Wennigsen conference in October 1945 when Schumacher's demand that a fusion of the KPD and the SPD could only take place on an all-German level was adopted. They protested against the 'undemocratic pressure on social democrats', harassment and preferential treatment of communists by SMAD. The conference resolution, however, looked forward to the 'fusion of the SPD and the KPD in a unified party'. The SPD leaders were not unhappy about the outcome; they fondly imagined that they had won some breathing space. The KPD, on the other hand, stepped up pressure for an immediate fusion. SMAD played its part by banning opposition speakers and arresting other opponents of rapid unity. The new course was more favoured at the local level than at the centre. In Thuringia, for example, the SPD executive was for immediate unity and warned the Berlin leadership that it would act unilaterally, if necessary. Other executives expressed similar views. This forced the central executive to stop prevaricating and to accept unity. Only social democrats in West Berlin could resist the tactics of the KPD and SMAD and they held a referendum on 31 March 1946. It had been planned as an all-Berlin poll but at the last moment the Soviet authorities banned it. Of the 32 547 members, 23 755 voted. In answer to the question: 'Are you in favour of an immediate merger of the two workers' parties?', 2937 (12 per cent) voted yes and 19 526 (82 per cent) no. However 14 883 (62 per cent) were in favour of an 'alliance which will guarantee co-operation and exclude fraternal strife' and 5559 (23 per cent) against (Kaden 1964: 256). Here was striking evidence that the will to cooperate was still extraordinarily strong but time was needed to iron out the differences. However Grotewohl brushed the referendum aside as an irrelevance. In order to make itself ideologically more attractive and to defuse some of the resentment about it being the 'Russian' party, the KPD launched the concept of the 'German road to socialism'. An article on this theme was published in *Einheit* in February 1946 by Anton Ackermann. He stated that there was no intention of forcing the Soviet system on the SBZ and that Germany's more developed economic and cultural life could make the building of a socialist economy and culture easier. A peaceful road to socialism was therefore possible and it was to be a democratic road. This won over many doubters in the SPD at the time and there were many in the KPD who looked forward to taking a German road to socialism. However the move was merely tactical. It was mirrored in other countries such as Poland, Czechoslovakia and Hungary which were also to follow their own road to socialism.

At the fifteenth and final congress of the KPD on 19–20 April 1946 Ackermann's thesis became official party policy.

The chief speaker at the congress was Walter Ulbricht and the main subject was the fusion. Of the 519 delegates, 130 were from West Germany. Simultaneously the SPD was holding its last congress. It also adopted a unanimous resolution to merge but some delegates opposed the communist practice, to be adopted by the SED, of basing cells in enterprises. The SPD had always been organised on an area basis (Weber 1980: 34).

The 'unification congress' of the KPD with 507 delegates and the SPD with 548 delegates took place in East Berlin on 21–22 April 1946. Wilhelm Pieck and Otto Grotewohl, the joint party chairmen, shook hands in the middle of the stage. As Grotewohl remarked, Pieck had come from the left and he from the right. The SED was not to be a linear development of the KPD. However the symbolism of the date was lost on many delegates: 22 April was the anniversary of the birth of Vladimir Ilich Lenin. The SED contained more social democrats than communists when it came into being and quickly recruited more members. By September 1947 there were 1.8 million members or 8.6 per cent of the population compared to 3 per cent in the CPSU at the same time. The SED was a mass party and according to the party statutes all posts were to be filled according to the parity principle. The unification congress elected a Central Committee (CC) of 80 members, 20 of whom were from West Germany. The CC, in turn, elected a central Secretariat, the top decision-making body. It was composed of seven communists (Wilhelm Pieck, Walter Ulbricht, Franz Dahlem, Anton Ackermann, Paul Merker, Walter Beling and Elli Schmidt) and seven social democrats (Otto Grotewohl, Max Fechner, Erich Gniffke, Otto Meier, Helmut Lehmann, August Karsten and Käthe Kern).

The First Elections

The SED was the largest and the most influential party in Germany in 1946. Its writ only extended to the Soviet zone and West Berlin, as the American, British and French authorities had refused to license it in their zones. Speaking for the workers and employees of the SBZ it could plausibly claim to represent the majority of the population. Without elections there was no way the other parties, the CDU and LDPD, could disprove this assumption. The SED placed great faith in the elections of the autumn of 1946, hoping that its optimism would be vindicated and that its leading role would be legitimised.

Again the SED chose to kick off in Saxony where its prospects appeared to be very favourable. The Soviet authorities played their part by holding up the registration of the CDU (only 593 out of 2402 local associations were in fact registered) and LDPD local associations. Only those organisations registered could put up candidates and this meant in effect that only about half of the Christian and liberal democrat candidates could stand. The SED received much more paper than the other parties and was favoured in the allocation of transport. Gemeinde or community elections were held on 1 September 1946 and the SED polled 1.6 million votes (53 per cent), the LDPD 671 000 (22 per cent) and the CDU 655 000 (21 per cent) (Weber 1980: 36). Mass organisations such as the Association for Mutual Peasant Aid and women's committees accounted for the rest. The SED had turned out to be the strongest party but in cities such as Dresden and Leipzig, the CDU and LDPD taken together had received more votes. Gemeinde elections took place in Thuringia and Saxony—Anhalt on 9 September 1946: once again the SED had a plurality of votes but once again it failed to obtain half the votes in some cities. Voters went to the polls in Bradenburg and Mecklenburg on 15 September 1946 and here the SED was most gratified by the results. In the former the party received 60 per cent and in the latter 69 per cent of the votes. Why should the SED have done so well in largely rural constituencies? The main reason must be that the CDU and LDPD were as yet poorly represented organisationally there. Bismarck's quip about moving to Mecklenburg when the world came to an end since everything there was at least 20 years behind the times was no longer apt. In 1946 Mecklenburg was ahead of the times! Kreis and Landtag elections took place on 20 October 1946 (see Table 1.1).

Compared with the Gemeinde elections, the SED gained 73 000 votes in Saxony and in Thuringia but the CDU polled 253 000 more and the LDPD 133 000 more. Elsewhere the SED lost votes. In Brandenburg it was 185 000 down, in Mecklenburg 125 000 and in Saxony—Anhalt 165 000 down. The CDU and the LDPD together saw their vote in these Länder rise by 890 000. All told the SED secured 47.5 per cent of the vote,

Table 1.1: *Kreis and Landtag election results, 20 October 1946*

	SED	CDU	LDPD	VdgB	Kulturbund
Brandenburg	634 786	442 206	298 311	83 271	—
	(43.9%)	(30.6%)	(20.6%)	(4.9%)	
	[44]	[31]	[20]	[5]	
Mecklenburg	547 663	377 808	138 572	43 260	—
	(49.5%)	(34.1%)	(12.5%)	(3.9%)	
	[45]	[31]	[11]	[3]	
Saxony	1 595 281	756 740	806 163	57 229	18 565
	(49.1%)	(23.3%)	(24.7%)	(1.7%)	(0.6%)
	[59]	[28]	[30]	[2]	[1]
Saxony—	1 063 889	507 397	695 685	56 630	—
Anhalt	(45.8%)	(29.9%)	(21.8%)	(2.5%)	
	[51]	[24]	[33]	[2]	
Thuringia	816 864	313 824	471 415	55 093	—
	(49.3%)	(18.9%)	(28.5%)	(3.3%)	
	[50]	[19]	[28]	[3]	
Total	4 658 483	2 397 975	2 410 146	295 483	19 565

VdgB   Association for Mutual Peasant Aid
( )   percentage of votes cast
[ ]   seats obtained in Landtag
Source: S. Doernberg *Kurze Geschichte der DDR*, 4th edn (Berlin, DDR, 1969) p. 101 and H. Weber, *Kleine Geschichte der DDR* (Cologne, 1980) pp. 36—7.

the LDPD 24.6 per cent and the CDU 24.5 per cent. One reason why the SED lost 400 000 votes and the other parties gained 1.2 million was that whereas the Gemeinde elections were tied to registered party branches, these elections were not. In no Land parliament did the SED have a plurality of seats although only in Brandenburg and Saxony—Anhalt could it and its ally, the Association for Mutual Peasant Aid, be outvoted by the combined forces of the CDU and LDPD. If the SED was disappointed by its performance outside Berlin, voting in the capital must have shocked it. In Gross Berlin the SPD polled

48.7 per cent, the CDU 22.2 per cent, the SED 19.8 per cent and the LDPD 9.3 per cent of the votes. These elections took place in all four sectors since the SPD was legal in the Soviet sector and the SED in the Western sectors. The most painful news was that the SPD was the most popular party in the Soviet sector with 43.6 per cent of the votes compared to 29.8 per cent for the SED. These elections taught the SED a lesson. Henceforth voters could not choose between parties but were presented with a single list of candidates from all parties. They could only vote for or against all the candidates. In early December Land governments were formed with the chairmen of the existing Land or provincial administrations being made Prime Minister. That meant that four of the five Prime Ministers belonged to the SED. The other, Professor Hübener, belonged to the LDPD. (He was dismissed in 1949.) Of the ministers, 21 were SED members, 9 LDPD members, 8 CDU members and one was from the Association for Mutual Peasant Aid. Four of the five Ministers of the Interior were SED members and all five Ministers of Culture belonged to the SED. These governments enjoyed a level of authority and legitimacy which the previous administrations, confirmed in office by SMAD, could not aspire to. The inability of the SED to secure a clear majority in the Landtage encouraged the CDU and the LDPD. This led to many conflicts which forced the SED to rely more and more on the centre and SMAD. This struggle was also reflected in the anti-fascist bloc. Jakob Kaiser used the election results to refute SED claims that it had the right to lead since it was the dominant party and instead championed Christian socialism. This was adopted by the CDU at its first congress in East Berlin in June 1946 when it confirmed Kaiser as its leader and Ernst Lemmer as its deputy leader. The CDU took over the role of the SPD as the 'bridge between east and west'. The LDPD under the quiescent leadership of Dr Wilhelm Külz caused the SED less trouble but as the international situation worsened so the CDU and the LDPD found that their room for manoeuvre began to diminish.

The Cold War and the Division of Germany

The Soviet Union believed in 1945 that she had been granted a

sphere of influence in Eastern and South-eastern Europe. However Roosevelt died in April 1945 and Churchill was removed as
Prime Minister in July 1945. President Truman and his Secretary of State James Byrnes genuinely wanted an agreement with
the USSR but they wanted the Soviets to acknowledge that the
USA was the stronger power and they sought access to Eastern
and South-eastern Europe in return for American aid towards
post-war Soviet reconstruction. At the centre of the problem
lay Poland. Stalin had looked in vain for bourgeois politicians
who would collaborate with communists. Since a neutral or
pro-Soviet government could not be found Stalin was forced
to impose a communist one on the country. This exacerbated
East—West relations and Polish voters in the United States
vociferously defended the right of Poland to choose her own
form of government. The fact that American credits and surplus
stock were not forthcoming increased the significance of reparations to the Soviet Union. Western fears of Soviet expansionism
were greatly exaggerated and it gave rise to the doctrine of containment which was enunciated in February 1946 but was not
adopted until a year later with the formulation of the Truman
Doctrine and the Marshall Plan. Containment offered the United
States a world mission and promised to provide the overseas
markets necessary for the expansion of the US economy. Since
the Allies could not agree on Germany they could not agree on
a settlement in Europe. Germany was unfortunate in finding
herself to be the apple of discord but she was held to be too
important by both sides to allow her to pass within the orbit of
the other side.

The conference of Foreign Ministers met in Moscow in
March—April 1947, in Paris in June—July 1947 and in London
in November—December 1947 but the only thing the feuding
ministers could agree on was the next venue. By this time, however, the foundations of a new political, economic and social
system had been laid in the SBZ. The setting up of Bizonia on
1 January 1947 and the appearance later of the Parliamentary
Council in West Germany and the formation of the German
Economic Commission (DWK) in the Soviet zone were further
indications of separate development. An attempt was made in
Munich in May 1947 at a conference of Land Prime Ministers
to halt the division of Germany but those from the east wanted
the first point on the agenda to be the formation of central

German administrations which would make the creation of a unified German state possible. After only a few hours' discussion the eastern representatives left Munich, since no agreement had been reached on the agenda.

The increasing strife between the Land governments and the central administrations led SMAD to establish the DWK on 14 June 1947. The DWK was to coordinate all the activities of the central administrations and to draw up an economic plan for the zone which had to be agreed by SMAD before publication. The DWK was to supervise the delivery of reparations and ensure that the needs of the Soviet occupation forces were met. A permanent bureau was established consisting of the chairman of the DWK, his deputy, the chairmen of the FDGB and the Association of Mutual Peasant Aid and of the central administrations of finance, agriculture, trade and food. The parity principle was openly breached for the first time since communists dominated the new body.

Although the creation of the DWK had contributed to the division of Germany, the second congress of the SED in September 1947 met under the banner of the 'struggle for German unity' and called for a referendum on the formation of a 'unified German democratic State with decentralised administration'. Since the SED claimed to be the leading political party in Germany it reiterated that it was following a specifically German road to socialism. However Walter Ulbricht also stated: 'We are on the way to becoming a party of a new type.' The Communist Information Bureau was also founded in September 1947 and Andrei Zhdanov, speaking for Stalin, divided the world into two camps with countries such as India and Indonesia outside. The democratic camp, led by the Soviet Union, was confronted by the imperialists, headed by the United States. The SED was one of the communist parties not invited to the founding congress but it quickly became apparent that it was to follow the Cominform line. The Cominform's main function was to supervise the transition of Eastern and South-eastern Europe into people's democracies by stressing the debt that the region owed the Red Army, Soviet experience and the advisability of emulating the Soviet economic model.

The inability of the Council of Foreign Ministers to agree led to the two parts of Germany going their separate ways. When Marshal Sokolovsky left the Allied Control Council on 20

March 1948 four-power administration effectively came to an end. The final blow was the currency reform of 20 June 1948 which introduced the Deutsche Mark (DM) to West Germany and in so doing ended the economic unity of the nation and also split Berlin. Soviet representatives left the Kommandatura which administered the capital on 16 June 1948 and in response to the Western currency reform the Ostmark was made the new currency on 24 June 1948. It was extended to the whole of Berlin but the Western Powers overruled this and declared that the DM was the legal currency in West Berlin the following day. The Berlin city government, whose headquarters were in East Berlin, voted to permit two currencies in the city over the protests of the SED. (A separate city government for East Berlin was set up in November 1948 after the Berlin city government had been forced to move to West Berlin.) The only weapon the Soviets had left was an economic blockade of West Berlin; this began on 19 June 1948 and lasted until 12 May 1949. The air lift which kept the West Berlin population alive had a decisive psychological effect on Germans under Western occupation. Until then they had been seen as victors but the feeling began to grow that they and the German population were engaged in a common battle to defend Western interests and values against the onslaught of the communist east. The blockade made it much easier to establish a separate West German state and it was the decisive factor in overturning SPD opposition. It is ironical that the blockade speeded up the formation of the Federal Republic given that the ostensible Soviet aim was to force the Western Powers to abandon preparations for such a state. In the beginning some American politicians were thinking of abandoning Berlin to the Soviets but such was the response in the United States that provisioning West Berlin became a crusade. Henceforth any concession to the USSR could be construed as a betrayal of Western interests. Inept Soviet diplomacy had produced this situation.

Towards a People's Democracy

The division of Germany became visible in 1948 as both the eastern and western parts of the country began politically, economically and socially to appear more like their occupying powers. A new mass phenomenon, the People's Congress movement, came into being in the Soviet zone, the chief object of which was to strengthen the Soviet position at the Conference of Foreign Ministers in London in November 1947. Another object was to exert pressure on the non-socialist parties. The first German People's congress convened in Berlin on 6—7 December 1947 with most of the 2215 delegates being either SED members or fellow travellers. It was billed as an all-German congress but only the KPD in the Western zones was represented. The congress called for the formation of an all-German government and the election of a national assembly. There were CDU members in the congress but they had broken ranks since Jakob Kaiser and Ernst Lemmer, the party leaders, had rejected the whole affair as a *démarche* by the SED. Colonel S. I. Tyulpanov of SMAD thereupon removed them and the new leader turned out to be Otto Nuschke, a supporter of the congress. He it was who opened the second congress on 17 March 1948 and Wilhelm Pieck (SED), Dr Wilhelm Külz (LDPD) and he became joint chairmen of a presidium, elected by a People's Council of 400 members, of whom 100 were from the western zones. The council was to act in the name of the congress when it was not in session.

The LDPD lost its leader in April 1948 when Külz died. The main consequence was that the party leadership began to slip into the hands of those who wished to collaborate with the SED. Those who opposed this tendency, such as Arthur Lieutenant and Leonhard Moog, were forced eventually to flee the country. Generally speaking at the Land and Kreis level CDU and LDPD members opposed the creeping influence of the SED. The two non-socialist parties were greatly weakened in 1948 by the creation of two new parties and the participation of mass organisations, on an equal footing, in the anti-fascist democratic bloc. On 29 April 1948 the Democratic Peasants' Party of Germany (DBD) came into being and its first head was Ernst Goldenbaum, a former member of the KPD. The DBD was to recruit those in the countryside who had bridled at joining the SED. On 25 May 1948 the National Democratic Party of Germany (NDPD) was founded and was led by Lothar Bolz, also a former KPD member. This party was aimed at former officers, ex-national socialists (the CDU and LDPD were not permitted to recruit former Nazis) and members of the middle classes. The

NDPD came up with the startling campaign slogan: 'Against Marxism — For Democracy'. However on closer inspection its placards carried an inscription in small print: 'With the permission of the Soviet Military Administration' (Leonhard 1972: 400). The People's Council of the congress movement immediately admitted the two new parties to its ranks but the CDU and LDPD put up a doughty fight in the bloc to prevent this happening. Nevertheless the DBD became a member of the bloc on 5 August 1948 and the LDPD followed on 7 September 1948. The mass organisations followed soon afterwards.

On 19 June 1948 the People's Council claimed to be a representative body for the whole of Germany and on 3 August 1948 a draft constitution of the 'German Democratic Republic', drawn up by a subcommittee, was adopted. It bore a striking resemblance to an SED draft produced in November 1946 and on 22 October 1948 the People's Council unanimously adopted the draft constitution (Weber 1980: 41).

The SED quickly won the upper hand in the mass organisations. Although the trade union organisation (FDGB) was referred to as being above party when it was founded it gradually fell under communist influence. Indeed communist trade unionists played a vital role in pushing through the fusion of the KPD and SPD in April 1946. At the second congress of the FDGB in the same month the SED obtained a majority of the 47 seats on the central executive. Plan fulfilment became the chief objective of the FDGB in November 1948. The works' councils, the workers' chief negotiating body, were fused with the enterprise trade union committees. This signalled the end of collective bargaining at the plant level and the trade unions concentrated, as in the Soviet Union, on raising labour productivity, seeing it as the key to plan fulfilment. The unions were to become 'transmission belts' — Lenin's phrase — for communist policies. When the FDGB joined the democratic bloc it provided the SED with further opportunities for control.

The pattern in the other mass organisations was somewhat similar. Although the youth movement (FDJ) was stated to be above party, communists played a leading role from its founding in 1946. So disillusioned did the CDU and LDPD become that they withdrew their representatives in the central council of the FDJ in January 1948. The Cultural Association for the Renewal of Germany, comprised of intellectuals and those involved in culture, came into being in July 1945 and the Democratic Women's Association of Germany (DFD) was founded in March 1947; both supported the SED.

The key to SED control, however, was the economy. If the relations of production could be made socialist, the party would dominate. Hence planning was of great significance since it could replace the market economy. The vitality of the market economy was being sapped from 1945 onwards as increasing pressure was applied to enterprise owners. This was especially noticeable in 1948. Some were tried for 'economic crimes', others harassed and many simply fled. Nationalisation embraced more and more concerns. The German Economic Commission (DWK) had its powers extended on 12 February 1948 by SMAD and when it was reorganised on 9 March 1948 it was able to issue orders which were binding on all other organisations. It had become the *de facto* government of the Soviet zone. Its chairman was Heinrich Rau (SED) and four of his six deputies were also SED members. A half-year plan, drawn up by the DWK, was adopted for the second half of 1948 but it only covered raw materials. A two-year plan, covering 1949 and 1950, was adopted by the Central Committee of SED on 30 June 1948. It had been drawn up by the DWK and the State Planning Commission. Central planning had come into being. The nationalised sector of industry only accounted for 39 per cent of gross production in 1948, the same as the private sector. The remaining 22 per cent came from Soviet (SAG) enterprises. Although practically all large factories, especially in heavy industry, were in the hands of the state, there were still 36 000 privately-owned enterprises. These dominated light industry and large-scale farmers still owned a quarter of the agricultural land (Weber 1980: 43).

The plan envisaged production rising by 35 per cent or 81 per cent of the 1936 level by the end of 1950. Labour productivity was to climb 30 per cent but wages only 15 per cent. The stimulus was to be an activist movement. These workers were to show the less enthusiastic the way. There were about 15 000 activists already at work in early 1948. Just what could be done was demonstrated by the miner Adolf Hennecke who mined 24.4 cubic metres of coal on 13 August 1948. This overfulfilled his norm by 287 per cent. In other words he did the work of almost four men in one shift.

The currency reform of June 1948 brought little improvement and in an attempt to counter the black market, the DWK announced the founding of a State Trade Organisation (HO). It set up 'free' shops in which the public could buy food and consumer goods at very high prices. This double system has continued to the present day but it sharply increased the proportion of goods sold in state shops. Shortly afterwards a state wholesale organisation was set up.

The SED becomes a Party of a New Type

The expulsion of the Communist Party of Yugoslavia, led by Tito, from the Cominform in June 1948 had a dramatic effect on other communist parties in Eastern and South-eastern Europe. Communist and social democrat parties were fused into united workers' parties and the Communist Party of the Soviet Union (CPSU) became the model to emulate. This meant that the SED had to become a party of a new type, a Marxist—Leninist party. This change of course was not to the liking of all party members, especially former social democrats and some pre-1933 communists. A party purge was decreed in July 1948 to cleanse the party of such elements. The leading role of the Soviet Union was acknowledged; if anyone bridled at this he was guilty of 'anti-Soviet propaganda'. The punishment for this was imprisonment as an 'imperialist agent'. In September 1948 the party's police, the Central Party Control Commission (CPCC) came into being. Similar organisations were created at the Land and Kreis levels. The CPCC supervised the party purges and between September 1948 and January 1949 about 400 SED members were expelled and arrested as agents of the Eastern Bureau of the SPD. Critically thinking communists were also hard hit (Weber 1980: 46).

Intensive study of Stalin's *History of the CPSU – Short Course* (1936) was ordered by the central Secretariat on 20 September 1948. The first SED conference in January 1949 completed the process when it stated that the chief task was to transform the party into a party of a new type. Democratic centralism was adopted as the principle of organisation. The formation of factions or groups was strictly forbidden. The duty of every party member was to defend the Soviet Union with all his strength. Control commissions reviewed every member's record. The net result of this transformation was the end of the parity principle for the filling of party offices, the abandonment of the special 'German road to socialism' in September 1948, the removal of a large number of 'undesirables' and a marked centralisation of SED affairs. The SED became organisationally more like the CPSU at its first conference (January 1949) when a Politburo was elected. It took over from the central Secretariat as the key party body and the Secretariat elected at the conference contained a majority of former KPD members for the first time. The Politburo was also firmly in the hands of ex-KPD members. It had taken the KPD four years — three of these under the cover name of the SED — to revert to its old organisational structure and political tactics.

Culture

The leading figure in the cultural world of the post-war era was Johannes R. Becher. He was chairman of the cultural commission of the KPD in exile in Moscow in late 1944 when the guidelines for the post-Nazi period were laid down. However Becher argued strongly in favour of a decidedly socialist cultural and educational policy and evidently expected the dictatorship of the proletariat to be proclaimed at the war's end. These views were rejected in favour of what can be called a popular front policy, one which would unite all anti-fascists in the struggle for democratic renewal in Germany. This was supervised by the department of information of SMAD and one of its ten sections was devoted to literature. There was also a SMAD publishing house which concentrated mainly on making available the Soviet classics at low prices. The German contribution was made through the Cultural Association for the Democratic Renewal of Germany which appeared on 4 July 1945 with Becher as president.

A veritable stream of talent flowed into the SBZ from exile after 1945. From the USSR, for example, came Becher, Erich Weinert and Friedrich Wolf; from Mexico came Anna Seghers, Bodo Uhse and Alexander Abusch; from the USA, Bertolt Brecht, Ernst Bloch and Stefan Heym; from Palestine, Arnold Zweig and from Switzerland, via West Germany, Stephan

Hermlin (Emmerich 1981: 41–2). Other writers who did not settle in the Soviet zone were nevertheless given prominence. Heinrich Mann (who died in the USA in 1950), Lion Feuchtwanger (who also remained in the USA until his death in 1958), Leonhard Franks, who moved to West Germany from the USA in 1950, and Thomas Mann, who settled in Switzerland in 1952 after leaving the USA, were the most significant. None of these writers was a member or even supporter of the SED but as 'bourgeois humanists' they were welcomed during the cultural 'popular front' period.

The literary output of the period 1945 to 1949 was almost exclusively devoted to the national socialist past. Here *Die Toten bleiben jung* by Anna Seghers is the most important. This novel covers the years 1918 to 1945 and despite the tragedies looks forward to a brighter future.

Bertolt Brecht, who moved to East Berlin in October 1948 but who had spent the post-war years in the USA and Switzerland in 'preparation' for his return, dominated the theatre. He was associated with the group which became the Berliner Ensemble at the end of 1948 and the beginning of 1949 but his *Mutter Courage und ihre Kinder* did not please the cultural functionaries although audience reaction was very positive.

2 The Impact of Stalinism, 1949–53

Central Europe before 1945 was dominated by Germany but afterwards it became more and more usual to speak of Eastern and Western Europe — Germany had been cut up and part of it belonged to Eastern and part of it to Western Europe. As Germany was torn asunder, traditional links were disrupted and new ones forged with the respective Great Power. As time passed the division of Germany began to take on an air of permanence as the political, economic and social development of the two states — one striving to become a liberal democracy, the other socialist — pulled them further and further apart. The poor resource base of the GDR meant that she had to import much of her energy and essential raw materials. Since the Western Powers had imposed an embargo on the export of strategic and other important goods the GDR was forced to look increasingly to the East for her imports and exports. As time passed she added economic as well as political dependence on the Soviet Union. If the years 1947–9 had seen the Soviet model trumpeted abroad, then the following four years saw an attempt to impose full-blown Stalinism on the GDR. However when the Soviet dictator died in March 1953 the GDR had still not become totally Stalinist. Political and economic decision-making was not concentrated in the hands of one man nor could the security police be used to implement anyone's latest whim. The multi-party system, although the non-socialist parties had been shorn of all decision-making power, was still intact and the private sector was still significant in industry, especially consumer goods and services. Full collectivisation was a thing of the future. Nevertheless the SED, led by Walter Ulbricht, had by 1953 taken over the instruments of control — the government, the trade unions, the youth movement, for example — but the instruments of coercion — the armed forces, the security and civil police — were only there in embryo. Indeed the uprising of 17 June 1953 was to reveal that the hold of the SED over the police was still not complete. Hence the instrument of coercion which dominated the GDR was still the Soviet Army. The concept of a ruling party exercising a dictatorship was not new to Germany; the SED claimed, as of May 1952, that it was building socialism, using as its medium the dictatorship of the proletariat. The construction of socialism effectively undermined the bourgeois democratic constitution of 1949 and the demands made on the working class proved too much for some sections of it in June 1953. The increased sovietisation of the GDR led to more and more detailed copying of Soviet practices. The first Five Year Plan was launched in 1951 and it inevitably led to the development of a central planning apparatus and an ever-increasing state sector in industry and trade. The leading role of the SED was enhanced by the planned economy and indeed in all other spheres of activity, such as government, culture, the mass organisations and education, the party magnified its role and exercised control through democratic centralism, which in essence meant that the arena of decision-making decreased as the power of the SED *apparat* increased. Stalin became the genial guide of the people; those who were imbued with his spirit would build a new, democratic, peace-loving Germany — or so the SED gave everyone to believe. The period 1949–53 saw the most abject negation of things German and the greatest glorification of things Soviet — to be more precise Stalinist — in the GDR's history.

The Founding of the GDR

By 1949 the transition to a people's democracy had been completed in the Soviet zone. Guided and moulded by SMAD, the SED had scaled the peaks of power and was consciously refashioning itself as a 'party of a new type', a Marxist–Leninist party, with the CPSU as its model. The commanding heights of the economy, heavy industry, mining and transport, were in the state's hands and thereby the social structure had been fundamentally altered. The next move was to establish a Marxist–Leninist state. East Germany was the only country in the socialist bloc where a new state had to be created. In all others, communists could work within the existing frontiers; no one questioned that Hungary or Bulgaria was a state. Hence the German Democratic Republic was artificial and if its legitimacy was questioned within its own boundaries, it was treated as an illegitimate offspring of Soviet great power ambitions outside. The only approximate parallel is Korea but there the communists laid claim to the whole peninsula in the name of their state.

The clear evidence that a West German state was going to come into existence overcame any doubts the Soviets might have had about founding a separate state to build socialism in Germany. The Soviets would have preferred to reach agreement with the Allies on an all-German state and government. Two states on German soil was a setback to their hopes of a socialist Germany and was a decidedly second best solution. A divided Germany was bound to be a source of tension in Europe and if the GDR was to become a pole of attraction for West Germans it would have to be economically successful, something which would take years to achieve. Concomitantly if West Germany should take off economically it would become very attractive to GDR citizens. The chief Soviet objective in Germany was to prevent the whole nation slipping into the capitalist orbit. This would undermine its sphere of influence in Eastern and Southeastern Europe. The Soviet Union was actively interested in fusing the two German states during Stalin's last year of life but such was the mutual mistrust that no agreement could be reached.

The elections to the Third German People's Congress took place on 15—16 May 1949 and voters were asked if they were for or against the unity of Germany and a peace treaty. Appended was a single list of candidates representing all the bloc parties and the mass organisations. Voters were given a choice: yes or no. This clear manipulation of the vote managed nevertheless to secure 66.1 per cent of the votes cast — but four million, or one third, voted no. The congress then elected from its members a German People's Council consisting of 330 persons: 96 of these belonged to the SED; 46 to the CDU; 46 to the LDPD; 17 to the NDPD; and 15 to the DBD. The others came from the mass organisations or were non-party. Since those representing the mass organisations (FDGB and FDJ, for example) belonged overwhelmingly to the SED, that party had a clear majority.

The primary task of this People's Council was to establish the German Democratic Republic. The details had to be agreed in Moscow before the proclamation was made, so during the second half of September 1949 Wilhelm Pieck, Otto Grotewohl, Walter Ulbricht and Fred Oelssner repaired there to discuss the steps that it was necessary to take to 'found a German democratic republic' (*Geschichte der SED* 1978: 218).

The People's Council met in Berlin on 7 October 1949, called the German Democratic Republic into being and transformed itself into a provisional Volkskammer or parliament. Johannes Dieckmann (LDPD) was elected chairman. The vice-chairmen were Hugo Hickmann (CDU), Jonny Löhr (NDPD) and Hermann Matern (SED). On 10 October the five Landtage elected a 34-man provisional Länderkammer (17 were members of the SED, 9 of the LDPD, 7 of the CDU and one belonged to the Association for Mutual Peasant Aid). Reinhold Lobedanz (CDU) was elected chairman. The next day the provisional Volkskammer and Länderkammer met in joint session and elected Wilhelm Pieck president of the GDR. On 12 October the provisional Volkskammer confirmed Otto Grotewohl as Prime Minister and his government in office. Walter Ulbricht (SED), Otto Nuschke (CDU) and Hermann Kastner (LDPD) became deputy Prime Ministers. Eight of the eighteen ministers belonged to the SED, four to the CDU, three to the LDPD, one to the NDPD, one to the DBD and one, Hans Reingruber, Minister of Transport, did not belong to any party. The key ministers, those of the interior (Karl Steinhoff), education (Paul Wandel), planning (Heinrich Rau), justice (Max Fechner), industry (Fritz Selbmann), intra-German and foreign trade (Georg Handke), were all in SED hands and the state secretaries in the ministries of foreign affairs, interior, planning, finance, agriculture and labour were also SED members. Hence the SED occupied a dominant position in the first GDR government.

The arrival of the GDR meant the departure of SMAD. It was dissolved and replaced by a Soviet High Commission whose tasks were to supervise the implementation of the Potsdam Agreement and all the Four Power directives which affected Germany. General Vasily Chuikov stayed on and headed the new organisation.

The Prime Minister, in presenting his government's programme, declared that due to the liberating role of the Soviet Army it had proved possible to establish a new German government. This fact 'obliges us in the future to be more active than before in fostering friendship with the Soviet Union. Peace and friendship with the Soviet Union are the prerequisites for the development, indeed for the very national existence of the German people and state' (*DDR* 1975: 158). The GDR government would do all it could to promote the 'unity of Germany'. The government would be bound by the constitution which had already been adopted by the People's Council in March 1949 and passed by the provisional Volkskammer on 7 October 1949. Since the GDR was still traversing its bourgeois democratic stage of development it reflected this. Germany was declared to be an 'indivisible democratic republic; it is based on the Länder' (art. 1). The Volkskammer – the parliament – was declared to be the supreme organ in the state (art. 50) and the members were to be elected by general, equal, direct and secret ballot and according to proportional representation. Freedom of speech, the press, assembly and religion were guaranteed as was the privacy of mail. Trade unions were afforded the right to call their members out on strike (art.14). Incitement against those belonging to other religions, races and nations was outlawed as was war-mongering (art. 6). However this article also banned incitement to boycott 'democratic organisations and institutions . . . and all other activities which are directed against equality for all'. These were declared to be crimes punishable at law. This article was interpreted by the authorities in such a way as to permit legal action against any form of opposition in the GDR.

On 7 December 1949 the Volkskammer passed the law on the establishment of a GDR Supreme Court and a Department of Public Prosecutions. The LDPD faction had submitted its own proposals about a Supreme Court which were closely related to the traditions of the Weimar Republic. The Volkskammer's legal commission then agreed on a draft which was very close to the government's text. The Supreme Court was to try all cases of 'great significance' and was also to act as an appeal court. The Department of Public Prosecutions was independent but bore a striking resemblance to the Soviet Prokuratura. The Supreme Court played an important role in establishing the authority of the state and was involved in many show trials as well as giving authoritative interpretations of the constitution, especially article 6. One estimate puts the number of those sentenced in 1950 alone for their political activities and views at over 78 000, including 15 death sentences (Weber 1980: 54).

The Ministry of the Interior was expanded and a Central Commission for State Control, responsible to the Prime Minister, was set up. The People's Police (Volkspolizei or Vopos), as the 'centrally directed armed organ' of the new state, grew in numbers and importance. The police were backed up by the People's Police in Barracks (Kasernierte Volkspolizei) who numbered about 50 000 in 1950 — they were to become the nucleus of the future National People's Army.

The establishment of the Ministry of State Security (the Stasi), by a Volkskammer decree on 8 February 1950, completed the process by which the SED gave tangible expression to its dominance in the state. The chief administration for the protection of the economy, a part of the Ministry of the Interior, became the nucleus of the new ministry. A striking fact about the decree was that it did not list the duties of the Stasi. In reality the Stasi escaped parliamentary control and was accountable to the Politburo of the SED. The Stasi was to detect all opposition to the state internally and to conduct espionage abroad. It also conducted the investigations in all cases where the accused was thought to have' acted in a manner 'hostile to the state'. The Stasi also looked after the security of leading officials and protected key installations. In order to do this it had its own guards regiment. However it fared badly during the uprising of 17 June 1953 and suffered a minor eclipse thereafter.

An example of a law which was politically motivated was the law on the protection of peace, passed by the Volkskammer on 15 December 1950. It had been proposed by the Second congress of the World Peace Council, a body which was under communist influence. The preamble set the tone. It was stated that the American, British and French governments were planning another world war which threatened to involve Germans in murderous fractricidal strife. The punishment for those found guilty of harming good international relations — this meant in practice speaking up for the West or criticising the East — was imprisonment or death (Fricke 1979: 198). Since the GDR claimed the right to speak for all Germans — the

West German leaders were held to be hell bent on fomenting another world war — any opposition to those in the GDR who were for peace was regarded as a criminal offence. This decree in effect made it illegal to criticise any utterance or policy of any GDR official on matters concerning war, peace and international relations. The GDR courts could define these terms as elasticially as they liked.

In the state apparatus the goal of the SED was to have its members in all key positions. Already in 1948 44 per cent of all state functionaries belonged to the SED, the CDU and the LDPD each claimed 5 per cent and the NDPD and the DBD each had 0.3 per cent. The rest did not belong to any party (Weber 1980: 54). As time passed the dominance of SED members became more visible. An official GDR source puts it was plainly: 'Just as in government, experienced SED members who had proved themselves in the class struggle occupied the leading positions in the state and economic apparatus' (*DDR* 1975: 160). The first loyalty of these functionaries was however not to the governmental or the state apparatus but to the party. The party 'stressed that all SED members in state organs were subject to party discipline and were duty bound to carry out party decrees. SED party organisations were set up in the new state organs' (*Geschichte der SED* 1978: 226). In this way the new governmental and state apparatuses were moulded along the lines of the SED apparatus.

The German People's Council on 15 February 1950 set up the National Front for a democratic Germany. The committee of the People's Council at Land, Kreis, city and village level were renamed committees of the National Front. The National Front claimed to be an all-German body and embraced all parties and organisations in the GDR. Hence it was much more comprehensive than the Democratic Bloc which included the political parties and the mass organisations. The SED faced considerable hostility from members of the CDU and LDPD who feared that the Front would swallow up their parties and from some of its own members who, at first, refused to collaborate with factory owners, pastors and ex-members of Nazi organisations. (Ex-Nazis and Wehrmacht officers who had not committed any crimes had their civil rights restored in 1950.) The National Front can also be seen as a kind of pre-parliament. Elections to the Volkskammer (it remained provisional until these elections) and the Landtage were held on 15 October 1950. It was the National Front which put up the single list of candidates. Prospective candidates had to speak at a selection meeting (dominated by workers) and only if accepted were they allowed to stand. Many of the CDU and LDPD leaders opposed this procedure since they regarded it as an SED tactic to eliminate all candidates who were at all critical of the leading role of the communists. In Saxony alone about 400 prospective candidates were rejected. The final electoratal list contained none of the 32 LDPD members and only 4 of the 20 CDU members of the Thuringian Landtag. Only 9 of the 100 members elected to the Brandenburg Landtag in 1946 faced the voters in 1950 and in the Mecklenburg Landtag only 10 of the 90 sitting members were readopted. In Saxony—Anhalt not a single member of the Landtag was permitted to stand for reelection (Weber 1980: 55).

At the elections 98.5 per cent of the voters came to the polls and 99.7 per cent of the votes cast were for the programme and the single list of candidates of the National Front. Contrary to the constitution some of the voters made their choice in public. The increasing stream of refugees from the GDR testified to the fact that these elections did not very accurately reflect the political loyalty of the population.

In the Volkskammer the SED had 100 seats, the CDU and the LDPD 60 each, the NDPD and the DBD 30 each, the FDGB 40, the FDJ 20, the Kulturbund 20, the DFD 15, the association of those persecuted by the Nazi regime 15, the Association for Mutual Peasant Aid 5 and the cooperatives 5. In addition East Berlin had 66 representatives who could speak but not vote due to the city being under Four Power control. According to social origin, 269 deputies were from the working class and 28 from the peasantry. Despite the fact that only a quarter of the voting members belonged to the SED the party had a majority of the seats since most of the members representing the mass organisations were communists. The new government clearly revealed the advance of the SED. Otto Grotewohl was Prime Minister and eleven ministers were SED members, four were from the CDU, two each from the LDPD and the NDPD and one was a member of the DBD. The Minister of Transport, Hans Reingruber, who was non-party, remained in office. Two of the deputy Prime Ministers were from the SED, Heinrich

Rau and Walter Ulbricht; the others being Lothar Bolz (NDPD), Hans Loch (LDPD) and Otto Nuschke (CDU).

The Land governments were completely reshuffled. The Prime Minister and Minister of the Interior in all five Länder belonged to the SED and the majority of the ministers were communists. The same happened at the Kreis and village level but even more significant was the ongoing centralisation of decision-making which reduced the importance of lower organs. The results meant that the 'process of the establishment of worker and peasant power — the dictatorship of the proletariat in the state — was more or less complete' (*DDR* 1975: 191).

The SED and the Non-socialist Parties

The third SED congress which met in East Berlin between 20–24 July 1950 was the first party congress after the founding of the GDR. The presence of leading representatives of fraternal parties from east and west underlined the direction the SED wished to take. The key man in the SED, Walter Ulbricht, was at last given recognition and was elected Secretary General (Stalin's party title between 1922 and 1934). The congress adopted the ambitious first Five Year Plan (1951–5). Compared to the other people's democracies the GDR was a year late in agreeing on its first Five Year Plan. Ulbricht stated that the early completion of the Two Year Plan (1949–50) had made this possible but the main reasons were the peculiar German situation and the heavy reparations burden. The 1946 goals of the SED were declared out of date and a new party programme was promised. (It was only adopted in 1963.) A new party statute, corresponding to the needs of a party of a new type, was also passed. Its core was democratic centralism which came to mean that decision-making was systematically concentrated at the centre, turning the concept into bureaucratic centralism. The statute underlined the fact that the SED was the 'party of the working class, its conscious and organised avant garde and the highest form of its class organisation'. Party members were to imbibe the 'teachings of V. I. Lenin', to learn from the 'experience of the CPSU and the history of the German labour movement' and to implement them in their own work. In reality it was Stalin's thought which took precedence. The Party leadership was very self-confident and saw Marxism—Leninism as truth. Since the laws of historical development could be perceived, their conscious application would usher in the new society. Hence studying the works of Stalin and the CPSU — held to be eminently successful in the Soviet Union — was a fundamental necessity. Their application would guarantee the SED's success in the GDR. It was a myth, however, to claim that the CPSU ruled the Soviet Union. Stalin was above the party, indeed he was above the government and the security police, the other two pillars of his power, as well. However, the party could claim a monopoly of political power and Stalin's role in the USSR encouraged the emergence of like figures in the ruling communist parties.

The congress elected Wilhelm Pieck and Otto Grotewohl joint chairmen of the CC. The members of the new Politburo were: Franz Dahlem, Friedrich Ebert, Otto Grotewohl, Hermann Matern, Fred Oelssner, Wilhelm Pieck, Henrich Rau, Walter Ulbricht and Wilhelm Zaisser. Anton Ackermann, Rudolf Herrnstadt, Erich Honecker, Hans Jendretzky, Erich Mückenberger and Elli Schmidt became candidate members. Only Ebert, Grotewohl and Mückenberger had previously belonged to the SPD; all the others were ex-KPD.

Despite the progress achieved, the leadership was far from satisfied by the speed of the transformation of the SED into a party reminiscent of the CPSU. Intensive ideological schooling was *de rigueur* for party members and during the first party study year — 1950—1 — almost a million members gathered in about 60 000 circles to learn about Marxism—Leninism, the history of the CPSU and the German labour movement. The congress also launched the first purge: 150 700 people, 7.3 per cent of the membership, were expelled. Over 30 000 trusted functionaries and members conducted interviews to root out members of the 'Tito clique', 'agents' of the Eastern Bureau of the SPD and 'anti-soviet' and 'anti-communist' elements. A special target of the investigators were former social democrats but many pre-1933 members of the KPD were also excluded. The first purge of the SED leadership took place at the same time. Paul Merker, a member of the Politburo, was not re-elected at the third congress and in August 1950 the CC expelled him, Leo Bauer, Bruno Goldhammer, Willi Kreikemeyer, Lex Ende, Maria Weiterer and several other long-standing communists from the party. They had all been in exile during the national socialist era but none had spent that time in the Soviet Union. They were all 'connected' with Noel H. Field, an American 'agent' who had played a key role in a show trial of leading Hungarian communists in Budapest. Most of those expelled from the SED were arrested — Kreikemeyer died in prison — but no major GDR show trial was staged. (It later transpired that the accusations made against Field were groundless.) The aim of the purge was to intimidate potential critics of SED policy and this meant that any misgivings about Stalinism or the dominance of the Soviet model would be summarily dealt with.

A party delegation, led by Paul Verner, travelled to Moscow in April 1950 to study how the 'party of Lenin exercised its leading role in the Soviet Union'. The tangible result of this visit was an SED decree of 3 June 1950 on 'measures to improve the organisational work of the party'. It was a blanket application of CPSU procedures.

In the GDR, as in other people's democracies such as Poland, the adoption of Soviet practices did not lead to the elimination of all non-socialist parties. These parties served three main functions: they gave the impression that pluralistic democracy existed and this masked the fact that the SED was claiming a monopoly of political power; they provided other channels of contact with West Germany — indeed the CDU and the LDPD had sister parties there; and they could be used as transmission belts for the promotion of SED policies in other strata of the population (Weber 1980: 58).

The claim that the SED alone had the right to transform society according to its desired goals was bound to be resented, especially by many members of the CDU and the LDPD. The SED applied three measures to overcome this opposition. The NDPD, DBD and the mass organisations were gradually drawn into more active participation in the Democratic Bloc; the formation of the National Front, ostensibly an all-German organisation, widened participation of pro-SED elements ever further; and then those politicians who would not bend to the prevailing wind could be simply removed. The Democratic Bloc, on the instigation of the SED, pressed for closer cooperation at all levels and this isolated those CDU and LDPD politicians and members who challenged the leadership role of the SED. In February 1950 the Central Committee of the

Bloc demanded the 'removal of those who disregarded joint decisions'. Mass demonstrations were initiated by the SED against these politicians and the recalcitrants were removed from their positions in the Land governments. The leadership of the CDU passed to Otto Nuschke, Georg Dertinger and Gerald Götting and that of the LDPD to Johannes Dieckmann, Manfred Gerlach and Hans Loch — all men who accepted the *Gleichschaltung* of the non-socialist parties.

The National Front took over from the Democratic Bloc as the main forum for political debate and at its first congress in August 1950 1000 of the 2500 delegates were from West Germany. The Front thus became the most important instrument for the transmission of SED views in West Germany and the main goal of the Front was declared to be the unity of Germany. The Front's analysis of the international situation was similar to that of the Cominform, which in turn was Soviet dominated. The Americans were held to be the heirs of national socialism and to be actively engaged in preparing for the third world war. Those former Nazis who sided with the SED were now welcomed with open arms and the SED proposed an amnesty for all except those serving sentences. Parallel with this went bitter SED attacks on former Nazis who held leading positions in West Germany (Weber 1980: 60).

Besides the party and governmental apparatuses the SED relied on the mass organisations to play a vital role in the transformation of society. The FDGB counted 4.7 million members in 1950 and at its third congress in August—September 1950 it acknowledged the 'leading role of the revolutionary party of the working class (SED)', the primacy of Marxism—Leninism and advocated 'closer ties with the Soviet Union' (*DDR* 1975: 182).

The youth movement, the FDJ, had over 3 million members, 1.6 million of whom belonged to the Young Pioneers in 1950. At its third parliament in June 1949 the FDJ had declared the goals of the SED to be its own and its fourth parliament in May 1952 adopted a constitution which recognised the leading role of the SED, the teachings of Marx, Engels, Lenin and Stalin as its guide and democratic centralism as its principle of organisation.

The DFD had about one million members; it brought together women of all political persuasions and outlooks. The society for German—Soviet friendship contained 1.9 million members and the Kulturbund had 200 000 in 1950.

The SED provided all the functionaries in the FDGB and the FDJ and the overwhelming majority in the other mass organisations, thus allowing these bodies to be dominated by communists. The SED first secretaries at Land, Bezirk, Kreis and village level were responsible for all activities in their area of responsibility and hence they supervised the development of the mass organisations. The secretaries of the mass organisations at each level were, in turn, responsible to the SED first secretary and were required to file systematic reports on the work of their organisation.

The Construction of Socialism

Even before the launching of the first Five Year Plan on 1 January 1951 the GDR was linked to the economies of the Soviet bloc. The Council for Mutual Economic Aid (Comecon) had been set up in Moscow in January 1949 and the GDR joined this socialist economic grouping in September 1950. Besides this many bilateral trade and scientific—technical agreements had been signed. The Cold War had led to a revolution in GDR trade flows. Whereas in 1947 only 8 per cent of trade was with the socialist bloc and 75 per cent with West Germany, in 1948 the former rose to 44 per cent and the latter dropped to 43 per cent. This trend continued and in 1951 76 per cent of GDR trade was with the socialist bloc and only 7 per cent with West Germany.

Industrial expansion was at the heart of the plan. By 1955 it was to be 90 per cent above the level of 1950 or double the output of 1936. Living standards were to 'exceed significantly the pre-war level' by the end of the plan. This was to apply especially to food and consumer goods. National income was to grow by 60 per cent and labour productivity in industry by 72 per cent. Agriculture was to raise output by 25 per cent. The favoured sectors were metallurgy — to grow by 153.6 per cent — and heavy machine-building — to expand by 114.8 per cent. Machine-building was to receive 15 per cent of investment, light industry 6.4 per cent but energy and raw materials 58 per cent. One of the goals of the plan was to expand the socialist sector

of the economy at the expense of the private entrepreneurs
and farmers. In 1950 26.5 per cent of industrial output, one-
third of field crops and one-quarter of marketed animal
products still came from the private sector.

The plan was ill suited to GDR conditions. It followed Soviet
experience and as such was based on abundant raw materials,
a large internal market and the dominance of the energy, steel,
iron, machine-building and chemical industries. Little attention
was paid to economies of scale since it was held advisable to
produce as wide a range of industrial products as possible. International specialisation was not encouraged since expansion of
foreign trade was not afforded priority. Given the poor resource
base of the GDR — only lignite was abundant, although potas-
sium, uranium and copper ore were also available — the country
was ill-equipped to expand heavy industry. Only 1.3 per cent of
pig iron, 7 per cent of steel production and 2 per cent of coal
output in pre-war Germany originated in the territory which
formed the GDR.

Nevertheless outstanding achievements were recorded in pig
iron production, which rose from 337 000 tonnes in 1950 to
1 517 000 tonnes in 1955 (7.5 times the 1936 output); in steel,
where over the same period the expansion was from 999 000
tonnes to 2 508 000 tonnes (twice the 1936 production); and
in chemicals. However these and other successes were achieved
at the expense of light industry and living standards. Officially
it was claimed that the industrial plan was fulfilled, and that
for national income overfulfilled, but the rise in living standards
was very modest and this increased the flow of refugees to
West Germany. Butter, meat and sugar were still rationed and
most consumer goods were in short supply. The average monthly
wage of a worker in socialist industry rose from 311 marks in
1950 to 432 marks in 1955 but those in post and communications in 1955 only received 345 marks. (Unless otherwise
specified, 'marks' refers to GDR marks.)

Between 1948 and 1951 the management of the socialist
sector of industry — the nationalised enterprises (VEB) —
was in the hands of about 75 associations of nationalised concerns (VVB). The VEB in each branch of industry were grouped
together in a VVB. About half the VEB were responsible directly
to the central ministries and the other half to the Land government. In 1952 the VVB were transformed into administrations

of nationalised enterprises (also known as VVB) and thereby lost their managerial functions. The new VVB had merely supervisory duties and the VEB became independent economic entities but still received detailed instructions derived from the national plan. About 70 per cent of the most important VEB were placed directly under the relevant technical ministry. About half of the VEB which were administered at the Land level were linked to the centrally-directed VEB. The other VEB, together with small local nationalised concerns, were classified as 'locally managed industry'.

The socialist sector also included the SAG. They accounted for 13 per cent of workers and 32 per cent of industrial output in 1951. These Soviet enterprises produced all the country's uranium, iron ore, oxygen and synthetic rubber and 80 per cent of watches, motorcycles and petrol. In 1952 a further 66 SAG were handed back to the GDR and this increased the number of VEB.

The building of socialism entailed the collectivisation of the countryside. If a holding was too small to be economically viable a cooperative held out the prospect of a better life, but the more prosperous the farmer was, the less likely he was to see collectivisation as an advance. Some modest successes were recorded by the state. In 1953 there were 4700 LPG or collective farms containing 128 500 members. They farmed 11.6 per cent of the agricultural land of the GDR.

The anomaly of an economy heading for socialism in a society which was still pre-socialist was resolved at the second party conference of the SED in July 1952 when Ulbricht proclaimed that socialism was to be constructed in the GDR. This was possible as socialist and semi-socialist enterprises were to produce 80.7 per cent of the industrial output of 1952. One of the consequences of this decision was to put even greater emphasis on labour productivity — work norms rose accordingly. A far-reaching administrative reform was enacted on 23 July 1952 when the five Länder were replaced by fourteen Bezirks. The number of Kreise rose from 132 to 217. This meant the end of the federalism which had been practised since 1945. Any independence from the centre was now eliminated as the Land governments and their traditions were swept away. The Bezirk-stag replaced the Landtag and the Bezirk council the Land government. Sixty to 90 members sat in the Bezirkstag and carried out their functions in 'permanent commissions', such as those on the budget, culture and youth. The Bezirk council performed legislative and executive functions. The chief Bezirk official was the secretary of the council who was always an SED member. Democratic centralism, the guiding principle of the party, was now extended to the state apparatus.

A field of major importance in the construction of socialism was education. A Politburo decree of 29 July 1952 on raising the level of instruction and improving the quality of party work in schools set new goals. Pupils were to develop into all-round personalities, able and willing to build socialism. School and production work were to go hand in hand and all activities were to be based on the principles of Marxism—Leninism.

The party was even more dissatisfied with the situation in the universities. The CC decided in January 1951 to embark on fundamental changes and a state secretariat for university education was set up to undertake this task. The following month it decreed ten months' study per year; Marxism—Leninism became an obligatory subject, thus making it easier for the SED to transmit its ideology, and everyone had to study Russian. SED and FDJ organisations in the universities conducted a vigorous campaign against 'hostile and obsolete views, especially against bourgeois cosmopolitanism and nationalism' (*DDR* 1975: 217).

The number of institutions of higher education more than doubled. During 1953 and 1954, 25 new universities or institutes were founded including three medical schools, six pedagogical institutes and a Hochschule or university for electrical engineering, finance, and heavy machine-building. Student numbers rose from 28 000 in 1951 to 57 500 in 1954 and many others took correspondence courses. Those of worker or peasant origin accounted for 53 per cent of the student population in 1954 (Weber 1980: 65).

The 'socialist cultural revolution' got under way in 1951 when the centralisation of all cultural activities began. A bureau for literature and publishing was established and a state commission for cultural affairs was founded. In 1952 a state film committee and a state broadcasting committee came into being. The activities of these organisations were outlined in a CC decree of 17 March 1951: 'The struggle against formalism in art and literature, for a progressive German culture.' The guiding principle was to be socialist realism. The main task of a socialist culture was to portray the battle to increase production in such a way as to inspire everyone to achieve even more. Many artists and writers were not committed to socialism so there was certain to be conflict between them and the SED. Others such as Alexander Abusch spoke of the 'writer and the plan' as early as 1948. Johannes R. Becher, who early on was keen to turn the artist into an activist, gradually came to the conclusion that a new, socialist culture could not be decreed from above and sarcastically referred to the attempt as a 'hyperformalistic experiment'. Walter Ulbricht expected the 'new man and woman, the activist, the hero of socialist labour' to emerge from the printed page. Culture was seen by the party as a force of production which would help to raise labour productivity.

Whereas the early post-war years had seen art and literature accorded some latitude — reminiscent of the pre-1929 Soviet Union — the onset of the construction of socialism meant that the party claimed the right to define and direct culture — again rather like the early 1930s in the USSR. It meant that Western writers such as Proust, Joyce and Kafka who could not be fitted into the socialist realist school had to cede primacy to Soviet writers such as Sholokhov and Ostrovsky. The consequence was that many works were sharply criticised; for example Paul Dessau's music to Bertholt Brecht's libretto *Das Verhör des Lukullus*. Brecht rewrote the libretto to counteract criticism of his own work. An exhibition of work by Ernst Barlach (died 1938) had to be quickly withdrawn after the SED had declared that his sculptures were 'mournful, depressing and pessimistic' in nature. This labelled it decadent, formalistic and anti-socialist (Emmerich 1981: 80). A film based on Arnold Zweig's *Das Beil von Wandsbek* was withdrawn after its première. In 1951 it was commonplace for books to be pulped, plays to be banned and paintings to be defaced — all in the name of socialist realism.

Paradoxically socialist realism also included great emphasis on the German classics. One of the accusations made against formalism was that it led to a loss of contact with the national culture and thereby to the disappearance of national consciousness. In so doing it promoted 'cosmopolitanism which directly supported the war policy of American imperialism'. Realistic art and culture was to spring from contact with the great classical masters such as Goethe, Schiller, Heine and Tolstoy. Geothe, after his jubilee in 1949, served as the 'model of a perpetually working man'. His Faust was the prototype of a man who was 'continually proving himself socially'. The party sought out those authors whose enthusiasm for work would prove contagious. In music Beethoven filled this role. Along with this concern for the giants of the past went the desire to restore some of the great buildings. The Staatsoper in Berlin and the Zwinger museum in Dresden, for example, were rebuilt.

The transition from the anti-fascist democratic to the socialist revolution involved less tolerance towards non-Marxist views. Christians, for example, had strong views on morality and ethics. The SED wished to propagate the view that morality was a class concept: anything which furthered the building of socialism was moral and anything which hindered it was immoral. The census of 1950 registered 14.8 million Protestants and 1.2 million Roman Catholics in 'a population of 18.4 million; hence it was primarily the Protestant churches which the party selected as its religious target. Contrary to the provisions of the 1949 constitution, religious instruction was banned in schools, and the church tax became a private matter. All church activities outside church premises were made very difficult or prevented altogether. Pressure was put on young Christians in schools to abandon their faith and to leave the *Junge Gemeinde*, the Christian youth movement. Some 300 high school pupils who refused were expelled. The severest pressure was exerted in 1953 when some pastors and lay members were arrested. The Protestant churches protested against the intolerance of the authorities and strongly rejected the accusations made against believers that they constituted a terrorist group who were trying to sabotage German reunification.

The Soviet Union and the German Question

The longer the Berlin Blockade lasted, the keener the Western Allies became to ensure that Soviet influence was confined to Eastern and South-eastern Europe. When the Foreign Ministers of the Four Powers convened in Paris in May 1949 — it was their sixth conference — the Basic Law (Grundgesetz) of the Federal Republic had been published. Preventing the establishment of a separate West German state had been one of the objectives of the blockade. Dean Acheson (United States), Robert Schuman (France) and Andrei Vyshinsky (Soviet Union) came fresh to the conference table; only Ernest Bevin (Great Britain) had any previous experience. Vyshinsky proposed that the Control Council be revitalised and that a peace treaty be negotiated but he also suggested that an all-German Council of State be formed. The Soviet Foreign Minister was not proposing the formation of a central German government, merely a central German authority. Elections, based on a single list of candidates, had just taken place to the German People's Congress but they were not seen as democratic by the West. Acheson suggested that free elections be called in all four zones to a German national assembly. The occupying powers could then negotiate a peace treaty with this body's representatives. Since the SED would not permit free elections (in the sense of each party fielding its own candidates) there was little likelihood of the Soviets agreeing to them since there was the risk that their influence in the GDR could decline precipitously. The conference broke up on 20 June 1949 without reaching agreement on any substantive matters. The Soviet Union came to accept that the Federal Republic would come into being but duly protested in a note on 1 October 1949 which Andrei Gromyko, deputy Foreign Minister, handed to the three Western ambassadors in Moscow. A more dangerous development, from the Soviet point of view, was the emergence of NATO which obliged the United States to maintain a physical presence in Western Europe. Washington, in turn, looked for closer cooperation among the non-socialist states so that they might become stronger economically and militarily. On the other hand, the concept that the capitalist and the socialist worlds could live together without resorting to war originated at this time.

The Federal government saw itself as provisional until the Basic Law could be extended to all parts of Germany. Strictly speaking it lacked the sovereignty to engage in foreign policy but the first Chancellor, Konrad Adenauer, saw reconciliation with France and the integration of the FRG in the Western world as ways of increasing the sovereignty of his country and the security of Western Europe. West Germany had become a member of the Organisation for European Economic Co-operation (OEEC) in 1948 and in late 1949 the first FRG—

US treaty, concerned with Marshall Plan commitments, was signed. In June 1950, in Paris, France, Italy, West Germany, Belgium, the Netherlands and Luxembourg, began discussions about a European Coal and Steel Community — the Schuman Plan — and the agreement became operational on 25 July 1952. The FRG became a member of the Council of Europe on 20 July 1950. The security of West Germany only became a major concern after the outbreak of the Korean War in June 1950. Parallels were drawn between Korea and Germany and the People's Police in Barracks were viewed with some apprehension since the FRG possessed no equivalent force. One solution proposed by Winston Churchill, for example, in August 1950 was to form a European army. Adenauer, later the same month, spoke of a voluntary force of 150 000 men along the lines of the People's Police and was willing, if a West European army was formed, to provide a German contingent. He promised this in the teeth of the opposition of the SPD. On 19 December 1950 the three Western Foreign Ministers accepted a German contribution to the defence of Western Europe. Negotiations which led to the formation of the European Defence Community took place throughout 1951. The fact that the FRG was playing a role in the defence of Western Europe meant that its relationship with the occupying powers changed. As a result, on 9 July 1951, France, Great Britain and the United States declared the state of war with Germany to be at an end and on 14 September 1951 the Western Foreign Ministers proposed that 'democratic Germany' be admitted as an equal member to a continental European community. The Bonn Treaty which ended occupation and returned most of German's sovereignty was signed on 26 May 1952. The FRG became an equal partner in a community of free states. The next day the Treaty of Paris which established the European Defence Community was signed (Vogelsang 1973: 134).

How were the Soviets to react to these developments? Adenauer placed the incorporation of the FRG in the Western alliance ahead of reunification and always reacted negatively to approaches from the East. However not everyone in his party was convinced of the wisdom of this policy: Kurt Schumacher, the SPD leader, was strongly opposed to it, especially to German rearmament. The SED and the Soviets, provided they acted skilfully, thus had considerable room for manoeuvre. On 30

November 1950 Otto Grotewohl proposed in a letter to Konrad Adenauer the formation of an 'all-German constituent council'. He called for 'Germans around the same table' and a referendum against remilitarisation and for peace in the whole of Germany struck a responsive chord. Adenauer turned the proposal down on 15 January 1951 and blamed the division of Germany on the GDR government. The Western Powers and the parties in the Bundestag, including the SPD, regarded free elections as the prerequisite for talks and as the prelude to the establishment of a democratic all-German state. Grotewohl responded in September 1951 by proposing 'all-German discussions', mainly about holding elections in all four zones. Again the Bundestag demanded free elections to a constituent national assembly. In preparation for this the Bundestag invited a UN commission to supervise the preparations for such elections but in early 1952 the GDR refused it entry. After the GDR government had again proposed a peace treaty on 13 February 1952 the USSR intervened and forwarded the first of two notes to the Western Powers on 10 March 1952. This note contained the most far-reaching concessions by the Soviet Union since Potsdam. It proposed the withdrawal of occupation troops one year after a peace treaty was signed, at the latest; parties and organisations to be free to develop; no alliance against Second World War opponents; the frontiers agreed at Potsdam; no economic and trade restrictions; own national armed forces; and to be recommended for UN membership. The timing of the note was significant. It arrived shortly before the signing of the European Defence Community treaty. Adenauer dismissed the note as an attempt to prevent Western unity but Jakob Kaiser (CDU) — the former leader of the sister party in the Soviet zone — wanted the offer to be carefully looked into. The concession that there should be free elections, however, was not mentioned but Grotewohl remedied the situation on 14 March 1952 when the Volkskammer passed a law on all-German elections. Since the Soviet note was only addressed to the Western Powers they responded on 25 March 1952 reiterating the fact that free elections were the only basis for an all-German government. They also stated that the UN commission should ensure that such elections were free. The Soviets proposed in their second note on 9 April 1952 that discussions about the proposed elections take place but refused to allow the UN commission into the GDR. The West did not make any concessions and gradually the exchanges petered out after the Soviets had reverted to their previous policy of requiring a peace treaty before elections could be held. A key figure in framing the Western reply of 25 March was the West German Chancellor. He stated that he had participated as an equal in the drafting of the reply and added: 'I was able to have several passages removed and to add a few of my own' (Vogelsang 1973: 139—40). Thus Adenauer was one of the voices which ensured that the Western Powers did not take up the Soviet offer seriously. Soviet policy was not resolute enough. If they regarded German rearmament and the integration of the FRG in the Western Alliance as a serious threat to their interests they should have been more flexible instead of backing away after making the initial concessions. They appear to have been unclear about their objective and this may have been related to Stalin's failing health in 1952. A unified Germany would surely not have posed a military threat to the Soviet Union but a well-armed FRG might. Neither East nor West was willing to put the other to the test by negotiating seriously.

The Uprising of 17 June 1953

The centralisation of planning which gathered pace during the first Five Year Plan inevitably reduced the negotiating rights of workers at the plant level. The wage fund, for instance, was fixed by the centre as part of its plan and workers were not consulted about its size. In the collective agreements between the enterprise management and the labour force, wages and workers' rights received little attention while much attention was devoted to the obligations and duties involved in fulfilling the plan. 'Technically-based norms' were introduced everywhere. The enterprise trade union organisations and the national FDGB began to concentrate on plan fulfilment and to neglect the rights of their members which they should have been defending. Along Soviet lines, trade unions were ceasing to represent the interests of their members and were becoming 'transmission belts' between the working class and the party. A hierarchy was emerging: the party and state avant garde was claiming the right to express the general interest. This in turn meant that it defined what was socialist. This pattern had first emerged in the Soviet Union where working-class traditions had had little time to develop before the rapid industrialisation of the 1930s. The GDR, on the other hand, had well-embedded traditions.

By early 1953 the preference given to heavy industry during the construction of socialism had perceptibly depressed living standards. Consumer goods were in permanently short supply and food was short. The situation was exacerbated by the policy of the party and the government which aimed at undermining the vitality of the private sector. Heavy taxes were levied on private farmers — the state spoke of 'large arrears' of taxes being due. The consequences were dramatic: the number of large farms in 1953 declined by 16 000, or one-third. The collective sector was in no position to take over the running of so many farms at short notice. The official statistics concede that the food industry only met 90 per cent of its planned targets in the first quarter of 1953. The persecution of the churches was stepped up and 'bourgeois' specialists throughout the economy were labelled 'saboteurs' — again reminiscent of the Soviet Union during the early 1930s — and private factory owners were harassed and their number declined by 2000 in 1953 alone. In November 1952 almost all self-employed persons and their families were deprived of their ration cards.

Stalin's death on 5 March 1953 placed the SED leadership in a quandary. There was no way of knowing what the new Soviet leadership's policy towards Germany would be. When Ulbricht was in Moscow for the funeral he asked for economic assistance but was informed by the new leaders of the CPSU, Malenkov, Molotov and Beria, that no help would be forthcoming. The New Course, soon to be adopted in the Soviet Union, should be followed in the GDR. This implied that the building of socialism would be slowed down. Ulbricht was reluctant to follow and this allowed Wilhelm Zaisser, the Minister of National Security — his superior was none other than Beria — and Rudolf Herrnstadt, the editor-in-chief of the party's organ, *Neues Deutschland*, to press for a more flexible policy whose ultimate goal was the removal of Ulbricht. The decree on the New Course was adopted by the Politburo of the SED on 9 June 1953 and the Council of Ministers followed suit two days later. (This incidentally underlined the fact that the party took precedence over the government.) The party and government admitted having made 'a string of mistakes in the past' (*Neues Deutschland* 11 June 1953) and consequently cancelled many of the severe measures taken against private industry and agriculture and the intelligentsia. Price rises were rescinded. Promises were made to increase the availability of consumer goods, to improve conditions for artisans and farmers and to improve intra-German relations. Only one section of the population did not benefit from this volte-face in policy — the working class. The Council of Ministers decree of 28 May 1953 calling for the raising of norms in industry and construction by at least 10 per cent by 30 June 1953 was still valid. It was defended in the trade union newspaper *Die Tribüne* on 16 June 1953 and this provided the spark which led to the uprising. The strike by construction workers on the Stalinallee in East Berlin was mirrored in 271 other cities and towns throughout the land and 300 000 workers were involved, according to Otto Grotewohl. Only a small proportion of the GDR's labour force took part in the demonstrations; Grotewohl's figures represented 5.5 per cent of the workforce. It was the industrial and construction workers, actively supported by the youth of the GDR, who were responsible for the events of 17 June. The peasants, the middle classes and the intelligentsia played little or no part in the proceedings. The industries most affected were construction, mining, machine-building, chemical and iron ore extraction — the very core of the heavy industry which had been given such preference and which was regarded as the *sine qua non* of socialism. The demonstrations had almost run their course when the Soviet Army declared a state of emergency and together with the People's Police in Barracks cleared the streets. However on 18 June, demonstrations continued in Halle—Merseburg and Magdeburg and the SED lost control. Originally economic demands dominated but then political slogans appeared. One of them was for free elections. No precise information about the number of casualties is available. Estimates range from 25 to over 300 dead. The uprising revealed how wide the gulf between the party and the working class had become and how little substance there was to the claim that the GDR was a workers' state and the SED a workers' party. The SED needed the physical presence of the Soviet Army to keep its power and this demonstrated how tenuous its legitimacy was. The uprising also produced the first serious differences of opinion within the ruling Politburo as the party attempted to increase its legitimacy by making concessions to the population.

3 Completing the Building of Socialism, 1953–61

The New Course imposed by the Soviet leadership and the June 1953 uprising forced the SED to become more flexible in its battle to build socialism. This led to heated discussions in the Politburo about which policies should be adopted. These differences continued until 1958 when Walter Ulbricht emerged as the victor. He was concerned to follow Soviet practices closely and this led to many changes of course. His opponents favoured policies more in tune with the peculiar needs of the GDR. Put another way, Ulbricht wished to retain the Stalinist schema as far as the official ideology was concerned whereas his opponents wanted to reduce the gap between Stalinist ideology and reality. Both German states received their sovereignty in 1955 but both were dependent on their respective Great Power. Khrushchev's attack on Stalin at the twentieth congress of the CPSU in February 1956 was unwelcome to many ears in the Soviet Union and in the socialist bloc. The events in Poland and Hungary stopped de-Stalinisation for a time and made it easier for Ulbricht, who was a reluctant de-Staliniser, to prevent any serious discussion of the SED's past mistakes. In the GDR the process was restricted to denouncing the cult of the personality and the arbitrary use of force. The decentralisation of the economy in the Soviet Union in 1957 led to the GDR following suit in 1958 and collectivisation was completed in 1960. This latter *démarche* – which was necessary to complete the victory of socialism in the GDR – led to considerable resentment and swelled the stream of refugees. Intellectuals were also disciplined and this caused many to leave the GDR. The regime's troubles were exacerbated by the open frontier in Berlin and eventually Khrushchev acceded to Ulbricht's request that it be closed. The building of the Berlin Wall on 12–13

August 1961 was a gamble but it paid off as the West only replied with verbal protests. Thereupon the GDR population had to come to terms with their own state and this transformed the situation of the SED.

The New Course

Immediately after the uprising of 17 June the SED announced that the New Course would continue and announced wage increases. The minimum pension also went up. The party placed the blame for the uprising on Bonn's shoulders but conceded that it had also made mistakes. 'If large numbers of workers do not understand the party's position, then it is the party which is at fault, not the workers' (*Dokumente* IV 1954: 441).

Hand in hand with these concessions went the desire of the SED leadership to settle scores with those involved in the uprising. At least 18 death sentences were carried out. GDR courts were responsible for some and the Soviets for the rest. In Magdeburg, for instance, two men were tried by a Soviet military tribunal and shot on 18 June 1953. An estimated 1383 were sent to prison (Fricke 1979: 288, 290). The most prominent person arrested was Max Fechner, the Minister of Justice, and a former social democrat. He had defended the right of workers to strike and had protested against the numerous arrests. He was dismissed and the CC accused him on 25 June 1953 of 'activities hostile to the state'. His orders had led to the release of 'American agents and ringleaders' of the uprising and he bore responsibility for 'numerous illegalities and unjustifiably high sentences on some workers'. Fechner had been out of step with the SED for some time on justice. His views belonged to the bourgeois-democratic stage of development whereas the SED by 1953 was building socialism. Vociferous voices were raised for a more 'party-minded' and 'class' approach to be adopted towards justice. One of the proponents of this line, Hilde Benjamin, succeeded Fechner as Minister of Justice.

The fifteenth plenum of the CC on 24–26 July 1953 passed a resolution entitled 'The New Course and the Tasks of the Party'. The goal was to raise living standards: to achieve this during the second half of 1953 the output of consumer goods was to be 30 per cent above that of the first half of the year.

The expansion of heavy industry in 1953 was to drop from 13 to 5.5—6 per cent. This involved the switching of investment to light industry. The increase of the means of production — capital goods — was to be 5 per cent and consumer goods 10 per cent in 1954 and 1955 (*Dokumente* IV 1954: 458). Despite acknowledging its mistakes, the party still held to the view that its 'general line was and is correct'. To strengthen its position in the factories, armed detachments (Kampfgruppen) were formed.

In October 1953 the government reduced the price of food products but the price of bread, butter and sugar remained the same. These price cuts had been made possible by a Soviet decision to deliver an extra 231 million roubles of food and raw materials on credit during 1953. Even better news was the fact that the USSR waived all reparation payments from 1 January 1954 — a saving of US$ 2537 million, it was claimed — and the cost of Soviet troops stationed in the GDR was not to exceed 5 per cent of the GDR state budget. The last 33 SAG, including the Leuna Works, the Buna chemical works and the Thale foundry, were handed back to the GDR without payment of the estimated value of DM2700 million. The DM430 million still due on the 66 SAG transferred to GDR ownership in 1952 was cancelled (*Dokumente DDR* 1957: 39).

Although the New Course improved living standards, the numbers of those leaving for West Berlin and the FRG increased. Whereas in 1952 182 000 left, this increased to 331 000 in 1953, dropping to 184 000 in 1954 but rising again to 253 000 in 1955. These figures only refer to those registered as refugees: others settled in West Germany without going through the reception camps. One estimate puts the number of these 'illegal immigrants' in 1954 at 51 000 (*DDR-Handbuch* 1975: 401). The situation was even more serious for the GDR since the overwhelming majority of these refugees were of working age and younger. These workers, farmers and members of the intelligentsia were precisely those the GDR needed to build socialism.

The uprising strengthened Ulbricht's position as leader since had he gone it would have created a dangerous precedent. He was fortunate in that he had been able to strip his strongest opponent, Franz Dahlem, of all his offices in May 1953. Herrnstadt and Zaisser lost their positions at the CC plenum in July

1953 and at athe seventeenth plenum of the CC in January 1954 both were expelled from the party. Anton Ackermann, Hans Jendretzky and Elli Schmidt were dropped from the CC and Franz Dahlem was barred from holding party office. Ulbricht's position was enhanced by the arrest of Lavrenty Beria in June 1953. (He was executed in December 1953.) This removed Zaisser's 'protector' in Moscow.

Changes at the top soon affected those lower down in the apparatus. By 1954, of the members of the 15 SED Bezirk committees elected in 1952, 62.2 per cent had been removed and 71 per cent of the first and second secretaries of the SED Kreis committees, in office in June 1953; 53.6 per cent of the other members of the committees were relieved of their duties (Schultz 1956: 259). At the primary party level over half the functionaries were changed. The Politburo came to the alarming conclusion in September 1953 that a great many of the 1.2 million members had 'no political education or party resolve'. There were also many passive members. Social-democratic views were common and there were 'openly hostile and foreign elements who opposed the execution of party policy' in the party's ranks (*Dokumente* IV 1954: 509). This state of affairs had come about because the SED leadership had gone over to the construction of socialism — and, moreover, to a socialism with a Soviet face — which did not find favour with many party members. Former social democrats, for instance, did not accept that politics should invade all aspects of life while some communists would have preferred a socialism with a German face or one which was born of German economic and political parents. The SED leadership wanted every member to become an activist, someone who would convince others that the leadership's views and goals were in the best interests of the GDR.

Many rank and file members were expelled or demoted to candidate status in the course of the interviews conducted by trusted party functionaries between July and October 1953. Resignations and expulsions changed the composition of the party. Whereas in May 1947 47.9 per cent of the membership had been workers and in April 1950 41.3 per cent, this dropped to 39.1 per cent in April 1954 (Schultz 1956: 244).

There were wholesale changes in the trade union organisation (FDGB). In the elections held after the June uprising 71.4 per cent of the functionaries were ousted. The purge in the FDJ was relatively mild, most changes coming at the Kreis level. However Erich Honecker, the first secretary, was embarrassed by the number of his members who had sided with the demonstrating workers on 17 June. The main casualty was Heinz Lippmann, Honecker's deputy, who evaded arrest by moving to West Germany.

Ulbricht was in a confident mood at the fourth congress of the SED in March—April 1954. He announced that the New Course was at an end and that the immediate task was to recommence the building of the foundations of socialism. In other words the emphasis placed on consumer goods' production was at an end.

The renewed march towards socialism led the party to come out in favour of collectivisation. Some private farmers had returned to the GDR after the harsh legislation of 1952—3 had been modified but for them it was a false dawn. Only about one farmer in six belonged to a collective farm (LPG) in 1954. There was no pressing economic need to collectivise, hence it was a political decision. However this decision had little impact until 1959 when full collectivisation was ordained.

A new party statute, the third, was adopted by the congress. Karl Schirdewan spoke about the changes which, in effect, brought the SED organisationally closer to the CPSU. It was stated in the preamble: 'The party is the leading force in all organisations of the working class and employees, in social and state organisations and is guiding successfully the building of socialism.' Entry to the SED was made more difficult; the minimum age of newcomers was raised from 16 to 18 years. The length of the candidate stage reflected the preferred social composition of the party. Blue-collar workers of five years' standing remained at the candidate stage for six months; other workers and collective farmers, for one year; and white-collar workers and members of the intelligentsia for two years. The state conferred on the party organisations in the economy the right to inspect the activities of plant management, thus increasing political control in the enterprise.

In line with developments in the CPSU, the SED called for a collective leadership and Friedrich Ebert, Otto Grotewohl, Hermann Matern, Fred Oelssner, Wilhelm Pieck, Heinrich Rau, Karl Schirdewan, Willi Stoph and Walter Ulbricht were elected to the Politburo with Erich Honecker, Bruno Leuschner, Erich

Mückenberger, Alfred Neumann and Herbert Warnke as candidate members. (This meant in effect that they could attend Politburo meetings, take part in the discussion but could not vote.) Walter Ulbricht was reelected First Secretary, the same title as his counterpart in the CPSU, Nikita Khrushchev.

Ulbricht never took to the New Course but it found favour with many SED functionaries and the population at large. Such were the hopes raised that an article by Professor Otto Reinhold, a leading party political economist, was published in *Neues Deutschland* on 2 June 1954. He conceded that many state and economic functionaries thought that heavy industry, within the framework of the New Course, was to play a subordinate role. He held this view to be fundamentally false and pointed out that the production of capital goods, as before, was to grow faster than gross output. However many of the top economic functionaries were in favour of the New Course and were searching for more sophisticated planning mechanisms to cope with the GDR's formidable economic problems. The debate continued until 1958 when Ulbricht and his supporters were able to force through their solution. The New Course was officially abandoned at the twenty-fourth plenum of the CC on 1 June 1955 when Ulbricht claimed: 'It was never our intention to choose such a false course and we shall never choose it.'

There were elections to the Volkskammer and the Bezirkstage again in October 1954. Of the 98.4 per cent of the voters who went to the polls, 99.5 per cent voted for the single list of candidates of the National Front. Secret voting was rare. Over 70 per cent of the candidates were from the working class and peasantry. Since the previous elections the LDPD, for instance, had acknowledged the leading role of the SED; the CDU had declared that it was in favour of the 'new social order' since it offered the best opportunity to live a Christian life; the DBD was active among the farmers and the NDPD concentrated on winning over the self-employed and the intelligentsia to socialism. This trend was reflected in the fact that of the 400 sitting members only 180 were reelected to the Volkskammer. Six members of the LDPD faction in the Volkskammer had been arrested during the life of the parliament; 17 other non-socialist members had moved to West Germany and 44 others had been forced to give up their seats (Weber 1980: 83).

The composition of the new government revealed the dominant position of the SED. Of the 28 ministers, 20 belonged to the SED and 9 of the 13 members of the presidium of the Council of Ministers were communists. Five of the ministers were also members of the Politburo and eleven others were members of the CC. This fusion of top party and government posts demonstrated how successful the SED had been in its desire to dominate government administration. The SED's control was enhanced by having a cell in every government and state organisation. This cell was expected to lead and guide activities so that party decisions could be put into effect at all levels throughout the country. The SED was firmly in command of the instruments of control in the GDR. Its main task now became the raising of the efficiency of the various apparatuses which turned out to be much more complex than the conquest of power.

The GDR and Sovereignty

With Stalin dead, Winston Churchill, the British Prime Minister, moved quickly to propose a conference 'at the highest level' of the Great Powers. He had in mind one along the lines of the wartime conferences when he spelled out his suggestion to the House of Commons on 11 May 1953. However nothing came of the proposal in 1953; it was 1955 before the summit meeting took place. The Soviet Union's self-confidence was boosted by the explosion of its own hydrogen bomb on 12 August 1953. Eventually it was agreed to convene a conference at foreign minister level to discuss Germany, Austria, Korea and Indochina. The Berlin Conference — the seventh meeting of the Foreign Ministers of France, Great Britain, the Soviet Union and the United States — took place between 25 January and 18 February 1954. Anthony Eden, the British Foreign Secretary, on Germany, proposed free elections, a national assembly, a constitution, adoption of the constitution and the formation of a government and the conclusion of a peace treaty, in that order. Molotov countered by suggesting that a peace treaty should come first and the formation of an all-German government last of all — he agreed with the order proposed for the other measures. It became clear that the Soviets wanted the GDR to enter a united Germany replete with all its political, economic and social achievements. The Soviet Foreign Minister also made it clear that his country would not countenance an all-German state entering into an alliance with the West. The only positive result which emerged from the conference was an agreement to convene a conference in Geneva on Indochina to which the People's Republic of China would be invited.

On 25 March 1954 the Soviet government published a statement on its relations with the GDR. 'The GDR will have the freedom, on its own initiative, to plan its own internal and external relations, including the question of relations with West Germany' (*Dokumente DDR* 1954: 304). The High Commissioner no longer had the task of supervising the activities of the state organs in the GDR; he was henceforth to confine himself to implementing the Four Power agreements as they affected the GDR. Thus the total dependence of the GDR on the USSR was brought to an end.

The Soviet Union did not abandon its hopes of preventing the rearming of West Germany and on 6 October 1954 Molotov, in a speech in East Berlin, spoke in favour of free elections in the whole of Germany and expressed willingness to accept the plan proposed by Anthony Eden in Berlin, provided that the rearmament of West Germany was terminated.

West Germany became a sovereign state when the Paris treaties were ratified on 5 May 1955. The High Commissions then ended their activities. On 7 May the FRG became a member of the West European Union and on 9 May it took part in a NATO council meeting as a full member for the first time. The response of the East was to conclude a military agreement which brought into existence the Warsaw Pact on 14 May 1955. The GDR was one of the founder members but as yet it had no army. It was proposed that the People's Police in Barracks be expanded into an army but Ulbricht and Colonel General Willi Stoph, the newly appointed Defence Minister, met considerable Polish and Czechoslovak opposition. Eventually an upper limit was agreed and it was accepted that the GDR forces be under the direct contol of the Warsaw Pact commander-in-chief. A political consultative committee was formed and the command structure was made subordinate to it. Stoph became one of the seven deputies of the Soviet commander-in-chief when the GDR Army entered the pact on 27–28 January 1956. The National People's Army (NVA) had come into existence on 18 January 1956 along with a Ministry of National Defence. Since the NVA is commanded by the Warsaw Pact commander-in-chief the NVA has no general staff. It is worth noting that in the treaty with the USSR on the stationing of troops, signed on 12 March 1957, the GDR came off worse than the other Warsaw Pact members. The GDR had no jurisdiction over Soviet troops moving into or out of the GDR. (This applied also to Czechoslovakia after the Warsaw Pact intervention of August 1968.)

The Geneva summit meeting of the four Great Powers took place between 18 and 23 July 1955, and in his concluding remarks, on 23 July, Marshal Bulganin, Malenkov's successor as Prime Minister, maintained that since the end of the war two Germanies had emerged, the GDR and the FRG, each with its own economic and social structure. A mechanical unification of Germany could under no circumstances be entertained any longer. Despite this Bulganin agreed with the directive, also dated 23 July, to the foreign ministers to attempt a solution to the German problem through unification of the country and free elections. Khrushchev blandly informed President Eisenhower that the German people had just not had enough time to appreciate the great advantages of socialism. All that would change in a few years. On his way home Khrushchev stopped off in East Berlin and announced on 26 July: 'The German question cannot be solved at the expense of the GDR . . . Can GDR workers countenance the loss of all their political and social achievements and all their democratic reforms? We are convinced that GDR workers will never agree to such an eventuality' (*Neues Deutschland* 27 July 1955). Thereby the Soviet Union changed her stance on Germany. She now adopted the concept of two German states and thus ended hopes that free elections would lead to a united Germany. After a conference in Moscow the GDR and the USSR entered into diplomatic relations on 20 September 1955 and thereby the GDR became a sovereign state. As a member of the socialist bloc, of course, she acknowledged the leading role of the Soviet Union. The USSR also retained control over Allied traffic to and from Berlin and the Four Power Agreements on Berlin still applied.

Hence the provisional nature of the Soviet zone of Germany and the GDR lasted ten years. In 1955 it was on a par with other members of the socialist bloc and was a member of Comecon and the Warsaw Pact. The USSR was the undisputed leader of the bloc and this restricted each socialist country's room for manoeuvre. Although the SED exercised power in the GDR its authority or legitimacy was not very high. Probably a majority of the population was not in favour of the direction in which the SED was heading and this meant that the role of the instruments of oppression — the NVA, the civil and security police and the border troops — increased. The stream of refugees showed no sign of drying up and this revealed that the SED was not winning the battle for the hearts and minds of the young and skilled. Unless it did so it could not create a viable state.

Social Change

By 1955 all the key sectors of the economy were in the hands of the state. In that year nationalised concerns accounted for 85.3 per cent of gross industrial production leaving only 14.7 per cent for the private sector. There were still about 13 000 private concerns but these were all small, employing in all about half a million workers. In the construction industry the state sector accounted for 53 per cent of output. All sources of energy had been nationalised and in raw materials and metallurgy about 90 per cent of employees and output came from state concerns. The private sector was strongest in the light and food industries where three concerns in four were still private. However the state sector embraced two-thirds of workers and 70 per cent of the output (Weber 1980: 85). Wholesale trade was almost totally in the hands of the state, as was 68 per cent of retail trade.

Plumbers, electricians and other artisans were mainly self-employed in 1955 but in agriculture the socialist sector was growing slowly. In 1955 it accounted for 27 per cent of global agricultural production; the LPG farmed 18.6 per cent of the agricultural land, the state 4.4 per cent and other state concerns another 4.4 per cent (*DDR* 1975: 286).

The first Five Year Plan ended in 1955 and in several sectors it was fulfilled. However it was conceded that it had not been possible 'in the short space of five years to overcome the general disproportions of the GDR economy'. Labour productivity rose by 54 per cent instead of the planned 60 per cent. Living standards rose but in comparison with the FRG, the GDR cut a poor figure.

By 1955 the GDR had only travelled some of the way towards becoming a Soviet-style state. Politically it resembled the USSR except that a multi-party system still existed, although the instruments of control were firmly in the hands of the SED. In the Soviet Union there were three forms of ownership: state, cooperative and private. In the GDR, too, these three existed but the structure was different. In the Soviet Union the whole of agriculture was in the state or cooperative sector whereas in the GDR the private sector was still dominant. All Soviet industry was state controlled but the private sector still produced much of the food products and consumer goods in the GDR. The dominance of private artisans was again unknown in the USSR. The GDR had always been a highly developed state; indeed a higher percentage of its labour force, 40 per cent, was employed in industry in 1945 than in the Soviet Union. As the economy grew so did the labour force: in 1949 there were 7 million employed and the number rose to 8.2 million in 1955.

The social structure also changed. In 1950 there were 4 million workers, 1.7 million employees, 1.1 million self-employed and another million family members who helped in the family farm or business. In 1955, however, there were 6.5 million workers and employees (78 per cent of those employed), about one million private farmers, 300 000 private artisans, 150 000 private shop owners, 190 000 collective farmers (LPG) and 35 000 in the free professions (doctors and lawyers, for example). The self-employed had dropped to 900 000 and the number of those who helped in the family business or farm was down to 650 000 (Weber 1980: 86). The corollary of this was that an increasing proportion of the gainfully employed were employed by the state — in industry, agriculture and administration — and it came to just over 68 per cent in 1955.

The social transformation in the GDR was so abrupt that 1 443 000 citizens left between 1949 and 1955. This is the officially reported figure but perhaps another 10 per cent moved to the FRG without registering. Then there were those who returned to the GDR after discovering that life in the West was not to their taste. About 10 per cent of refugees returned but many of them later left the GDR. Since over half the refugees were under the age of 25 the battle to win people over to socialism was going to be long and hard.

A social structure similar to that of the Soviet Union: two classes — the working class and the collective farmers — and a stratum — the intelligentsia — was gradually taking shape in the GDR. A ruling stratum was forming consisting of leading officials in the party, state and the economy with party officials playing the key role. Besides the functionaries at the centre there were those at the Bezirk, Kreis and village level. In 1955, according to the statistical yearbook, there were 110 000 employees and 30 000 workers engaged in political, social and economic organisations and 317 000 civil servants overall. Industrial and agricultural management in the state sector enjoyed considerable material privileges. Others who belonged to the new elite were officers in the army, police and security forces and lawyers. All in all this new 'upper crust' of functionaries may have amounted to about half a million (Weber 1980: 87). If their families are included they made up about 10 per cent of the population. These men and women gradually separated themselves from the rest of the population both in status and privilege. Those recruited to this stratum were predominantly from working-class and farming families — 60.5 per cent of top functionaries in the central state apparatus were of working-class origin in 1955 — whereas in the Soviet Union during the 1930s the new stratum was recruited mainly from the peasantry. Hence the GDR revealed itself to be a more developed economy but since the main criterion for recruitment was the same as in the USSR, namely reliability, the same problems arose. Evolving a more efficient bureaucracy soon became a major concern of the SED leadership.

The Impact of the Twentieth Party Congress on the GDR

The dethronement of Stalin at the twentieth congress of the CPSU in February 1956 was a landmark in communist affairs. Until then it had never been officially conceded that the CPSU could make mistakes. Its infallibility was shattered once and for all. It should be borne in mind that Khrushchev did not

attack Stalin's record before 1934; in other words the demono-
logisation of Trotsky, Zinoviev, Bukharin and the others had
been justified. Also Khrushchev's main complaint about the
'cult of the personality' concerned the depradations it had
wrought on loyal party members and officials, many of whom
had been executed or imprisoned unjustly. The sufferings of
the man and woman in the street were largely ignored by the
First Secretary. Since de-Stalinisation took place in the Soviet
Union, every socialist state was duty bound to follow. If it
proceeded in fits and starts in the Soviet Union it never
got under way in Albania, for example. Also the Chinese took
umbrage at the character assassination of Stalin, partly because they had not been consulted beforehand. In Poland and
Hungary it led to a change in leadership and in the latter country
a revolution.

Ulbricht knew about Khrushchev's anti-Stalin speech in
advance. The Soviet leader had sharply criticised his old men-
tor in a speech in Sofia in the summer of 1955 (Jänicke 1964:
72). Khrushchev, in early 1956, had also invited several East
European leaders, including Ulbricht, to an informal meeting
and had discussed the forthcoming congress with them. No hint
of what was to come however was given by *Neues Deutschland*
on 14 February 1956, the opening day of the congress. It spoke
of the target, set a decade before by Stalin, of overtaking the
per capita output of the capitalist world, being adopted by the
congress as the primary task. Then the message of greetings,
signed by Ulbricht, ended with the words: 'Long live the
invincible teachings of Marx, Engels, Lenin and Stalin.' However Ulbricht ended his speech to the congress with the words:
'Long live Marxism—Leninism.' After the congress it became
clear that Ulbricht wanted to minimise the impact of the
revelations on the SED. On 26 February 1956 *Neues Deutschland* attacked Trotsky, Bukharin and the other opponents of
Stalin for choosing a 'course which had led undeniably to
treason'. It was also in favour of avoiding 'any semblance of
a personality cult'. SED members were confused and dissatisfied. Then Ulbricht, on 4 March 1956, changed tack.
'Stalin cannot be regarded as one of the all-time greats of
Marxism—Leninism', he wrote in the party organ. He 'caused
the CPSU and the Soviet Union considerable damage when
he placed himself above the party and engaged in the cult of

the personality'. Shortly afterwards at a Bezirk conference of the East Berlin SED he criticised Stalin for committing 'serious errors in agriculture, unpreparedness in the face of Hitler's attack in June 1941, altering in his favour his own biography and for demonstrating towards the end of his life an increasing tendency for personal arbitrariness' (*Neues Deutschland* 18 March 1956).

The third SED conference which convened between 24 and 30 March 1956 avoided a debate on Stalin's errors by concentrating on economic affairs. The only member of the leadership to touch the sensitive knot of de-Stalinisation was Karl Schirdewan. 'We must revise our previous assessment of Stalin during the last fifteen years of his leadership. Mistakes and errors occurred which caused damage to the cause of socialism' (*Protokoll* 1956: 315). This implied that the Stalinist model of development was faulty and as such was a direct criticism of the planned economy as it had developed in the GDR. The writer Willi Bredel, who was also a member of the CC, conceded that the revelations about Stalin at the twentieth congress of the CPSU had led to many sharp exchanges inside the SED and with workers. He made it clear that some of the blame rested with his own generation.

> If our young comrades imbibed Stalin page by page and word for word is it their, indeed only their fault? Is it not above all the fault of the older generation, of our generation? The study of the party has been conducted uncritically for many years as comrade Ulbricht made clear. I think instead of ridiculing younger comrades for doing this we should engage in more self-criticism ourselves. (*Protokoll* 1956: 542)

Bredel's advice went unheeded by the party leadership. The ice of their own legitimacy was so thin that they rallied around Ulbricht. The main task of the conference was to adopt the second Five Yar Plan covering the years 1956 to 1960. Emphasis was again placed on heavy industry at the expense of light industry and consumer goods' production. Overall industrial growth was to be at least 55 per cent. This was to be achieved mainly by raising labour productivity by 50 per cent. This was seen as feasible if technical progress was fully utilised. In return real wages were to rise by 30 per cent, the seven-hour day was to become the norm and the 40-hour week, with no loss of pay, was to be introduced in selected sectors of industry. Since the goals set labour productivity over the plan period turned out to be too ambitious the other targets could not be achieved. The socialist sector was to be enlarged by the state taking a 50 per cent or even larger share in those private concerns regarded as economically significant. Whereas at the end of 1956 there were 144 semi-private concerns employing some 14 000 workers and employees, this had jumped to 4455 and 291 000 respectively in 1960. Their contribution to the industrial economy rose from 0.4 per cent in 1956 to 7.5 per cent in 1960. Correspondingly private concerns dropped from 12 278 employing 412 233 in 1956 (11.1 per cent of industrial output) to 6476 employing 174 000 in 1960 (3.8 per cent of industrial output). In 1955 the private sector produced 26.7 per cent of the output of the national economy but this was down to 10.1 per cent in 1960 (*Statistisches Jahrbuch* 1968: 37, 115).

The downgrading of Stalin did not mean that less attention would.be accorded Soviet practices. Indeed speakers at the third SED conference went out of their way to underline the close connection between the two countries. This went as far as following Khrushchev's fads, for example maize. Since the Americans fattened their stock mainly on maize, the Soviet leader decided that Soviet farmers should do the same. What was good for the Soviet Union was good for the GDR and so it was decided to pay maize particular attention. A learned handbook was to be published which would explain how to grow the crop. In his concluding speech Otto Grotewohl declared: 'The GDR is an integral part of the great camp of peace, democracy and socialism which is led by the Soviet Union. This irreversible state of affairs makes possible a beautiful and happy future for us' (*Protokoll* 1956: 1017).

Although economic questions dominated the conference, measures to stimulate democracy at the local level were also adopted. Local organs were to be given more rights and were to decide matters of importance to the locality. The Volkskammer debated the draft law in September 1956 and it was conceded that state organs had ridden roughshod over local representative institutions. In fact local assemblies had only met sporadically and it had been the Kreis or village councils which had taken the decisions. The draft law envisaged new assemblies at all levels with greater powers to control the activities of the councils which, after all, had been elected by the assemblies. In the discussions about the draft law citizens were encouraged to propose amendments and over 10 000 were handed in. The Law on the Local Organs of State Power was passed on 17 January 1957 and regulated the activities of the Bezirkstage, Kreistage, city, city borough and village assemblies. Members were to be elected by secret ballot. Each body was to elect its own council and to operate according to the principles of democratic centralism. Since the party apparatus took precedence at the local level these new institutions were not autonomous.

Socialist legality was accorded priority in the Soviet Union and this led to a review of sentences passed in the GDR. In June 1956 11 896 persons were pardoned and a further 10 000 were released by October 1956. Among those released were the former Minister of Justice, Max Fechner, the former state secretary in the Ministry of Trade and Supply, Paul Baender, Dr Karl Hamann (LDPD) and Dr Leo Herwegen (CDU) (Fricke 1979: 332–3).

Ulbricht was forced to give some grounds against his party opponents. He was able to prevent a review of the cases of Herrnstadt and Zaisser but the twenty-eighth plenum of the CC decided to rescind the judgement against Franz Dahlem and to rehabilitate him. The judgements against Anton Ackermann, Hans Jendretzky and Elli Schmidt were also rescinded by the party. The CC did not go as far in the case of Paul Merker. 'The Central Committee has ascertained, after investigating the case of Paul Merker, that the accusations made against him were largely of a political nature which did not warrant criminal proceedings' (*Neues Deutschland* 31 July 1956). Nevertheless Merker was not rehabilitated (nor indeed were others such as Kreikemeyer) nor did Dahlem or those cleared of anti-party behaviour receive their old posts back. Indeed none of these functionaries ever made a political comeback. Such was Ulbricht's influence that he was able to halt de-Stalinisation before it had time to undermine his own position. His attitude was summed up by a remark he made at the twenty-second congress of the CPSU in October 1961. 'We do not have Stalinism, hence there is no need for de-Stalinisation.'

Ulbricht Defeats his Critics

The First Secretary faced two groups of opponents who had well thought out views which posed a serious threat to his supremacy between 1956 and 1958: the intellectuals and the party economists. The working class, in contrast to 1953, remained relatively calm as living standards rose and workers' committees came into being. These committees, proposed at a CC plenum in November 1956, were a response to events in Poland and Hungary. They were to perform an advisory role but were only set up in 18 VEB. In early 1958 they were dissolved and their functions passed to the trade unions. Opposition in the party and the universities to the rough methods and the constant interference of the party bureaucrats in intellectual life was considerable, especially since the intelligentsia had been accorded substantial leeway in the early 1950s. Intellectuals in the party and the institutions of learning eagerly grasped the opportunity of venting their frustration and Ulbricht's hopes that the discussions could be kept 'scientific' were soon dashed. The main demands can be listed as follows: the right to free discussion without the fear that coercive methods would be employed; an end to the interference of the SED in academic life; the cleansing of Marxism of Stalinist falsifications; and the abolition of dialectical materialism as the dominant tool in scientific disciplines (Weber 1980: 90).

The leading figures in the intellectual opposition were the philosophers Wolfgang Harich and Ernst Bloch. Bloch had returned to the GDR from the United States in 1949 and had, at first, been treated magnanimously by the SED. His freedom of expression had been gradually restricted until he ceased lecturing at the University of Leipzig in 1957. In 1961 he moved to West Germany and forwarded a bitter letter of complaint to the chairman of the Academy of Sciences in East Berlin in which he maintained that after the building of the Berlin Wall there was no room in the GDR for 'independent thinkers'.

The gulf between the society which the teachings of Marx, Engels and Lenin was to bring into being (as defined by the SED) and the real state of affairs in the GDR aroused disquiet among many young Marxists. Ironically the SED was training an opposition within its own ranks. Brought up to believe that the highest goal of mankind is to construct a 'communist' society in which all exploitation, inequality and differences between individuals have been eliminated, young people could see that inequality was growing and that the party bureaucracy was detaching itself from the rest of the population. If the working class was the ruling class why could it not formulate its own goals with the party as arbiter? The difference between the world as the SED wished it to be and reality had led to a credibility gap developing between the party and the population. To many people the party was given to telling lies. This encouraged cynicism and careerism which, in turn, appalled many young people. They thought that the remedy was to return to Marx and to establish a socialist society according to his precepts. They did not want to return to capitalism which they regarded as obsolescent. Hence they wanted an end to Stalinism and the bureaucratic rule of the SED. In Czechoslovakia this became known as 'socialism with a human face' which accepted that the communist party had the right to rule. However the party's rule should be based on legitimacy and not on coercion. It should be added that this view of the party's role is fundamentally un-Leninist. Lenin always held that the party should lead the working class and never be led by it. In the GDR, as elsewhere, the blame for all the deficiencies of the party was heaped on Stalin and in so doing failed to see that Stalin built his power on a Leninist party base. For instance, the Harich group advocated freedom of thought and discussion, the rule of law, an end to the political police and the dominance of the SED apparatus over the membership. This involved a specific German road to socialism. It was also a direct threat to the SED leadership and it responded quickly since its power was not based on legitimacy but on primacy in the instruments of control and coercion. During 1957 Harich — Professor of Marxist Philosophy and editor-in-chief of the *Deutsche Zeitschrift für Philosophie* — and other leading intellectuals and 'revisionist' party officials were sentenced to long gaol terms.

On 11 December 1957 the Volkskammer passed a law which amended the criminal code and made it easier for the state to act against political opponents. Among the definitions of treason was the 'desire to incorporate a part or the whole of the GDR in another state'. Someone who passed 'information or research findings to another state or its representatives, to organisations or groups which conduct a struggle against worker and peasant power' was guilty of espionage for which the penalty was not less than three years in prison. This effectively meant that no GDR citizen could legally have contact with non-communist organisations or their members. Anti-state propaganda and incitement were defined and slandering the state was also a crime. A by-product of this was that political jokes could be taken seriously by the uniformed apparatus. Helping someone to flee the GDR became a crime. In serious cases terror, espionage, wrecking and sabotage carried the death penalty (*Gesetzblatt* 1957: 643 ff.).

The decisive factor in the struggle between Ulbricht and his economic opponents was the First Secretary's Soviet connections. After Poland and Hungary Khrushchev did not want any experiments — other than those initiated by himself, of course.

Among the academic economists who wanted to turn away from the Soviet-style planned economy to greater reliance on market forces, especially banking, were Professor Fritz Behrens, director of the Central State Administration of Statistics, Arne Benary, head of the Socialist Economy section, and Dr Günther Kohlmey, director of the Institute of Economic Sciences of the German Academy of Sciences, all of whom were influenced by Yugoslav self-management methods. Behrens stated: 'Economic management should be the marriage of a minimum of central institutions to a maximum of initiative and independence from below, all based on economic laws, especially the law of value.' Wages, in turn, were not to be related to the output of an enterprise but to its profitability. In agriculture the most notable advocate of market socialism was Kurt Vieweg, who wanted all farmers, private and cooperative alike, to operate on an equal footing.

The most powerful supporter of market-socialist views in the party and government was Fred Oelssner, a member of the Politburo and the party's leading ideologist, and Fritz Selbmann, a deputy Prime Minister. Others who wanted real de-Stalinisation were Karl Schirdewan, a member of the Politburo and CC secretary for cadres, who proposed that the 'policy of the international relaxation of tension should be accompanied by the relaxation of tension in our state organs', Gerhart Ziller, CC secretary for the economy and Ernst Wollweber, Minister of State Security. This group wanted to slow down the race towards socialism and to run the economy by using 'economic' criteria. This implied that politics should not impinge on economic decision-making.

The thirtieth plenum of the CC (30 January–1 February 1957) declared that the decision of the GDR to become a part of the 'socialist camp' was irreversible. The thirty-fifth plenum of the CC in February 1958 expelled Schirdewan for 'factional activities' and Wollweber from the CC and Oelssner was removed from the Politburo for 'repeated infractions of Politburo discipline and refusal to become part of the collective of the Politburo'. Ziller had committed suicide in December 1957. Behrens lost his post as chief statistician and the others were sacked. Vieweg left the GDR in 1957 when criticism became too pointed but returned in 1958. He was then arrested and sentenced to a term of imprisonment. Whereas much of the debate among the academic economists had been in the open, that between Ulbricht and his opponents had been conducted behind closed doors. Nevertheless all SED primary organisations received a letter attacking the 'opportunist policy of the factionalist group of Schirdewan, Wollweber and others'. No details of the opportunistic policy were appended.

Heinz Brandt has written that Schirdewan told him that he had had a talk with Khrushchev soon after the twentieth congress of the CPSU during which the Soviet party leader accepted him as Ulbricht's successor. Ulbricht, however, was saved by the difficulties which confronted Khrushchev after the Polish and Hungarian events, which had led to a change in leadership in both countries. Khrushshev was in no mood to countenance another leadership change and all the changes that would entail since he had to concentrate first and foremost on securing his own position. Ulbricht skilfully made use of the opportunity afforded him (Brandt 1977: 328).

Ulbricht also settled accounts with Paul Wandel, CC secretary for culture, who was dismissed for 'insufficient hardness in carrying out the cultural–political line of the SED leadership'. It fell to Kurt Hager to discipline the universities. There had been 'signs of revisionism' in the trade unions as well and about one-third of the full-time officials at the Bezirk level were removed.

The fifth congress of the SED which met between 10 and 16 July 1958 saw Ulbricht the master of the situation. Never before had he been so dominant in the party; by now all opposition had been banished. During his speech Ulbricht repeated his appeal to West Germany to enter into a confederation so that a peace-loving, democratic and independent united German state could be established. He had first proposed a confederation on 30 January 1957 with an all-German council being formed to prepare 'free, all-German elections'. During the discussions on the first Rapacki Plan for a nuclear-free zone in central Europe, the GDR Council of Ministers, on 26 July 1957, brought the matter up again but this time spoke of the all-German council only having 'consultative status'. On 2 August 1957 the USSR saw a confederation as only the 'first step' towards the ending of the division of Germany and on 20 January 1958 a Soviet note to the FRG government lent further support to the SED proposal. On 13 February 1958 Ulbricht made moves towards the reunification of Germany dependent on the FRG supporting the Rapacki Plan. At the fifth party congress Ulbricht hardened his position still further. Whereas previously the 'socialist achievements of the GDR' were to be protected during the period of fusion they were now to be 'permanently inviolable'. Previously the First Secretary had spoken of 'two sovereign German states' but now the GDR became the only 'legitimate, sovereign German state'. Ulbricht was all for political and economic competition between the 'socialist and the monopoly capitalist' systems. This led him to propose as the chief economic task of the GDR the overtaking and surpassing of the West German per capita consumption of food and important consumer goods by 1961. The reason for choosing 1961 was because Ulbricht maintained that the West German government and NATO intended to complete the arming of the Bundeswehr with atomic weapons by the end of 1961. Hence the 'forces of peace must attain their goal by the end of 1961, i.e. prove the superiority of our social order so as to win over the broad masses of West German workers, the West German trade unions and the West German intelligentsia to the cause of peace' (Ulbricht 1953 — 71: v 440). The goals set for the GDR population reveal Ulbricht's optimism but here he was mirroring Khrushchev's optimism. The latter had set Soviet farmers similar goals but in their case they had to surpass the Americans. Neither country attained its goal.

Ulbricht was able to seize the initiative in all-German affairs and to appear as a leader who wanted to reduce tension because of Bonn's refusal to negotiate with East Berlin, thereby conferring diplomatic recognition on the GDR, and to budge from the view that free elections were the first step on the road to German unification. This 'policy of strength,' with the wisdom of hindsight, was ill-advised since the GDR could resist Western pressure as long as Soviet willpower to defend it lasted. The FRG government and the West simply did not take advantage of the many opportunities offered. However it is possible that had Bonn started to negotiate seriously East Berlin would have erected further obstacles to progress. The GDR's goal may merely hve been to secure diplomatic recognition. Nevertheless the exercise should have been undertaken.

The fifth party congress passed many resolutions including the ten commandments of socialist morality. The aim was to reflect the new relations in the GDR, not only in production but in everyone's private life. The ten commandments were:

1. Thou shalt always defend the international solidarity of the working class and all employees as well as the permanent ties which unite all socialist countries.
2. Thou shalt love thy fatherland and always be ready to defend worker and peasant power with all thy strength and ability.
3. Thou shalt help to eliminate the exploitation of man by man.
4. Thou shalt perform good deeds for socialism since socialism produces a better life for all working people.
5. Thou shalt act in the spirit of mutual support and comradely cooperation during the construction of socialism, respect the collective and take its criticisms to heart.
6. Thou shalt protect and increase the property of the people.
7. Thou shalt always seek ways to improve thy performance, be thrifty and strengthen socialist labour discipline.
8. Thou shalt bring up thy children in the spirit of peace and socialism to become citizens who are well educated, strong in character and physically healthy.
9. Thou shalt live a clean and decent life and respect thy family.
10. Thou shalt demonstrate solidarity with all those people who are fighting for national liberation and defending their independence. (*Protokoll* 1959 I: 160–1).

The fifth party congress set the goal of completing the victory of socialism in the GDR, thereby bringing the transition period to an end. This implied that the socialist relations of production would have to permeate the whole economy and in so doing the private sector in agriculture and industry would have to be phased out. Along with this went the need to expand the economic base of socialism and to carry through a socialist cultural revolution. Optimism was in the air as the economy grew by 7.9 per cent in 1957 and industrial production expanded 11.3 per cent in 1958 and 12.6 per cent in 1959. In 1957 the 45-hour week was introduced throughout socialist industry. A currency reform was carried through on 13 October 1957. It was directed against 'currency speculators' in West Berlin and the FRG. It was ostensibly political in motivation but in reality it was economic due to the need to reduce the surplus purchasing power which then existed as a result of the shortage of consumer goods. Citizens could exchange one old mark for one new but had to produce their identity card. The reform effectively eliminated the cash overhang and most affected those who had amassed large sums of cash. In May 1958 rationing of butter, sugar and meat ended and this signalled the end of rationing. The two-tier pricing system whereby rationed goods were much cheaper came to an end. The new prices lay between the old rationed and free prices. However the subsidised prices for bread and potatoes still remained and the increase in the cost of living was to be met by higher wages. Not surprisingly the number of refugees in 1958 dropped — 204 092 compared to 261 622 in 1957 — and in 1959 the number dropped to the lowest level since 1949.

An international division of labour was arranged at a Comecon meeting in July 1957. The GDR was to concentrate on the mining of lignite, on mining and textile industry equipment, on building refrigerator wagons and presses up to 10 000 tonnes in weight.

The slowdown in the economic growth of the USSR led Khrushchev to launch the Seven Year Plan 1959—65. This obliged all the other socialist countries to follow suit and at a Comecon meeting in Moscow in May 1958 the GDR's plan was accepted. It placed particular emphasis on energy, chemicals, electrical engineering and machine-building. It envisaged labour productivity rising by 58 per cent or between 9 and 9.5 per cent annually. This plan revealed the significance of the GDR economy in Comecon – the second largest after the Soviet – and it also underlined the fact that the GDR was becoming more closely integrated into the socialist economic grouping.

When a major new political line is adopted in socialist countries it is necessary to alter the organisational structure of the state. This is to ensure success for the political leader who has launched the new initiative. When Khrushchev defeated the Anti-Party group in June 1957 in the Soviet Union – it meant the victory of the party over the state apparatus – administrative changes had to follow. These in turn were mirrored in the other socialist countries, including the GDR. One of Khrushchev's goals was rapidly to increase industrial and agricultural growth and to this end he decentralised the planning system. In the GDR, between the end of 1955 and April 1957, the economy was supervised by three commissions. Fritz Selbmann was responsible for industry and transport, Fred Oelssner for consumer goods' production and supply and Paul Scholz for agriculture. In April 1957 an economic council was established consisting of Bruno Leuschner, Fritz Selbmann, Heinrich Rau, Fred Oelssner, Paul Scholz and Willy Rumpf, all of whom were members of the presidium of the Council of Ministers. The battle over whether economic or political criteria should have priority in the economy had been won by Ulbricht and this led to the council being dissolved in 1958. Following the Soviet pattern it was decided to reform fundamentally the economic apparatus. In February 1958 eight industrial ministries were dissolved and their functions passed mainly to the State Planning Commission. About 70 Associations of Nationalised Enterprises (VVB) came into being but unlike the pre-1952 VVB the new variant was an administrative rather than an economic organ. At Kreis level, plan commissions were set up and at Bezirk level, economic councils were formed. They and the VVB were to ensure the proper functioning of the centrally managed enterprises and also to run local industry. The upgraded State Planning Commission was the central organ of the GDR Council of Ministers for planning the economy and supervising plan fulfilment. On the party side, the economic commission of the CC was replaced by an economic commission of the Politburo in early 1958. The head of this new commission was Erich Apel, a highly competent engineer and economist and its secretary was Günter Mittag, a very able technical administrator.

The main function of the non-socialist parties was to act as 'transmission belts' for SED decisions. After the fifth congress of the SED the other parties acknowledged the leading role of the SED in the GDR. Their task was to carry out successfully the tasks allocated to them by the SED. The LDPD, for instance, recommended their members to accept state participation in their enterprises and by October 1959 714 private owners had signed over part of their concern to the state. The DBD played an important role in the completion of collectivisation in 1960. By the end of 1959 over 22 000 members were working in collective farms. The CDU, LDPD and NDPD played their part in convincing private artisans that they should group together into cooperatives and private traders that they should work for the state on commission. The diminished role which the non-socialist parties were playing in national life was reflected in their memberships. Whereas in December 1947, the CDU had 218 000 members, this fell to about 70 000 in 1961. The LDPD had 183 000 members in 1948 and this dropped to about 70 000 in 1961. In the same year the NDPD and the DBD each had about 80 000 members.

If the significance of the non-socialist parties declined, that of the mass organisations rose. The youth movement, the FDJ, had the task of helping the GDR youth to 'work, learn and live' as socialists. The sixth parliament of the FDJ in May 1959 drew up the 'programme of the younger generation to secure the victory of socialism'. Youth was to become more involved in industrial and agricultural production and key aspects of 'socialist construction' were to become 'youth projects'. Building the Friendship oil pipe line and the airport at Berlin—Schönefeld were among them. The FDJ was also to play a more important role in leisure activities. Among its tasks was combating West German and other sources of bourgeois culture. It organised festivals of 'young talent', literary and art festivals and theatre performances — all for young people. The sixth parliament also elected Horst Schumann first secretary of the Central Council of the FDJ.

Sport received special attention for two main reasons. It promised to gain international prestige for the GDR and it provided the opportunity of giving young males some pre-military training. The Society for Sport and Technology (GST), a mass organisation, was formed in 1952 and its task was to train young men in sporting and technical skills and thereby to raise the defence capacity of the GDR. The German Gymnastics and Sports Federation (DTSB) was founded on 27–28 April 1957 as a successor to the German Sports Committee. All sports bodies are affiliated to it and it also has schools for training sportsmen and women, coaches and officials. It had over a million members in 1960.

As the GDR moved towards socialism so the role of the trade unions increased. The fifth congress of the FDGB in East Berlin in October 1959 summarised its activities under the heading: 'The tasks of trade unions during the struggle for the victory of socialism in the GDR and the securing of peace.' In practice this meant raising labour productivity by raising socialist conscious-ness and the technical and educational level of the workers. Trade unions were also to develop into 'schools of socialism'. At the congress it was stated that the movement had 6.1 million members.

Elections to the Volkskammer were held on 16 November 1958 under the slogan 'Plan, work and govern with us.' The single list of candidates received 99.8 per cent of the votes cast and left the impression that there was no opposition in the GDR. Some citizens wondered why an opposition party could not be founded. 'Opposition in the GDR could only be directed against the policy of our government . . . It would favour the promotion of fascists and militarists to positions of great power . . . and would favour the preparation of an atomic war' (*Neues Deutschland* 17 May 1957). Therefore from the SED's point of view it was quite simple: an opposition (which meant in effect opposition to the SED) would lead to an atomic war and the annihiliation of mankind; hence every sign of opposition in the GDR had to be dealt with harshly in order to avoid a nuclear holocaust.

Education

Educational reforms in the Soviet Union in 1958 promoted polytechnical education and permitted one-third of the curri-culum during the last four years of schools to be devoted to the theoretical and practical problems of industry and agriculture. The fifth congress of the SED regarded the introduction of polytechnical education as a central problem. In January 1959 the CC published its 'Theses on the Socialist Development of the School System in the GDR.' In order to achieve higher educational standards the eight-year Grundschule was to be replaced as the normal compulsory school by the 'general polytechnical ten-class higher school'. It was to have a single curriculum which was to be obligatory for all children by 1964. The aim was to eliminate the distinction between academic and vocational training and to start vocational training at a higher educational level than hitherto. Pupils enter at the age of six and in the last four forms have to spend one day a week in industry or agriculture. By calling the new establishments high schools (Oberschulen) the party was implying that they were stepping stones to the universities. Those going on to university spend a further two years at an expanded high school (Erweiterte Oberschule) and those going to technical college receive another two years of vocational training before entry. One reason for the reform was political. The head of the CC department of educational affairs conceded in 1958 that the party had made little headway in the existing Oberschulen which selected their pupils according to ability and hence were predominantly middle class. 'There are even whole schools where not a single teacher subscribes to *Neues Deutschland*' and where less than half the staff took the *Deutsche Lehrerzeitung*, the party sponsored teachers' newspaper (*Deutsche Lehrerzeitung* 13/1958). About two-thirds of the curriculum in the new polytechnical Oberschule was devoted to science and technical subjects. New subjects such as civics were also introduced. More staff had to be trained and between 1958 and 1962 some 62 000 new teachers began work. Of these, 21 000 took senior forms (*DDR* 1975: 350).

After creating the 'socialist school' it was necessary to transform the universities into socialist seats of learning and this was resolved at the third SED university conference which convened in February—March 1958. The aim was to effect the scientific—technical revolution in the universities and to produce highly qualified specialists who would be willing and able to build socialism. In 1958 there were 46 universities with 87 000 full- and part-time students, over double the number of 1951. In 1961 the student population had risen to 113 000 of whom 29 000 were female. As regards social origin, 50.3 per cent of the students were from the industrial working class, 19.4 per cent were employees (clerical workers, etc.), 5.3 per cent were from the peasantry, 15.4 per cent were from the intelligentsia, 6.2 per cent were from self-employed homes and 3.4 per cent were classified as 'others' (*Statistisches Jahrbuch* 1960–1: 141). Also in 1961 there were 142 000 students at technical colleges.

Culture

The New Course and the events of 17 June 1953 did not lead to any fundamental change in cultural policy. The SED did state that the 'possibility of free creative activity had to be guaranteed' and that party concepts should 'in no circumstances be imposed administratively' on artists. Nevertheless the party expected writers and artists to contribute to the building of socialism and the literature of the period 1948–56 can be called 'production literature'. It ran into the sand since it was lapidary, wooden, unconvincing and uninspiring. Writers came to regard the alternative to the officially imposed socialist realism as liberalisation, or in other words, more emphasis on the material they wished to write and publish. A concerted attack was launched on contemporary literature at the fourth Congress of Writers in January 1956. Impeccably socialist writers such as Eduard Claudius criticised the 'barren, petty-bourgeois' level and Stefan Heym the 'wooden primitiveness' of the literature of the day. The twentieth congress of the CPSU, which followed a month later, added impetus to the criticism and a thaw appeared to have set in. However the events in Poland and Hungary ended this phase and many of the views expressed were branded as revisionist. This affected especially György Lukács who had been a minister in the 'counter-revolutionary government' of Imre Nagy. He was condemned for his 'arrogant attitude' towards the 'young socialist literature' whose 'quite new historical quality' he had allegedly failed to recognise. This type of criticism became part and parcel of the 'second socialist stage of the cultural revolution' which was launched in 1957 and was to lead to Parteilichkeit, or party-mindedness, finally taking over in literature and art. Alexander Abusch, a leading SED functionary concerned with culture, conceded that the 'struggle between the two cultures', between the dominant bourgeois and the newly emerging proletarian, was a 'long way from being won'.

Attempts to bridge the gap between art and life and between production workers and artists had been made but no concerted campaign had been launched. The lignite miners of Nachterstedt made their plea in 1955. They wanted 'more books about the mighty construction of the GDR which was under way, about the activity and life of working people. Write and describe the working man as he is, as flesh and blood, the way he works, loves and struggles' (Emmerich 1981: 86). In 1957 Walter Ulbricht called on all artists to go out into the factories and on to the farms more often in order to feel 'at home' there and to link their lives and interests to those of the people. It was the fifth congress of the SED — no other congress has ever devoted such attention to culture — which called for the 'gulf between art and life and the alienation between the artist and the people' to be overcome. Ulbricht declared that since the working class was already 'master' in the state and the economy the time had come for it to 'storm the fortresses of culture and to take possession of them'. The educational reform which introduced poly-technical schooling for all was a parallel; it was designed to close the gulf between learning and production.

In the realm of literature the Bitterfeld conference which took place in April 1959 was decisive. About 150 professional writers and 33 amateur worker—writers took part and it was decided that writers should join factory brigades and learn all about working conditions at first hand. Miners were to seize 'their pens' and to document the everyday struggle for higher production. One worker summed up his feelings: 'The greatest contribution to our literary development is made by the worker himself when he becomes an author. Miners, reach for your pens, our socialist national culture needs you.' It proved quite difficult to get writers to exchange mental for physical work in the factories and lightning visits were common. On the other hand, factory writing blossomed and collectives began to write about their experiences and their needs. Brigades vied with one another to produce the most appealing diary of their everyday activities.

Another goal of the cultural revolution was to undermine the unity of German culture. A socialist German national culture was desired for the GDR to reflect the building of socialism there. The SED did not wish to make a complete break with the past but to join classical German culture to the new socialist culture. It wanted to eliminate the achievements and influence of the culture of the bourgeois stage of German development.

The only branch of culture in which the GDR made an impact internationally during this period was literature. Bruno Apitz's novel *Nackt unter Wölfen*, published in 1958, dealt with the travails of a young Jewish child who was smuggled out of Auschwitz to Buchenwald in a suitcase. The child was success-fully hidden from the camp guards, at considerable cost to those involved. While this was going on, an uprising by the prisoners was being planned. Communists played an important role in the leadership of the successful uprising, which took place before and during the American liberation of the con-centration camp. The title, 'Naked among Wolves', is symbolic; human beings are stronger than the fascist wolf. By 1965 the novel had sold over two million copies in 28 countries and had been translated into 25 languages. Dieter Noll's two-volume novel *Die Abenteur des Werner Holt* (1960–3) also aroused considerable interest. It is partly autobiographical and describes the horrors of war and the search for identity and fulfilment afterwards. On a different plane, Christa Wolf, who achieved recognition during the 1970s, published her *Moskauer Novelle*, which she saw as full of 'pious views' in her more self-critical later days, in 1961.

The SED took action against those writers and artists who were too outspoken in their criticisms: the writer Erich Loest was imprisoned in 1958. The conflict between the party and the cultural intelligentsia revealed that the vision of reality which the SED wished to project was totally different from that of many writers and artists.

The Decision to Build the Wall

Throughout 1958 the Soviet Union actively pursued the strengthening of its position in Germany and concomitant with this the international standing of the GDR. The successful flight of the first Sputnik in 1957 boosted Soviet morale and in

June 1957 Khrushchev consolidated his position by defeating the Anti-Party Group. He became Prime Minister in March 1958 at the expense of Marshal Bulganin but in reality he had been the decisive voice in shaping government policy since the summer of 1957. Khrushchev's new-found confidence that the world situation was improving daily from a Soviet point of view led him to unleash a Berlin crisis. A speech in Moscow on 10 November 1958 was followed by a note to the three Western Powers on 27 November 1958. The note was an ultimatum; Khrushchev wanted to end the Allied occupation of West Berlin and the Western rights in Berlin. The Soviet Union no longer spoke of a Berlin question but a West Berlin question — West Berlin should be transformed into a free city. The Allies could stay another six months but if an agreement was not reached within that time the 'Soviet Union would conclude an agreement with the GDR and put into effect the planned measures'. The Soviets hoped to force the Western Powers to recognise the GDR since the supervision of the routes to and from West Berlin were to pass into GDR hands. Although there were clear indications of what was afoot before November 1958 — especially from speeches by Ulbricht and Ebert — Western governments were caught off guard. An important factor was the serious illness of John Foster Dulles, the American Secretary of State. The Allies replied on 31 December 1958 and declared that they were willing to discuss the 'Berlin question in the wider context of talks on a solution to the German problem and European security as well'. The Soviet government replied on 10 January 1959 and proposed that the 28 nations which had been at war with Germany, the GDR and the FRG meet to discuss a German peace treaty. The two German states had to sign the treaty but as long as Germany was not united a 'free city of West Berlin' had to be set up and its existence guaranteed. The conference was to take place within two months in Warsaw or Prague. On 27 March 1959 the Soviet government made it clear that it would accept a meeting of foreign ministers beforehand. On 15 April 1959 Dulles resigned and was replaced by Christian Herter, a man who possessed much less authority than Dulles in foreign affairs. On 11 May 1959 the Geneva conference opened with the GDR and the FRG represented by advisers. The conference ended on 5 August 1959 without any agreement, not even an interim one on Berlin. Since the West stood fast on its rights in Berlin the problem was simply pushed into the future. The Geneva conference can be seen as the moment when the US government abandoned its policy of negotiating 'from strength' and began to search for an agreement with the Soviet Union. Since the Soviet government no longer spoke of elections leading to a united Germany, the West had to concede that this goal could only be forced through by war, something the Allies were not willing to embark upon. Geneva also signalled the fact that the first step in the recognition of the GDR by the West had been taken. Although no agreement was reached at Geneva the USSR came out of the Berlin crisis the stronger.

By May 1958 the number of collective farms had risen to 7780 and they farmed 29 per cent of the agricultural land. This was still, however, a long way from the goal of completing the victory of the socialist relations of production in the countryside. At the seventh plenum of the CC in December 1959 Otto Grotewohl, the Prime Minister, argued that cooperative agriculture was superior in output and productivity to medium- and small-scale farming. This led to a campaign to bring all private farms into the socialist sector, which reached its peak in the spring of 1960. On 5 March 1960 Bezirk Rostock became the first to declare itself 'fully socialist' and on 14 April 1960 Bezirk Karl-Marx-Stadt the last. The campaign was pushed through against all opposition and had to be completed before spring ploughing and sowing. Predictably it increased the number of those leaving the GDR. The intention of socialising agriculture restricted the expansion of private agriculture before 1960 and this affected national output. Over the years 1955–60 global agricultural output in the GDR only expanded by 9 per cent or less than 2 per cent annually. Rapid collectivisation was a further blow and this led to national income growth dropping to 4.5 per cent in 1960 and 3.3. per cent in 1961.

The same pattern occurred in services. Whereas in 1957 only 1.5 per cent of services were provided by artisan cooperatives this rose in 1959 to 21 per cent and in 1962 to 36.2 per cent. In the same year 90 per cent of retail trade was in the state sector.

Two changes in the structure of the state were put into effect in 1960. On 10 February 1960 the Volkskammer set up the National Defence Council. In the event of an internal or external emergency it concentrated all legislative and executive power in its hands. Walter Ulbricht was elected chairman and as such became commander-in-chief of all GDR armed forces — except, of course, those which were under the command of the Warsaw Pact — in the event of war. The secretary of the council was Erich Honecker. Its membership has never been revealed but it is assumed that it includes all the heads of the uniformed apparatus and the leading party figures. The First Secretary's position was strengthened even further when Wilhelm Pieck, the first and only president of the GDR, died on 7 September 1960. The office of president was abolished and replaced by a state council. It was to promulgate the laws, ratify international agreements and provide interpretations of existing legislation. The chairman, Walter Ulbricht, appointed and recalled GDR ambassadors, accepted the letters of credence of foreign ambassadors and presented the awards and medals conferred by the State Council. Hence the Council's functions were in many ways similar to those of the presidium of the USSR Supreme Soviet. However it was much more influential and during the 1960s it became the most important government body in the GDR. It effectively took most non-economic functions away from the Council of Ministers. It played a decisive role in the formulation of new legislation and it supervised the execution of SED decrees by the state apparatus.

These changes underlined Ulbricht's power in the GDR. He was First Secretary of the SED, chairman of the National Defence Council, chairman of the State Council and first deputy Prime Minister. The incumbent Prime Minister, Otto Grotewohl, however, was in no position to restrict his authority. Ulbricht's deputies in the State Council were Grotewohl, Johannes Dieckmann (LDPD), who was president of the Volkskammer, Heinrich Homann, chairman of the NDPD, Hans Rietz, a member of the presidium of the DBD and Manfred Gerlach and Gerald Götting, secretary general of the LDPD and the CDU respectively. The other 16 members of the State Council were party and state functionaries, workers, collective farmers and members of the intelligentsia. The secretary was Otto Gotsche, a confidant of the First Secretary.

Ulbricht's rise meant that others who did not share his

vision of how the party and the state should be run had to vacate their positions. Between 1958 and 1961 105 top functionaries were removed from the 15 Bezirk party organisations including 7 first secretaries and 16 other secretaries. The purge was especially thorough in Bezirk Dresden, where 16 functionaries were replaced, and in Bezirks Halle and Cottbus, where 10 officials were removed in each. In 7 of the 15 Bezirks the man responsible for the economy was changed and in 6 the secretary for agriculture was replaced (Jänicke 1964: 94). There was even a minor personality cult though a less charismatic figure than the First Secretary with his rimless spectacles, goatee beard and squeaky Saxon voice would be difficult to imagine. At the fourteenth plenum of the CC in November 1961 Otto Schön went so far as to say: 'Walter Ulbricht — he is the party' (*Neues Deutschland* 29 November 1961). Despite this, or perhaps because of it, Paul Verner, first secretary of Bezirk Berlin, stated the following day: 'Our party was and is a stranger to the personality cult.'

On 15 November 1960 the FDGB presented a draft Labour Law Code for discussion. Despite the fact that about 23 000 changes were proposed by workers the final version passed by the Volkskammer on 12 April 1961 revealed no significant changes. Most of the alterations suggested implied higher wage rates and better holiday provisions. Paul Fröhlich, a candidate member of the CC, made it quite clear on 28 March 1961 why such suggestions were being rejected. 'Demands have been made which cannot be entertained due to the level of production of our social life, especially labour productivity.' The right to strike, anchored in the constitution, was not mentioned. The FDGB newspaper had explained why this was. 'We do not need the right to strike in our labour law code because workers have no one against whom they would need to strike.' (*Die Tribüne* 23 November 1960). The right to work was laid down and labour was to raise productivity by applying the most advanced science and technology, and to fulfil the economic plan. Hence the primary objective of the new legislation was plan fulfilment in the enterprise: workers' interests took second place. 'Socialist labour discipline' was made more rigorous and enterprise directors acquired more authority. The new code legalised the conflict commissions which had existed in factories since

1953. They were to settle minor disputes and pass only the more serious to the courts.

The collectivisation of agriculture inevitably depressed production so that by June 1961 Willi Stoph, deputy Prime Minister, had to concede that it was proving difficult to supply the population with bread, butter and meat. Industry, too, was affected by the harsher line taken against the private sector. Reviewing the first quarter of 1961 the Council of Ministers spoke of serious shortfalls in plan fulfilment. The new Labour Law Code caused considerable disquiet and contributed to the increased flow of refugees to West Berlin. An added complication was that the SED had decided to make the GDR independent of West German imports as a result of Bonn terminating the interzonal trade agreement in September 1960. This latter move had been in response to the introduction by the GDR of a regulation requiring all West German visitors to East Berlin to acquire a pass. The FRG government annulled their cancellation of the interzonal agreement in December 1960 so as not to endanger trade with West Berlin but the GDR remained steadfast in her desire to eliminate all economic dependence on West Germany.

The uncertainty which Khrushchev had introduced about West Berlin's future and the economic difficulties listed above swelled the stream of refugees to a flood, so that in April 1961 defectors from the GDR were double the monthly rate of the previous year. Soviet–American relations became very chilly after the shooting down of a US reconnaisance plane over the Urals in May 1960 and the failure of the Paris summit meeting the same month — largely the result of the First Secretary's intransigence in demanding an apology from President Eisenhower, something which the British Prime Minister, Harold Macmillan, told Khrushchev that the President could not do. After the meeting of Khrushchev and the new US President, John F. Kennedy, in Vienna in June 1961 the Soviet leader felt more confident of his own country's strength and became more willing to press for a solution to the Berlin problem along the lines advocated by Ulbricht. The SED leader wanted to gain control over air, land and water transport to Berlin, something which would quickly lead to West Berlin falling under GDR control. One of the reasons why Khrushchev had been willing to torpedo the Paris summit was the need to demonstrate to the Chinese that the Soviet Union was still capable of confronting capitalism. The Chinese, of course, regarded peaceful coexistence as revisionism. When Kennedy, on 25 July 1961, made it clear that the United States regarded the presence of Western troops and their rights of access to West Berlin as essential, the Soviet Union had the choice of a head-on conflict or seeking to seal off West Berlin from the rest of Berlin and the GDR. Ulbricht conceded at the thirteenth plenum of the CC on 3–4 July 1961 that so far it had not been possible to 'explain the basic questions of the policy of worker and peasant power to the masses in such a way as to convince them [of their correctness] . . . Then there is the peace treaty and a final solution to the West Berlin problem.' As the number of refugees climbed so the GDR courts became more severe, especially against those it found guilty of being 'traders in human beings'. Instead of making concessions to dam the flood as it had done, for instance, in 1959, the SED held to its course. During August 1961 47 433 left. Since about half the refugees were young people under the age of 25 the effect, if not stopped, would have been catastrophic for the GDR economy. This very fact was one of the reasons why the first secretaries of the communist parties of the Warsaw Pact organisation, meeting in Moscow on 3–5 August 1961, acceded to the GDR wish for a wall. The Soviets had finally come to the conclusion that they were strong enough to force through this drastic solution. On 11 August the Volkskammer, on the advice of the CC, made the Council of Ministers responsible for taking all the necessary measures. During the night of 12–13 August 1961 units of the NVA, factory militias, the border troops and the People's Police, supported by Soviet troops stationed in the GDR, erected barbed wire fences and rough walls along the frontier between East and West Berlin. In the days that followed a proper wall was built. The open heart in Berlin had been stitched together and the GDR was finally isolated from West Berlin and West Germany.

4 State, Society and Developed Socialism

The building of the Berlin Wall was a watershed in the development of the GDR. Unlike citizens in other socialist states, those in the GDR had a choice: remain or emigrate. This prevented the full rigour of Stalinism being applied and may have been the main reason why spectacular show trials were not staged. The Wall, of course, signalled defeat in the battle to win over the recalcitrants to socialism. It conceded that peaceful competition between capitalist West Germany and socialist East Germany benefited the former rather than the latter. This was a surprise and a bitter blow to the SED leadership which had become used to appealing to the West German working class over the heads of its own government. The greatest impact of the Wall was psychological. That part of the population, probably a majority, which was not committed to building socialism had now to come to terms with the regime. There has always been tension between the German and Soviet traditions in the GDR. Until 1961 the SED placed greater emphasis on the Soviet tradition and succeeded in consolidating its power along Soviet lines. After the Wall it felt more secure and was able to adopt policies which owed more to the German tradition. A major concern for the party was economic policy. The disappointing results of the post-1958 period revealed that inefficient use was being made of the technical and educational potential of the working class and the intelligentsia. This led to the adoption of the New Economic Policy in 1963 but it was renamed the Economic System of Socialism in 1967. Too much faith in the potential of science and technology produced distortions in growth patterns and such was the disappointment experienced that the whole experiment was terminated in 1970. The desire to regenerate industry and agriculture made it incumbent on the party to bring ideology into step with advances in the technical world. Besides a new party programme and a new constitution, the SED added its own contribution to Marxism—Leninism. In 1968 it expounded the view that socialism was not a transient phenomenon but would last into the foreseeable future — thus taking communism off the agenda for a long time to come. These views now form the essence of developed or mature socialism in the Soviet Union and elsewhere. Ulbricht's self-confidence in dealing with Khrushchev's successors led to friction over ideological questions and Berlin. The increasing economic difficulties facing the GDR compounded Ulbricht's difficulties and eventually he was forced to step down in favour of Erich Honecker in May 1971.

The closing of the frontier led party officials to impose their authority on those who were critical of SED policy. Coercion was applied to those who challenged the official view that the building of the Wall was an historic victory for peace. It had, after all, prevented a West German invasion, or so it was claimed. One paper wrote: 'Some may have doubted lately if it is right to seize and beat enemies of our republic', but concluded that fists were necessary to bring home to enemies the real state of affairs (*Leipziger Volkszeitung* 23 August 1961.) The violence had been legitimised by the party organ, *Neues Deutschland*, in a leading article on 9 August 1961 when it had praised the action of a worker who had rammed his fist 'into the cakehole of a warmonger'. In October, Werner Krolikowski, first secretary of Bezirk Dresden and his counterpart in Bezirk Leipzig came out against the iron-fist policies of the period. The violence had ebbed away by the end of 1961. This was partly due to the activities of Nikita Khrushchev in the Soviet Union. He launched another wave of de-Stalinisation at the twenty-second congress of the CPSU in Moscow in October 1961 and one of the first tangible results was the removal of Stalin's body from the Stalin—Lenin mausoleum in Red Square and its burial nearby. Cities, factories, roads, farms and institutions named after the dead dictator were renamed and this spread to Eastern and South-eastern Europe. The Stalinallee was rechristened and the huge Stalin statue disappeared overnight. Ulbricht and the SED leadership had finally decided on de-Stalinisation. However some rank and file party members and young people judged this to be a tactical move by the First Secretary to satisfy the Soviet needs of the moment and Ulbricht came in for some harsh criticism. Such was the virulence of the outbursts that the party leadership was forced to condemn the 'baiting of comrade Ulbricht' (*Neues Deutschland* 12 November 1961).

The SED was fully aware that the chief way to enhance its legitimacy was through economic success. Since most people wanted to raise their standard of living and were keen to progress in their jobs the potential was there. The loss of so many persons of working age before August 1961 meant that all available sources of labour had to be tapped. There was really only one source left — women. A campaign was launched to recruit more females to the workbench. A Politburo communiqué of 24 December 1961 entitled 'Women, Peace and Socialism' declared that the economic problems facing the GDR could only be solved if every available pair of hands was utilised. Women, in fact, were to play a more important role in the building of socialism than hitherto. However the reservoir of available females was shallow: 68.4 per cent of all able-bodied women between the ages of 16 and 60 were already employed, accounting for 43.9 per cent of the labour force. Raising the skills of the employed women was of key importance. The demands of the scientific—technical revolution were such as to require an increasing number of women in skilled jobs and in the technical intelligentsia. Women made up 28 per cent of the student population but were mainly to be found in non-engineering and applied science fields. Some professions were dominated by females. In pharmacy, for instance, 71 per cent of students were women but in technical universities only 6 per cent of those enrolled were female (*Neues Deutschland* 10 February 1962).

The communiqué placed special responsibility on the women's committees in the factories and on the Democratic Women's Association of Germany (DFD). A more active stance was to be adopted to win over a greater proportion of the female population to socialism. Education was of key importance and it afforded the SED opportunities to influence the younger generation but any type of activity which attracted housewives away from the home was potentially beneficial. The DFD set up housewife brigades and called on all those of working age not gainfully employed to join them. Although there were 3.5 million women employed, the DFD only counted 1.3 million members. A women's congress was convened for the first time in June 1964 and of the 1100 delegates, only 643 were DFD members (Weber 1980: 111). Since it was recognised that the formative influence on a child is its home life and environment, getting mothers and housewives out to work served another purpose: it afforded the party the opportunity of winning them over to socialism. Their children could be looked after in crèches and kindergartens, thus permitting socialisation to begin at a tender age.

In the race for socialism, women had been left behind. Women played a more important role in political and social life during the 1940s and the 1950s than at the beginning of the 1960s. At the latter date not a single woman was a full member of the Politburo and there were only two female ministers: Hilde Benjamin, Minister of Justice, and Margarete Wittkowski, deputy chairman of the Council of Ministers and responsible for trade, supply and agriculture. Whereas about one-quarter of SED members were female, only 15 of the 121 full members of the CC elected at the seventh congress were women. Five of the 60 candidate members were female. The two female candidate members of the Politburo, Edith Baumann and Luise Ermisch — both elected in 1958 — were dropped at the congress but one of the new candidate members elected was a woman, Margarete Müller. It is of interest that no woman has ever been a full member of the Politburo. Hence it was clear that despite formal equality before the law, considerable educational opportunities and the goodwill of the SED, women still found themselves in a society which was clearly dominated by males.

The second wave of de-Stalinisation which began with the twenty-second Congress of the CPSU in October 1961 made it imperative to look for new sources of legitimacy. In the USSR the party turned back to Lenin and looked forward to communism beginning in 1981. In the GDR the time became opportune to stress the German tradition at the expense of the Soviet. A National Document was put out by the National Front in March 1962 and it articulated the SED view on the German nation. It was claimed that there was one German nation, divided into two states, one socialist and the other capitalist, and mutually hostile. The blame for the division of Germany was placed on the shoulders of Bonn; it was something that the SED 'did not desire and which could not be allowed to last'. Concomitant with this went a desire to establish the GDR as the legitimate heir of all that was good and progressive in German history. The CC in June 1962 discussed a project to produce an *Outline History of the German Labour Movement* and after some debate it was adopted in April 1963. The goal was to write a multi-volume work which would provide new working-class heroes to replace Stalin. Rosa Luxemburg, Karl Liebknecht and August Bebel were to inspire the younger generation with their deeds and raise the standing of the SED. Historians were given very clear instructions about what the SED required and were to be guided by the 'political requirements of the present struggle' and the directives of the party. Although de-Stalinisation was the order of the day, the attitude to the writing of labour history remained essentially Stalinist. It was to strengthen the position of the SED at a particular point in time. The SED would provide the interpretation and the task of the historian was to provide the evidence to confirm preformulated views.

The new history was also designed to promote the Ulbricht personality cult which was gradually gathering pace. The occasion of his seventieth birthday on 30 June 1963 was seized upon to publish some effusive prose but the fact had to be faced that Walter was not made of the stuff which produces charismatic leaders.

The New Economic System of Planning and Management of the Economy

The early 1960s were a chastening time for the SED economically. The 'chief economic task' of catching up and passing West Germany never developed enough impetus to promise success. The hope of becoming free of the need to import from the FRG was never very realistic and as growth rates slowed, the return on investment dropped. Whereas between 1951 and 1955 an investment of 32 000 million marks generated an increase in national income (net social product in the sphere of material production) of 21 000 million marks. Between 1956 and 1960 investment rose to 63 000 million marks but the rise in national income was only 21 000 million marks. Over the years 1961–4 investment was as high as 66 000 million marks but the increase in national income was a depressing 10 700 million marks. Various conclusions can be drawn from these figures. The GDR's initial industrial spurt was over and a new economic strategy was needed. Extensive growth was no longer adequate, a switch to intensive growth was imperative — the more so because of the scarcity of labour — and this could only be based on the latest developments in science and technology. Since the economic advance of the USSR and Czechoslovakia was also slowing down, there was a community of interest in economic reform.

An important contribution was made by Evsei Liberman, a professor of economics in Kharkov, in an article in *Pravda* on 9 September 1962 entitled 'Plan, Profit, Bonus'. He advocated a thoroughgoing reform of the enterprise planning system with the use of plant profitability as a method of assessing enterprise activity and calculating bonuses for the labour force. Liberman was particularly concerned to force enterprises to concentrate more on what customers wanted to buy and to break the habit of fulfilling their plans by producing too many unsaleable goods. The following month Ulbricht made it clear that there would have to be changes in the way the GDR economy was run and this initiated a lively debate about Liberman's proposals. On the whole the GDR reaction was quite critical but the First Secretary, speaking at the sixth congress of the SED in January 1963, in proposing economic changes, formulated his views in a way which revealed the influence of Liberman.

The goal set for the GDR economy was the 'all round construction of socialism' within the world socialist system. A rapid rise in labour productivity was of special significance as 'socialist relations' among citizens were cultivated. Increased cooperation among socialist states was envisaged and trade turnover with Comecon partners mounted.

Ulbricht's initial NES proposals were tested on a small scale — in ten enterprises (VEB) and four associations of nationalised enterprises (VVB) — and the results were discussed at a CC economic conference in June 1963. It transpired that a wholesale restructuring of the economy was to be attempted, going far beyond previous reforms and anything attempted in the Soviet

Union. Since the publication of the Liberman article in the Soviet party newspaper had legitimised economic reform not only in the homeland of socialism but also in other socialist countries, GDR economists were afforded the opportunity for the first time of devising a socialist economic model which owed more to German than to Soviet tradition. On 11 July 1963 the Council of Ministers approved the Principles of the New Economic System of Planning and Management of the Economy (NES). It was to consist of the scientific management of the economy, scientifically formulated long-term central state planning and the widespread use of economic incentives.

In order to gear the SED for its new duties it was split down the middle according to the 'production principle'. In February 1963 four new bureaux or commissions were established in the Politburo: the bureau of industry and construction; the bureau of agriculture; the ideological commission; and the commission for agitation. These organisations were also added at the CC level. At Bezirk level, a bureau of industry and construction, a bureau of agriculture and an ideological commission were set up. At Kreis level either a bureau of industry and construction or a bureau of agriculture was established. Previously the party had been organised along territorial lines; in other words the party organisation was responsible for all activities in its area of jurisdiction. Without abolishing the territorial principle, party economic endeavour in a given region was now divided in two. SED Bezirk and Kreis executives were responsible for the leadership of all bureaux and commissions in their area.

This reform was also extended to the state and economic bureaucracy. The goal was to bring officials into direct contact with the concepts of profit, price and profitability. This favoured those with technical and economic expertise. The older functionary who was long on ideological orthodoxy and short on technical *savoir-faire* was immediately placed at a distinct disadvantage.

The splitting of the party and the changes that entailed were directly related to the fact that the CPSU was the leading and guiding party in the socialist bloc. These changes made more sense in the Soviet Union where the territory was vast but little sense in the GDR where it is possible to traverse the country from north to south in one day and from west to east in half a day. Practically all enterprises can be reached in about half a day from East Berlin.

Since the reform was initiated by the party there was never any attempt to introduce a socialist market economy along Yugoslav lines. It was also not as radical as the reform attempted in Czechoslovakia in 1968 or the New Economic Mechanism in Hungary, also adopted in 1968. The NES was to make central state planning more efficient by paying more attention to individual and collective interests at plant level. It was an attempt to overcome the intractable problem of reconciling party control with economic efficiency. The SED was desirous of economic growth but not at the expense of party control. Since a perfectly functioning centrally planned economy pre-supposes perfect information, an incisive central will and the ability to implement completely all set goals, a certain level of uncertainty and imprecision is inevitable. Because it is impossible for the centre to take all important decisions, there is inevitably some devolution of decision-making to the enterprise. This can either be recognised officially or not. The NES made the decision-making at plant level official. The SED hoped that the NES would lead to a system in which central and local decision-making would complement one another. Indeed it was hoped that the NES would develop into a self-regulating mechanism which would permit the party to set central goals which the enterprises would then fulfil.

The key economic institution in the NES was the VVB. Previously it had been midway between the Council of Ministers and the plant, the VEB. Now it was endowed with economic functions and afforded some independence. Power was devolved to it from the industrial departments of the National Economic Council and the State Planning Commission. A VVB was res-ponsible for a particular branch of industry, plastics and shoes, for example, and was to form a 'long-term plan group' in order to improve the branch technically and economically. These planning groups brought together the available scientific and technical talent so as to evaluate the findings of research and development, in the GDR and outside, and thereby to advise on how the particular sector of the economy should develop.

The decision-making power of the managing director of the VVB was extended and his sphere of activity widened. He was to supervise his accountants, keep an eye on the profit and loss account, engage in some marketing, commission consumer research studies and establish closer relations with scientific and research institutes. Material incentives were to be accorded priority in the struggle to raise labour productivity. Wages and bonuses were to be tied to the profitability of the enterprise, with real gains in productivity, eliminating waste and increasing efficiency the goals to be aimed at. Longer holidays were promised to those who recorded outstanding achievement.

Initially the NES was applied to the following branches of the economy: chemicals, electrical engineering, metallurgy, machine-building, energy and transport. Then it was to be extended to building and construction, agriculture and domestic and foreign trade. Hence it was a structural policy, aiming to promote those sectors perceived to be of most value to the economy. Just what sectors should be chosen turned out to be a very complex problem to resolve. The GDR could follow foreign examples, West German or Japanese, for example, but such a policy would not necessarily be beneficial. Since the GDR had a small domestic market, exports were of key importance in ensuring long production runs. Without such runs production costs would be too high. Just how difficult it was to decide which sectors should be expanded can be illustrated by taking the experience of the aircraft industry. In 1954 it was decided to develop an aircraft industry, centred on Dresden. The Soviet Union provided the blueprints and the necessary equipment and there were enough engineers and skilled labour available. A two-engined passenger aircraft, the IL 14, was ready for testing in March 1956. It proved successful so a four-engined passenger aircraft, the 152, capable of covering 2500 kilometres at 800 km/hour, was undertaken. The engines came from the Soviet Union but it was planned to produce them eventually in Ludwigsfelde. The maiden flight took place in December 1958 but during the second flight in March 1959 the plane crashed. It was restructured and the 152-II made its maiden flight in 1960. The GDR began showing the plane to prospective buyers but on 31 December 1961 the whole venture was wound up and the manufacturing capacity turned over to other uses. No reason was ever given for the abrupt change of heart but it may be assumed that the aircraft turned out to be too expensive. With this white elephant as a reminder, GDR planners had to be very cautious about blindly following world trends in high technology.

Besides the long-term plan groups, another way the VVB could significantly influence the structure of the economy was by means of the product group. Product groups are groups of enterprises, either nationalised, semi-private or private, within a given sector of industy which produce technologically similar or related products or semi-fabricates. Besides norms, types, standardisation and the production process used are discussed. Also involved are forecasting, scientific and technical development, joint research, rationalisation, comparison of work experience, discovery and utilisation of spare and underused capacity and relations with subcontractors. The VVB had overall responsibility for the product groups and appointed a leading enterprise to supervise activities. Although this plant — it could be a VEB, a semi-private or private concern — had no legal authority to enforce its decisions, since they had to be reached by agreement, it exercised considerable influence over its part of the economy. Sometimes the organisational problems were immense. For instance the electrical appliance industry produced about 10 000 products in 1963 and was structured as follows: the VVB Electrical Appliances embraced 18 VEB which were divided into two product groups involving 31 other VEB, 38 locally-managed VEB and 270 semi-private or private enterprises and cooperatives.

As has been said, profit and profitability were accorded a more important role in the enterprise but other indicators such as those which prescribed factory inputs remained. Hence the NES contradicted the basic assumptions of Liberman.

Before examining the implementation of the reform it is worth casting a glance at the organisation of economic planning in the GDR.

The ultimate responsibility for the drafting and the implementation of plans rests with the Council of Ministers. The key institution is, however, the Politburo but during the Ulbricht era the State Council played a leading role in setting overall guidelines. Central state organs such as the State Planning Commission, the National Economic Council and its industrial departments and the GDR State Bank play significant roles. The most important local organs during this period were the VVB and the Bezirk economic councils.

The State Planning Commission is the central organ for economic planning and together with the Ministry of Finance it checks that financial indicators are being adhered to. There are planning commissions in each Bezirk and the VVB had long-term plan groups. All the activities of these bodies are co-ordinated and supervised by the State Planning Commission.

The National Economic Council only existed for a short time. It came into being in 1961 when it was discovered that the State Planning Commission was quite unable to cope with the huge volume of work entrusted to it. Following the Soviet example, industrial ministries had been dissolved in the GDR in 1958 and their functions transferred to the State Planning Commission. In 1961 they were transferred to the National Economic Council. With the removal of Khrushchev in October 1964, the industrial ministries reasserted themselves in the Soviet Union and on 14 January 1966 the GDR followed suit. During its short existence the National Economic Council was the main organ of the Council of Ministers for the planning and management of industry. Its chief task was to draw up the annual plan for manufacturing industry, coordinate it with ministries not involved in manufacturing industry, balance it and pass it on to the State Planning Commission. Since it was directly involved in the management of industry it set up departments for the various branches of industry and their heads were superior to the managing directors of the VVB.

The most significant organisational measure of the NES was to make the VVB economically independent. They were detached from the state administration, became legal persons and were responsible for the economic management of their particular branch of industry. Ulbricht, at the sixth congress of the SED, referred to them as a 'type of socialist corporation'.

The Bezirk economic councils performed the same functions *vis-à-vis* the VEB subordinated to them (those not part of a VVB) within their own Bezirk. Whereas the VVB operated according to profit and loss the economic councils have neither economic nor legal independence and their income and expenditure is channelled through the state budget. In order to promote cooperation between the VEB which were subordinate to a VVB and those run by an economic council, the economic councils were freed from responsibility to their Bezirk councils and made directly responsible to the National Economic Council. This led to considerable friction, for example, over housing for workers and transport, so that in 1965 the economic councils were again placed under the Bezirk councils. On the technical level they remained subordinate to the National Economic Council (Leptin and Melzer 1978: 29).

The concept of profit and profitability, without a thoroughgoing price reform, is only a bookkeeping one. If the GDR was to become internationally competitive then its prices had to reflect relative scarcity. The price structure in the early 1960s was such that raw materials were priced too low, leading to waste and a neglect of substitutes which were often too highly priced. This made little economic sense in a country which was poorly endowed with resources. The chief plan indicator had been output measured in physical terms. This had led to the production of goods whose cost to the economy was higher than enterprise costs. Economic and technical progress was held back since investment decisions were based on the existing price structure whereas rational prices would have led to different investment decisions being taken.

The first stage of the price reform, revaluing fixed capital, was completed on 30 June 1963. The value of gross fixed capital in manufacturing industry was increased by 52 per cent, on average, to 105 000 million marks. The next step, the more important one, of reforming industrial prices was carried out in three stages. Stage 1 began on 1 April 1964 and affected coal, energy, iron, steel and basic chemicals and increased prices, on average, by 70 per cent; stage 2 began on 1 January 1965 and concerned the paper industry, leather, skins, building materials and most of the chemical industry and raised prices, on average, by 40 per cent; stage 3 began on 1 January 1967 and involved machinery, electrical goods, electronics, final products of the chemical industry and the light and food industries and raised prices, on average, by 4 per cent. Profits were to be calculated on fabrication costs, i.e. value added by the enterprise. The new formula was devised to prevent an enterprise making large profits by producing goods with a high input of expensive raw materials. The reform also introduced a production fund tax, a charge on the gross fixed and circulating capital of the enterprise. This 'interest' charge came to 6 per cent.

In order to avoid any unrest among the population the prices of consumer goods were left unchanged and this meant that enterprises in this sector had either to suffer a reduction in profits or become more efficient.

With these prices in operation, profit became the most important incentive to improve performance. Since the concern could retain part of the net surplus it thus had an interest in increased efficiency. The role of money changed. Whereas previously the banks had been an executive organ of the state providing interest free transfers from the state budget, they were now to be permitted to extend loans on which interest would be charged, to support profitable investment projects and to charge higher rates of interest and refuse credit on projects which were not in accordance with plan objectives. Hence banks received considerable power to influence economic activity and in order to reach their decisions they had to be given access to the enterprise's accounts.

How long would it take NES to become fully operational? Ulbricht, at an SED economic conference, declared: 'It will take two to three years to elaborate and introduce NES' (*Die Wirtschaft* 14 September 1965). However at the ninth plenum of the CC, in April 1966, he revealed that the NES had not been fully introduced and that it would take a further two years to complete the process. However it was still not complete by 1968 when recentralisation began again. Why then was the process so slow?

The NES was a fundamental break with many past practices and enterprise managers and workers required time to take in its implications. Management had to learn to think as entrepreneurs. Going over to self-financing posed considerable problems for the enterprise, the combine and the VVB. Bank personnel had to acquire the skill to judge credit-worthiness. Although the guidelines about decision-making had been laid down for factories and the VVB there were still many unresolved problems in practice. The third stage of the price reform envisaged for 1 January 1966 had to be postponed for a year and this led to the 1966—70 plan being drawn up in 1967. Hence it was only after 1967 that enterprises could judge the effect of the new prices on their costs and rates of profit. In many instances it turned out that enterprises, including some new ones, were unprofitable due to high inputs of raw materials, poor organisation of production and location. A major problem was that enterprises were being asked for the first time to calculate accurately their costs, whereas previously cost accounting had been neglected. In many cases enterprises found it extremely difficult to measure their costs.

The 'second phase' of the NES was launched in early 1966 when the New Economic Council was abolished. Besides the seven ministries which reappeared, a Ministry of Material Supply and a Ministry for Bezirk-managed Industry and Food were set up. The State Planning Commission again became responsible for drafting and supervising annual and perspective (five-year) plans. A State Bureau of Labour and Wages and a Bureau of Prices were also established. The State Planning Commission was to reduce the number of central plan indicators and to liaise more closely with enterprises. The powers of the Ministry of Finance were increased. The net result was that the autonomy of the VVB managing director was cut back a little.

The labour force received some tangible benefits. The five-day week, every other week, was introduced in 1966 and a year later every week became a five-day week. Some bank holidays disappeared, however, as a result. Later the minimum holiday period was increased by three days to fifteen working days.

The 'second phase' of the NES lasted just over a year. It gave way to a 'new phase of development'. This was made public in a book by Walter Ulbricht with a preface by Günter Mittag, CC secretary for the economy, and a leading figure in the evolution of the NES. The First Secretary revealed that the NES was only the precursor of fundamental changes in GDR society. 'We intend to elaborate and introduce the NES not only in the economy but also in all social development' (Ulbricht 1966d: 9). Shortly afterwards the NES was renamed the Economic System of Socialism to underline the fact that it was viewed as permanent.

Changes in State and Society

National service was introduced by a law passed by the Volkskammer on 24 January 1962. Men between the ages of 18 and 26 years were to serve 18 months and to become members of the reserve afterwards until they reached the age of 50. The NVA numbered 90 000 at the time: it was not intended to increase the size of the professional army, but to improve its battle readiness. The NVA had always experienced difficulty in recruiting men and in the past SED party organs and mass organisations had often been given the task of recruiting a certain number of men. Although national service existed in West Germany the GDR had always shied away from introducing it. It would have increased the flood of refugees to West Berlin and it would also have run the risk of providing arms training to potential 'enemies of the republic'. National service would help to overcome the aversion many citizens felt towards anyone in a uniform. It would also provide the SED with an excellent opportunity to influence ideologically the nation's young manhood at an impressionable age. A greater proportion of the state budget would have to be devoted to defence and border control. Walling and fencing in the GDR population would be expensive but from the SED's point of view it was a good investment if it almost eliminated the prospect of fleeing the republic. In such a case the vast majority of the uncommitted would gradually come to terms with socialism if economic advance could be guaranteed. The goal of improving the quality of NVA personnel was given a boost in September 1962 when the first graduates from the Military Academy joined the forces. They had successfully completed a four-year course.

The border police were also restructured. On 15 September 1961 they were renamed the border commando unit of the NVA and thereby made part of the NVA. In so doing they were removed from the jurisdiction of the Ministry of the Interior. At the same time the police on stand-by (Bereitschaftspolizei) who had been serving in East Berlin and on the frontier with West Germany were made part of the border commando unit. In July 1962 a 'Coastal Brigade', designed to patrol the Baltic, was created. In 1974 the border commando unit of the NVA was renamed the border police (Grenzpolizei) and remained under the control of the Ministry of National Defence. Their strength was then about 46 000 men.

The Volkskammer elections due in 1962 were postponed until 20 October 1963 when the single list of candidates received 99.95 per cent of the votes cast — many of them in open rather than in secret balloting as the constitution prescribed. The fact that the GDR was now a socialist society led to a change in the representation of the various parties in the Volkskammer. Instead of 100 seats, the SED received 110; the CDU, LDPD, NDPD and the DBD each retained their 45 seats; the FDGB was accorded 60 instead of 45 seats; the FDJ obtained 35 seats instead of 25; the DFD 30 instead of 25; and the Kulturbund 19 instead of 15 places. Since most of the representatives of the mass organisations were SED members, the party further increased its overall majority. The jump in the number of members representing the mass organisations also indicated that these had increased in significane *vis-à-vis* the non-socialist parties.

Otto Grotewohl presented his new government of 30 ministers in November 1963. The new Minister of the Interior was Major General Friedrich Dickel, a deputy Minister of National Defence. Margot Honecker became Minister of Education. When Grotewohl died on 21 September 1964, Willi Stoph succeeded him as Prime Minister.

The occasion of the fifteenth anniversary of the GDR on 7 October 1964 was marked by an amnesty for criminals and political prisoners. In the same year judges acquired a little more autonomy but the SED was not taking any risks since probably all leading legal posts were filled by its members. The coming of socialism meant that the law had to be amended to take into account the socialist relations of the population. The Supreme Court became responsible for the whole legal process but the SED could act indirectly if it so desired. Changes were made to the labour code and in civil law and even a law on copyright was promulgated in September 1965. A new law on the family, the work of the Ministry of Justice, was adopted in December 1965. The draft law had been presented for public discussion and about three-quarters of a million citizens had their say. The new law promoted marriage and the family and underlined the role of the state in promoting the socialist family.

Youth posed the SED considerable problems. With the victory of socialism in the GDR the battle for the hearts and minds of the nation's young people was joined in earnest since they were the key to a successful socialist society. The future literally lay in their hands. The FDJ — which counted 1.4 million members in 1963 — had always resisted Western pop culture but began timidly to come to terms with it. The first secretary of the FDJ, Horst Schumann, led the way by dancing the twist, hitherto regarded as degenerate capitalist hip-weaving. The Politburo of the SED appealed in a communiqué on youth on 21 September 1963 to all youth leaders and teachers to lend a sympathetic ear to the experiences and problems of the younger generation. The practice was apparently widespread of dismissing 'uncomfortable' questions as provocative. The party desired the formation of socialist personalities and such problems could only evolve if pupils were 'treated with respect and their problems taken seriously'. It was normal for young people to hold back their views, to wait for instruction from above and to conform. Such persons, it was pointed out, were unlikely to achieve much in life. The party thus conceded that most young people lived in two worlds, the public and the private. In the public world they outwardly conformed, said the right things and concentrated on promoting their own careers. In private they regarded leading SED functionaries as peddlers of myths or half-truths, even cynics or hypocrites. Satisfaction in life came from cultivating the private life with its totally different value system. The SED's task was to bridge the gulf between the two worlds by coming closer to the hopes and aspirations of the younger generation. Developing a socialist consciousness and producing the new GDR man and woman to the SED leadership amounted to GDR citizens acting according to norms elaborated at the top. This, in turn, would strengthen the position of the ruling party elite. However many youngsters had no desire to be 'programmed' by the older generation of party officials. They wanted access to Western pop music, dance and life-styles. They preferred jazz to Soviet folk songs, and jeans and long hair afforded them a sense of identity. At the same time Soviet youth was awakening and had produced poets such as Evtushenko and Voznesensky. Where were their equivalents in the GDR? In its efforts to appear more relevant the SED slackened the reins of control and condemned the behaviour of the activists who acted in an oppressive and disrespectful manner towards members of the non-socialist parties, religious believers and farmers.

It was also discovered that all was not well in education. A commission was set up in 1963 to review the whole situation and its report brought little comfort to the SED leadership. The greatest weakness was discovered in those disciplines which were of greatest significance for the development of the GDR; mathematics, the natural sciences and political education. This led to the Volkskammer passing a new 'Law on the Unified Socialist Educational System' on 25 February 1965 which guaranteed all citizens an equal right to education. The new educational system consisted of: pre-school education; the ten-class polytechnic high school; vocational training; special classes for those who have finished school and are proceeding to university; engineering and technical colleges; universities; and further education for workers and employees. The unity of education and training was the guiding principle of the socialist educational system. This was to be achieved by linking theory and practice and learning and study with productive work. Pupils, apprentices and students were to 'be educated to love the GDR and to be proud of her social achievements and to be ready to place all their strength at the disposal of society, to strengthen the socialist state and to defend it' (*Gesetzblatt der DDR* 1965 I: 83).

The promotion of sport served several goals. It prepared the nation's youth for military service, it raised the level of physical fitness and it promised to break the isolation of the GDR in the non-socialist world. Since the GDR was not recognised diplomatically in the Western world, sporting success was a valuable source of prestige which could boost the legitimacy of the regime. The International Olympic Committee (IOC) did not recognise the GDR as a sovereign state and hence GDR athletes participated as part of an all-German team. The last occasion on which this occurred was at Tokyo in 1964 and the problem of staging trials for the all-German team was solved by holding them in Czechoslovakia. Then in October 1965 the IOC acceded to the wish of the GDR to participate under her own colours and this occurred for the first time at the Winter Olympics in Grenoble. In Mexico City in 1968 the nation's sportsmen and women achieved third place behind the USA and the USSR, a formidable achievement. Great efforts were made to discover and train young talent in other activities such as ice dancing. The great sporting success of the GDR was achieved by relentless effort and material incentives. A GDR sportsman or woman who breaks a world record receives an increased pension and if he or she breaks a world record again, the pension goes up again. From the GDR government's point of view it is money well spent because the prestige gained from such achievements brings the GDR to the attention of the general public throughout the world and results in favourable publicity.

A new electoral law was passed by the Volkskammer in July 1965 which afforded electors the possibility of choosing those on the unified list whom they preferred. Candidates who did not receive 50 per cent of the vote were deemed not to have been elected. During the elections to the Kreistage and the city councils on 10 October 1965, 186 107 candidates were declared elected with only two failing to be elected. Their names were not revealed (Weber 1980: 117). The greatest obstacle to those who wished to strike off names was the fact that most of the voting was open, not secret. This meant that those who wished to mark their ballot papers had to go to a booth to do so, thus making it clear who the voters were who objected to some of the candidates. A GDR voter does not need to mark his ballot paper so as to make it valid.

Second Thoughts about Reform

One of the sharpest critics of Stalinism was Professor Robert Havemann and he sought to make good use of the second wave of de-Stalinisation which began in 1961. A Professor of Physical Chemistry at the Humboldt University in East Berlin, he raised eyebrows in 1962 when he claimed that dialectical materialism, far from helping modern science, was in fact hindering it. In October 1963 he began a series of lectures at the Humboldt University on 'Scientific Aspects of Philosophical Problems' which turned out to be extremely popular with students. Havemann started from a fundamentalist Marxist point of view and argued that the dialectic should be left entirely to the scientists; the professional party philosophers were therefore superfluous. He touched on other sensitive subjects such as morals and politics but his lecture on 7 February 1964 turned out to be his last. He was expelled from the SED and lost his professorship a month later. Havemann's downfall was exceptional in 1964. Other wayward intellectuals and members of the cultural élite were afforded more latitude. However the prevailing liberal attitude had enemies in high places. Erich Honecker and other conservatives launched an attack on the permissive ideological climate at the seventh plenum of the CC in December 1964. They called for stricter party controls, a tougher line towards West Germany and closer ties with the socialist bloc. These demands had little impact at the time but Ulbricht's developing relationship with the new First Secretary of the CPSU, Leonid Brezhnev, favoured a more orthodox line by the party. Brezhnev came to East Berlin in November 1965 and a new trade agreement, covering the years 1966–70, was signed. Rumour had it that Erich Apel, one of the keenest supporters of the NES, committed suicide on 3 December 1965 rather than see the treaty accepted. Apel saw the NES as affording the GDR the opportunity of catching up with the leading industrial nations. 'Our sights are set on world standards. If in any given field the Soviet Union achieves world leadership we shall model ourselves on that pattern; if West Germany or Japan achieves a similar distinction, then we shall follow that example' (*Neues Deutschland* 21 February 1964). This new openness led to trade turnover between the GDR and the USSR, as a percentage of total trade turnover, declining from 49.3 per cent in 1962 to 43.4 per cent in 1965; trade turnover with members of Comecon declined from 78 per cent in 1963 to 73.7 per cent in 1966.

The eleventh plenum of the CC, which met between 15 and 18 December 1965, launched a full-scale attack on the prevailing liberal climate in ideology and culture. Erich Honecker delivered the Politburo report and he castigated those scientists, engineers and state managers who had not 'yet overcome the tendency to look immediately to the West in all questions of new technology, without having taken the trouble to find out what the Soviets were doing in these fields'. He informed these specialists that closer cooperation with the Soviet Union was to be afforded primacy. Many films, plays and literary works were openly 'sceptical and innovatory' and concentrated on the 'mistakes' in GDR society. The 'absolute freedom' being claimed by some artists only helped the enemies of socialism. The singer Wolf Biermann and the writer Stefan Heym were referred to as traitors for having published in West Germany. Another target was Havemann. He was dismissed from his post in January 1966 and shortly afterwards was expelled from the Academy of Sciences. Indeed many functionaries lost their jobs, the most prominent casualty being Hans Bentzien, the Minister of Culture.

As regards youth, Horst Schumann, the First Secretary of

the FDJ, admitted that his organisation had provided 'totally erroneous ideological guidelines'. Schumann recommended a return to previous norms and the relaxed attitude towards Western life-styles and views was abruptly terminated. Schumann later underlined the leading role of the SED in society and admitted that many young people had challenged and openly rejected such a role.

The Economic System of Socialism (ESS)

The seventh congress of the SED, which met between 17 and 22 April 1967, set the country new tasks. Whereas the sixth congress had stated that the chief task was the 'all-round construction of socialism', the seventh congress declared the 'completion of socialism' to be the target. 'The formation of the developed social system of socialism begins with the 7th Congress . . . Developed socialist society utilises to the full the economic system of socialism based on the scientific—technical revolution' (*Neues Deutschland* 23 April 1967). Thus the GDR was proclaiming that the experimental stage was over and that a socialist economic model in a developed socialist society had been evolved. The performance of the economy in 1966 had given considerable satisfaction. Industrial output rose 6 per cent and national income 5 per cent. The 1966—70 plan envisaged this being achieved every year. A 'socialist human community' was evolving in the GDR. 'The growth of the socialist human community is determined by science as a direct force of production in all sectors of material production, by organisation and management of complex processes . . . and by the evolution of socialist personalities, something which is clearly evident in all classes and strata.' This new concept of community blurred class distinctions as the boundaries of the working class were extended to include many who had previously been outside it.

The ESS was to be a centrally-planned socialist economy but the market was not completely eliminated. 'The socialist planned economy is neither an administered economy nor a so-called market economy which functions spontaneously. The socialist production of goods and the market play quite an important role in it. However the determining factor of its organic unity is and will remain social planning' (*Neues Deutschland* 18 April 1967).

Another administrative reform was introduced in 1967. The State Planning Commission was upgraded to become the economic general staff of the Council of Ministers. Some of its duties, at the same time, were transferred to the Council of Ministers. The increase in the functions of the Council of Ministers and the ministries is evidence of further recentralisation. A more significant change was the Council of State resolution of 22 April 1968 on the further development of the ESS. The planners had discovered that the instruments at their disposal were sufficent to guide the activities of the VVB but not sufficient to bring about the structural changes in the economy they were seeking. Since great emphasis was placed on 'structure-determining' sectors of the economy such as chemicals and electrical engineering, the Council of State ordered a return to central directives and the central allocation of resources. In many ways this was a decisive move away from the ESS but it did not affect those sectors not regarded as determining the structure of the economy. In those areas enterprises saw their independence *vis-à-vis* the central planners extended in that their annual plans were not so closely scrutinised, provided their activities were in accordance with long-term plan goals.

The ESS was extended on 1 January 1968 to embrace not only industry but trade and agriculture as well. The VEB were to try harder to become self-financing. Due to constantly changing technology, the VVB were to be allowed to initiate dynamic price changes. Data-processing was accorded more significance. The State Secretary for Data Processing was made a member of the Council of Ministers and his area of competence was extended. The number of computer outlets was to increase rapidly and the necessary computer expertise acquired. It was unfortunate for the technocrats that at precisely this moment relations between the Soviet Union and Czechoslovakia were deteriorating, something which boded ill for experimentation.

Industrial expansion during the 1960s was quite satisfactory but towards the end of the decade a crisis began to loom. The emphasis placed on the 'structure-determining' sectors saw growth in them surge ahead — they accounted for just over half of industrial output in 1970 compared to 36 per cent in 1955. However the rest of the economy suffered and this led to serious imbalance. The weather did not help either. The winters of 1968–9 and 1969–70 were long and severe and were followed in both cases by hot, dry summers. Long-term underinvestment in energy, transport and water supply resulted in these sectors not being able to take the strain. Agriculture was in an even worse plight. Compared to industry's 4.4 per cent real annual growth between 1960 and 1965, agriculture could only manage 0.3 per cent; between 1965 and 1970 industry recorded 5.8 per cent annual growth but agriculture only achieved 1.7 per cent annual growth (Mitzscherling *et al.* 1974: 69). The hot summers reduced the fodder available and hard currency had to be spent on importing fodder to maintain the animal population.

It transpired that indirect instruments were quite inadequate to achieve the enterprise behaviour the central planners wanted. Concerns often produced goods which conflicted with the planned goals of the economy due to the incorrect prices then in operation. The whole situation was reviewed at a meeting of the Politburo on 8 September 1970 and crucial decisions affecting the economy were taken. A decree of the Council of Ministers of 23 September 1970 substantially altered the goals of the 1971–5 plan which had just been worked out. A debate ensued during which the deficiencies of the ESS were aired. The fourteenth plenum of the CC, which met between 9 and 11 December 1970, was devoted to the economy and a major shift to recentralisation was announced. The decision-making power of the VEB was sharply curtailed: the VVB could no longer initiate price changes, all prices were frozen and an increase in the indicators handed down by the central planners made it clear that the NES—ESS had been laid to rest.

The Scientific—Technical Revolution

At the twenty-second congress of the CPSU in 1961 science was upgraded to become a force of production, thus transferring it from the superstructure to the base. It also spelled out the significance of the scientific—technical revolution. The use of atomic energy, man's probing of the cosmos, developments in chemistry and the automation of production were to transform life. The new Soviet party programme looked forward to communism and declared that only socialism was capable of fully exploiting the potential of the scientific—technical revolution. The SED reclassified science as a force of production in the programme adopted at the sixth congress in 1963. Furthermore the empirically oriented social sciences, such as planning, management and the natural sciences, were also classified as forces of production. Cybernetics, praised as the 'fundamental science of the coming age' by Khrushchev at the twenty-second congress, could now be applied to a socialist society. This discipline, which also includes systems theory, can be viewed as a theory of dynamic self-regulating systems. Its main proponent in the GDR was Professor Georg Klaus. One of his goals was to express dialectical and historical materialism in mathematical terms. Klaus saw systems theory as a force of production of the first magnitude which would provide the rationale for automation. He developed a cybernetic theory of society in which social organisations were to be self-regulating in a rational, optimally efficient fashion. Eventually the central organs of the state and the party would be 'controlled' through feedback from the working population. His theory, of course, aroused enormous interest and opposition, not least from those who clearly saw that their jobs would be downgraded or eliminated. Those who felt most threatened were the party ideologues. The battle for cybernetics was fought out between 1962 and 1965 and a major factor in its success was the support Ulbricht afforded it.

The scientific—technical revolution involved greater consultation and more contact between workers and management. More information was needed, everyone, including party officials, had to display greater technical proficiency and material self-interest was accorded a higher priority. As a consequence the SED set out to expand 'socialist democracy'. Permanent production councils, production committees, social councils based on the VVB, more commissions of representative institutions at local level and greater responsibilities for mass organisations, especially the FDGB, were initiated.

The courting of the technical intelligentsia meant that the SED had to pay more attention to purely empirical data. It conceded that purely ideological claims could be challenged by those with technical expertise. Great advances were made in education and the level of skill of the labour force was raised significantly. The number of graduate scientists, engineers and economists rose sharply.

The extravagant hopes held out for the scientific—technical revolution in the 1960s were not realised. The SED hoped, for instance, that it would lead to an economic take-off which would solve the German problem by demonstrating the superiority of socialism. Unfortunately for the party the whole operation turned out to be much more complex than anticipated. The price reform was never satisfactorily completed and a part of the planning mechanism, the input—output table, was never entirely drawn up. Instead of bringing society together the stress on expertise widened the gulf between the intelligentsia and the working class and did nothing to reduce the gulf between mental and physical labour. Those employed directly in production dropped from 74.4 per cent in 1962 to 67 per cent in 1970; those involved in research and development rose from 3.2 per cent in 1962 to 5 per cent in 1970; and those regarded as management rose from 6.5 per cent in 1962 to 10 per cent in 1970. Incomes of production workers rose noticeably faster than those of the labour force as a whole between 1965 and 1974. Since training takes time, too many workers embarked on courses to acquire higher qualifications only to see the promised jobs fail to materialise when they had completed their training. In one heavy industry plant, in 1976, 28.6 per cent of jobs intended for semi-skilled workers were being done by skilled workers. By the early 1970s about 10 per cent of the skilled labour force were performing tasks below their level of qualification. If this was true of the labour force it applied *a fortiori* to the technical intelligentsia.

The higher technical demands of the 1960s required expensive capital equipment to be worked longer every day. This led to more night work and shift working with an increase in nervous strain, boredom and tiredness. As processes became more automated, workers had to perform fewer functions. The need for assembly line work grew but, understandably, more and more workers resisted this. The pressure to raise labour productivity often led to worse working conditions; social side-effects such as a decreasing birth rate and an increasing divorce rate were due, in part, to these new circumstances.

Changes in the SED

Although the population of the GDR declined during the 1960s, party membership increased. In December 1961, the

Table 4.1: *Social composition of the SED*

	1961	1966	1971
Workers	33.8	45.6	56.6
Peasants	6.2	6.4	5.9
Employees	32.6	16.1	13.0
Intelligentsia	8.7	12.3	17.1
Others	18.7	19.6	7.4

Source: M. McCauley, *Marxism—Leninism in the German Democratic Republic* (London, 1979) p. 140.

SED counted 1 610 769 full and candidate members but in June 1971 this had risen to 1 909 859. The social composition of the party also changed over the same period (see Table 4.1).

A deliberate policy of recruiting more workers was undertaken during the 1960s to overcome the odd situation of a party which claimed to be the *avant-garde* of the working class being numerically dominated by non-workers. A special target during this period were skilled workers since they were seen as key personalities. As a member of the party they can be called upon to set an example to their colleagues and often to undertake unpaid endeavour. They must show a positive attitude to innovation and show the way to others. The SED grew by just over 150 000 between 1961 and 1966 but even if all new recruits had been workers the proportion of workers in the party in 1966 would not have been as high as 45.6 per cent. A possible explanation is that a large number of employees and members of the intelligentsia left the party, but there is no evidence to support this. Indeed the SED was very eager to recruit from the expanding technical intelligentsia. A more probable answer is that some members were reclassified as workers due to the implications of the scientific—technical revolution. Another difficulty in interpreting party statistics is that a member retains the classification he received on entry during his career. Hence Ulbricht was counted as a worker even though he had been a full-time functionary for years. The more able and ambitious workers graduate to white-collar jobs in the party, government and mass organisations. At the sixth congress in 1963 it was revealed that 55.5 per cent of the delegates were workers but that almost half of them were performing 'leading functions in party, government and mass organisations' (*Neues Deutschland* 21 January 1963). More information was given about workers in the party at the seventh congress in 1967. 'The character of our party as a party of the working class is expressed by the fact that 61.6 per cent of all members and candidate members were workers on joining the party. A large proportion of these comrades now occupy leading positions in the party, state, economy, police and armed forces, many are acquiring qualifications to become members of the intelligentsia or technical employees (*Protokoll* 1967: 226). This appears to mean that workers who acquire the requisite skills are reclassified as members of the intelligentsia. The proportion of workers in the SED given by Erich Honecker at the eighth congress in June 1971 was the highest ever attained. The new First Secretary also revealed that 76.8 per cent of all members were of worker origin.

The concept of intelligentsia is not very precise when used by the SED. This key stratum also doubled its proportion in the party during the 1960s. An increasing number of graduates were to be found in the party. The graduate population in 1966 was put at 557 000; this revealed that just over half of all graduates were SED members. As regards age structure in 1966, 20.3 per cent of members were under 30 years of age and 21.2 per cent over 60. Also 41.2 per cent of members had been in the party for 15—20 years and 6.9 per cent had previously been members of the KPD or SPD.

In 1967 it was stated that 77.7 per cent of first secretaries and 57.5 per cent of second secretaries of Kreis executive committees had been over ten years in the party apparatus. One reason for this was their high level of education: 83 per cent of Kreis secretaries (there are usually five or six per Kreis) were graduates and 64.2 per cent had passed successfully through the Karl Marx Party University. The same level of academic achievement was not reproduced at Bezirk level where only six of the fifteen first secretaries were graduates.

The Central Committee elected at the sixth congress in 1963 was much younger than its counterpart elected at the previous congress in 1958. Its technical and professional qualifications were also much superior to those of the 1958 CC. Of the 121 full members elected in 1963, 27 were graduates and another five were enrolled at the Karl Marx Party University and later graduated. Among the 60 candidate members in 1963, 35 were graduates. Hence candidate members were much more highly qualified than full members, reflecting concern for the economy, education, science and culture. By 1967 the qualifications of full members had improved when 53 per cent were graduates. The overwhelming majority of new full members elected in 1967 were graduates. In 1971, 59 per cent of full members and 89 per cent of candidate members had enjoyed higher education. The CC was, of course, dominated by the party functionaries. Next came the government apparatus, with the Council of Ministers increasing its representation as time passed. All the heads of the mass organisations were in the CC as were several managing directors of the VVB. On the other hand, the officially recognised minority, the Sorbs, was not represented in the CC.

Membership of the Secretariat was remarkably stable during the 1960s. There was a clear division between the older members, Hager (ideology), Honecker (security), Norden (agitation until 1967), Verner (German affairs) and the younger men, Grüneberg (agriculture), Mittag (economic affairs), Jarowinsky (domestic and foreign trade and supply), Lamberz (agitation and propaganda from 1967) and Axen (international relations from 1966). Walter Ulbricht was, of course, the leading secretary and when he was removed on 3 May 1971 and replaced by Erich Honecker, Paul Verner took over the latter's responsibilities for security.

There are about 40 departments of the CC, with about 2000 important functionaries, all responsible to a CC secretary. As its name implies, the Secretariat is concerned with the day-to-day running of the party. In 1971 all secretaries were full or candidate members of the Politburo with the exception of Horst Dohlus, secretary for party organs, but he became a candidate member in 1976 and a full member in 1980.

It is difficult to distinguish between the competence of the Secretariat and that of the Politburo. The Secretariat is mainly concerned with party affairs but supervises the activities of the government, the police and the military. The Politburo supervises all party activity, ensures that the key elements in the political system function efficiently and takes all the decisions of primary importance to the state and society. The Politburo has its own bureau which acts as an intermediary between it and the Secretariat. This bureau prepares the agenda for Politburo meetings. The Secretariat is also responsible for the nomenklatura. This is both a list of the appointments which cannot be filled without higher party authority and the individuals suitable to fill these posts. These posts are divided into three groups with the most senior posts on the nomenklatura of the Politburo.

The party statute states that the CC elects the Politburo as political head of the work of the CC between plenums which should take place at least once every six months. This disguises the real significance of the Politburo which is the key institution in party and state. Each congress elects a new CC and it in turn elects a new Politburo and Secretariat. The Politburo elected at the sixth congress in 1963 consisted of fourteen full and nine candidate members. By the seventh congress, Otto Grotewohl and Bruno Leuschner had died, Erich Apel, a candidate member, had taken his own life and Karl-Heinz Bartsch, also candidate member, had been exposed as a former member of the SS. Gerhard Grüneberg and Günter Mittag had become full members in September 1966. Horst Sindermann became a full member at the congress. Walter Halbritter and Günther Kleiber, both possessing technical expertise, became candidate members. Between the seventh and eighth congresses Paul Fröhlich and Hermann Matern, chairman of the Central Control Commission of the party, died. Hermann Axen was promoted to full membership in December 1970, replacing Fröhlich. Werner Lamberz became a candidate member at the same time. At the eighth congress, in June 1971, there were further changes. Erich Honecker had replaced Walter Ulbricht as First Secretary shortly before the congress. Ulbricht stayed in the Politburo but all his party responsibilities passed to Honecker. Lamberz became a full member as did Werner Krolikowski, first secretary of Bezirk Dresden, without having passed through the candidate stage. Harry Tisch, first secretary in Bezirk Rostock and Erich Mielke, Minister of State Security, were promoted to candidate membership.

The 1960s, in sharp contrast to the 1950s, was a decade of remarkable stability. No one left the Politburo over policy differences with the First Secretary. Young, well-educated cadres were drawn in to cope with the complexities of state and society. Naturally the candidate members had higher academic qualifications than full members of the Politburo. Two who stand out are Lamberz and Mittag. Lamberz deployed great skill in formulating Marxist–Leninist positions and in charting an ideological path in a technological era. Mittag, a very capable economist and administrator, also possessed political realism. In 1968 he came out unequivocally in favour of close party control of the economy.

Women have always been in a majority in the GDR but in a minority in the SED. Active recruitment of women improved the situation. In December 1966, 26.5 per cent of full and candidate members were female but this had risen to 28.7 per cent at the eighth congress in June 1971. Women were poorly represented in the party apparatus. In the 15 Bezirk executive committees elected in May 1971, 24.9 per cent of members were women and 42.7 per cent of candidate members were female. However of the 90 Bezirk secretaries, only four were female and of the 195 members of the Bezirk secretariat there were only nine women. Among the 121 full members of the CC, elected in 1963, 15 were female and 5 of the 60 candidate members were women. At the seventh congress in 1967, the 131 full members included 16 women and 6 of the 50 candidates were female. Women improved their standing at the eighth congress in 1971. Among the 135 full members, 18 were female and 7 of the 54 candidate members were women. No woman has been elected a full member of the Politburo since its inception in January 1949 although there have been candidate members. There were no female secretaries of the CC in 1971.

The picture was, not surprisingly, the same in the state apparatus in 1971 with only one Bezirk council being headed by a woman, Irma Uschkamp in Cottbus. Margot Honecker, the wife of the First Secretary, was the only woman in the Council of Ministers and Margarete Wittkowski, president of the State Bank, was the only other woman occupying a leading state post. Among the 150 or so state secretaries and deputy ministers only three were female but five of the 25 members of the Council of State were female in 1971.

It is of some significance that women played a more important role in the upper echelons of the party and state apparatuses while socialism was being built in the GDR than afterwards.

Developed socialism appears to favour the male. How can this be explained in a country which declares that equality of the sexes exists? Traditional prejudice against career women, the close connection between key posts in the SED and the government, a shortage of qualified women for responsible positions, the burden of work, children and the home and the fact that important posts often require considerable travel and time spent away from home and the striking lack of organisations which will promote the political interests of women — the DFD, for instance, reflects the policies of the male-dominated party leadership rather than the interests of women — are some of the reasons which spring to mind. During the 1960s women were concentrated in certain occupational groups and the women who occupied important party and state posts were grouped together in certain policy areas. No woman was head of a key sector of the economy. (A possible exception is Margarete Wittkowski, president of the State Bank.) Women are breaking out of their traditional occupations but are failing to acquire decisive positions. Until this situation changes the numerical strength of women in the GDR will not be reflected in policy-making.

Foreign Policy

When Cuba entered into diplomatic relations with the GDR in January 1963 she became only the thirteenth state to do so. No capitalist state recognised the sovereignty of the GDR. Due to her vigorous anti-imperialist policy, the GDR began to win friends in the Third World and in February 1965 the first success in foreign policy was registered. Ulbricht travelled to Egypt and was accorded all the honours due to a head of state. His invitation to visit Egypt had in part been due to the good offices of the Yugoslavs who had done much to pave the way. (Relations between the GDR and Yugoslavia had taken a turn for the better after the GDR had agreed to pay reparations amounting to about 100 million marks in early 1963.) An Egyptian general consulate was established in East Berlin and gradually it became possible to expand diplomatic links so that the GDR had either a general consulate or a consulate in nine countries and there were official trade missions in another ten states, some having limited consular rights. Attempts to gain admission to the United Nations in 1966 were blocked by the Western Powers.

Prior to 1958 the GDR had never objected to the presence of West German representative institutions in West Berlin. Indeed the GDR had welcomed the convocation of the Bundesversammlung, held to elect the president of the FRG, in 1954 and the Bundestag, or lower house, in 1955. As of 1958 the GDR altered course to pursue a policy of squeezing the West Germans out of Berlin. When a plenary session of the Bundestag was announced for 7 April 1965 in West Berlin, the USSR and the GDR acted in concert. The GDR stated that participants would not be granted permission to cross her territory but the warnings were ignored. Transit traffic was interrupted and army manoeuvres across the routes meant that all traffic to West Berlin was halted on several occasions. It ended suddenly on 10 April 1965 when the Soviet High Command called off the manoeuvres. The GDR had stated that they would end on 11 April and the reason for the abrupt end to the interference would appear to be connected with the decision by the United States to send additional armoured units to Berlin on 10 April.

At the tenth plenum of the CC on 24 June 1965, Otto Winzer, the newly appointed Minister of Foreign Affairs, went so far as to claim unrestricted sovereignty over the land, water and air of the GDR. He maintained that the USSR exercised 'control over the flights which were necessary for communications purposes and the supplying of the three Western Powers in West Berlin' only by virtue of the fact that this concession had been granted her by the GDR. If the Western Powers wished to overfly the GDR they would have to apply to the GDR government for permission to do so. This was a nice piece of bluff since everyone was aware that the Soviet Union did not need to ask for GDR permission to act in the GDR.

Until 1966 the GDR pursued a policy of 'all-German initiatives' so as eventually to persuade the government in Bonn to enter into negotiations, thereby affording the GDR diplomatic recognition. Contacts were frozen after the building of the Berlin Wall but over Christmas 1963 an agreement was reached with the West Berlin Senate which resulted in 1.2 million West Berliners being able again to visit their relatives in the eastern part of the city. Old age pensioners in the GDR received permission to visit their relatives in West Germany from November 1964 onwards. Other opportunities existed for exchanges of view in the press but were not taken seriously by the FRG. In May 1964 Ulbricht sent a letter to Ludwig Erhard, the Federal Chancellor, proposing gradual disarmament by both German states and the convocation of a German Council composed of an equal number of members from the Volkskammer and the Bundestag. The ostensible goal was a 'unified, peace-loving Germany'. The letter was returned to East Berlin unopened.

On 12 June 1964 the USSR and the GDR signed a treaty of friendship, mutual assistance and cooperation in Moscow. The 'decisive factor' governing relations between the two states was the 'principle of socialist internationalism'. The treaty was a substitute for the separate peace treaty which the USSR had been threatening to sign with the GDR. It spoke of West Berlin as an 'independent political entity' in which the FRG had no jurisdiction. The Western Powers replied on 26 June 1964 by rejecting the new definition of West Berlin's status and claiming that its links with West Germany were legitimate while stating that the FRG government spoke for the German people throughout the world.

In order to test feeling about reunification in the FRG, the SED, on 11 February 1966, forwarded an 'open-letter' to the delegates of the SPD congress, scheduled for Dortmund in June 1966. This was not a new *démarche*. The SED had sent twelve 'open letters' to the SPD during the years since 1951 but they had all gone unanswered. Likewise the SPD had also forwarded a dozen 'open letters' to the SED over the years 1951–63. In its latest letter the SED sought ways of establishing closer contact and cooperation with the SPD so as to overcome the division of Germany. The SPD replied on 18 March 1966 in the form of an 'open answer' and made it clear that it did not consider the SED to be a suitable negotiating partner as long as the declared policy of the SED was to 'replace the free democratic order with the rule of a monopolistic party' but asked if the SED was prepared to work towards making everyday life in divided Germany easier. On 26 March 1966 the SED replied in a second 'open letter' and proposed that representatives of the SED and the SPD should speak at a meeting in Karl-Marx-Stadt and that later both parties should discuss matters at an SPD meeting in Essen. The SPD immediately agreed and proposed meetings in Karl-Marx-Stadt and Hanover. Several meetings between Paul Verner and Werner Lamberz, for the SED, and two SPD representatives took place in East Berlin and eventually it was agreed to hold the meetings on 14 and 21 June 1966. However the debates never took place. The SED leadership withdrew using a new law passed by the Bundestag as a smoke screen — they argued that it was directed against them and that they would be liable to arrest when they entered the FRG — but the main reason would appear to be the party's concern about the great expectations aroused in the GDR population by the discussion of German unity. In other words the SED had misjudged the mood of the average GDR citizen and even of party members. The pull of West Germany turned out to be much greater than expected.

When the SPD entered the Grand Coalition with the CDU/CSU in December 1966 it put an end to any lingering SED hope that a wedge could be driven between social democrats and Christian democrats on the conditions for German unity. Willy Brandt, the SPD leader, became the new Foreign Minister. The coalition launched a much more active Ostpolitik, the goal of which was to establish better relations with the socialist states. The GDR read this as an attempt to isolate her and changed her Westpolitik or policy towards the FRG completely. The SED bitterly attacked the SPD and even renamed it the Social Democratic Party, dropping the 'D' which stood for Germany. This was also extended to the other West German parties, the argument being that they had ceased to represent Germany's real interests. Together with this went a campaign to convince GDR citizens that unification between the 'socialist fatherland' and the 'Federal Republic, ruled by monopoly capitalism' was quite out of the question. This led the SED to claim that there was no longer any common German culture, literature or science and consequently institutions were renamed. For instance, on 2 February 1967 the State Secretariat for All-German Affairs became the State Secretariat for West German Affairs. On 20 February 1967 a new GDR citizenship law was passed which repealed the Reich and State Citizenship Law of 1913 and removed the claim in the GDR constitution that there was a single German citizenship. At the same time a polemic was launched with Romania which had broken ranks and entered into diplomatic relations with the FRG on 31

January 1967. The GDR was incensed that another socialist state had not rejected Bonn's claim to speak for all Germans. The Romanians replied in kind pointing out that the GDR's comments represented 'interference in the internal affairs of another country'. With Bonn sounding out Prague about diplomatic relations, the GDR became alarmed that her standing in Eastern and South-eastern Europe could suffer. At a meeting of the Foreign Ministers of the Warsaw Pact in February 1967 Ulbricht won the support of the USSR and Poland. Tangible results soon followed. In March 1967 the GDR signed a treaty of friendship, cooperation and mutual assistance with Poland and Czechoslovakia, in May with Hungary and in September 1967 with Bulgaria.

At the conference of communist and workers' parties in Karlovy Vary in April 1967 (Yugoslavia and Romania declined to attend) the first steps on the road to the Helsinki Final Accord were taken. Collective security was the aim and it was to be based on the recognition by the West of the frontiers resulting from the Second World War. It was agreed that no state should recognise the FRG until she had accepted this. This in turn meant that the FRG had to recognise diplomatically the GDR before she could enter into diplomatic relations with the other socialist states. If the SED could derive some satisfaction from Karlovy Vary, other events in Czechoslovakia were arousing unease. When Antonin Novotny was replaced by Alexander Dubček as First Secretary of the Communist Party of Czechoslovakia, the long-delayed process of de-Stalinisation began. The SED immediately became one of the 'Prague Spring's' fiercest critics. To Ulbricht and the SED leadership every step along the democratic road in Czechoslovakia was tantamount to 'surrendering the positions gained by socialism to counter-revolution'. In other words the SED opposed the attempts of the Communist Party of Czechoslovakia to move from ruling by coercion to ruling by consent. Not everyone in the GDR objected to such a development. For example, Robert Havemann was an enthusiastic supporter of the Prague Spring.

The first meeting of the Warsaw Pact states to consider developments in Czechoslavakia took place in Dresden, in March 1968 with Romania absent. The Soviet Union, Poland the GDR, Hungary and Bulgaria at their next meeting in Warsaw on 14—15 July 1968 came out strongly against the path being taken by the Czechoslovak communists. They warned them that they would not stand idly by if socialism was under threat in their country. This became known as the Brezhnev doctrine which permits the CPSU to define socialism according to Soviet interests. Ulbricht did make one last attempt, at Karlovy Vary on 13 August 1968, to convince the Czechoslovak leaders that they should change course. The SED leadership consistently took a hard line against the Czechoslovak attempt to introduce 'socialism with a human face' but the decision to invade on 21 August 1968 was primarily a Soviet one. The five states which had met at Warsaw intervened and this involved German troops invading Czechoslovakia again after an interval of 20 years. They were quickly withdrawn but the GDR had made it clear that she would defend her system of government abroad as well as at home.

In order to improve relations with East Berlin it was necessary for Bonn to ameliorate relations with Moscow. Talks got under way in Janury 1970. Andrei Gromyko wanted the FRG to recognise the GDR in international law but Egon Bahr, for West Germany, argued that neither the GDR nor the FRG was a fully sovereign state. Only when a peace treaty was signed and the Four Powers had given up responsibility for Germany would the two German states become sovereign. These two German states — recognised by Chancellor Willy Brandt in October 1969 — existed under the umbrella of the Great Powers. Hence they were not foreign to one another and this meant that the FRG could not recognise the GDR in international law. At the same time the FRG was attempting to establish closer relations with the GDR. The East Germans were hesitant in responding to a note of 22 January 1970 which Brandt had sent to Willi Stoph, chairman of the Council of Ministers. However it was agreed to meet in Erfurt, just inside the GDR border, on 19 March 1970. Stoph immediately demanded that the FRG recognise the GDR in international law, something which the Soviets had conceded could not be done at that time. A second meeting took place at Kassel, just over the border in West Germany, on 21 May 1970. Stoph kept up his hard line, demanding 100 000 million marks as compensation for the damage occasioned the GDR economy before the building of the Berlin Wall.

The Moscow Treaty was signed on 12 August 1970 and while

in the Soviet Union Willy Brandt met Leonid Brezhnev. He made it clear to the Soviet leader that it would not be possible to secure a majority in the Bundestag for the ratification of the treaty unless an acceptable Berlin settlement were reached.

Four Power negotiations on Berlin had been under way since 26 March 1970 but the two sides adopted radically different approaches. Whereas the USSR regarded East Berlin as an integral part of the GDR, thus placing only West Berlin under Four Power control, the Western Allies took the whole of Berlin to be within the competence of the Four Powers. Transit rights, the Soviets proposed, should be negotiated with the GDR. She in turn insisted that transit rights could only be negotiated when the special political status of West Berlin was accepted. Later the Soviets altered their position and no longer insisted that recognition of the special status of West Berlin had to precede a transit agreement, but the GDR held to her hard line. The USSR was more interested in a Berlin settlement than the GDR, since she was keen to improve her standing in Bonn and in so doing she could encourage the West Germans to loosen their ties with the Western Alliance. Friction between East Berlin and Moscow contributed to Ulbricht's removal from office in May 1971. Afterwards progress was much more rapid with the vital breakthrough coming on 11 August 1971. This may have been connected with Henry Kissinger's visit to Peking and the news that President Nixon was to visit China. The Berlin Agreement was signed on 3 September 1971 but with the Western Powers stating that it applied to Berlin and the Soviet Union and the GDR speaking of a West Berlin Agreement. However everyone accepted that West Berlin was not part of the FRG but that the West Germans could maintain links with the city. Even this became unclear as the Russian word for links implies that no political ties are permissible whereas the English and French terms permit these. Transit rights were agreed between the two German states and an agreement was signed on 17 December 1971. This document became part of the Four Power Agreement. The way had been smoothed for the ratification of the Moscow Treaty by the West German parliament and this was achieved in May 1972. The Berlin Agreement came into force on 3 June 1972 with the signing of the final protocol. The Soviet goal, that of getting the Western

Powers to accept the post-war frontiers, was within sight. Helsinki was to finish the process which had begun in Karlovy Vary.

Developed Socialism

The ever-increasing stabilisation of the GDR and the bright prospects held out by the NES added to the growing self-confidence of Ulbricht and the SED leadership. This had an effect on the ideology and the First Secretary, on the occasion of the hundredth anniversary of the publication of Karl Marx's *Das Kapital*, in 1967, revised the father of scientific socialism's definition of socialism. Whereas Marx regarded socialism as a short transition phase on the road to communism, Ulbricht claimed that it was no such thing but a 'relatively independent socio-economic formation during the historical epoch of the transition from capitalism to communism'. Shortly afterwards Günter Mittag went one stage further. 'The formation of the developed social system of socialism, with its economic system as its core, permits us now to enter the second phase of the socialist revolution in the GDR in which socialism will henceforth develop on its own base' (*Neues Deutschland* 24 November 1967). This meant that money, prices and profit were not to be transitory phenomena but were to remain a long time. However under socialism they were to be of a 'qualitatively new type'.

The main reason why Ulbricht introduced his revisionism was that socialism had not been victorious on a world scale. Capitalism had proved surprisingly resilient and moreover labour productivity in many capitalist countries was higher than under socialism. Consequently the advent of communism was being pushed further and further into the future. Ulbricht's new definition of socialism was possible because of Khrushchev's ideological innovations in the Soviet Union where he had claimed that the foundations of communism would be in place by 1981. The SED leader was much more realistic. Nevertheless, in lengthening the life of socialism and putting it historically on a par with feudalism and capitalism, he was bracketing the USSR and the GDR together. He was also indirectly saying that the Soviet Union's attempt to reach communism by 1981 was misguided. In other words he was claiming the right to develop creatively Marxism—Leninism and this challenge Moscow could not ignore. Ulbricht's growing self-confidence *vis-à-vis* the CPSU can be seen in the message which the Politburo of the SED sent the CC of the CPSU on 17 October 1964, shortly after Khrushchev's removal. It judged the previous First Secretary's implementation of Marxist—Leninist policy to be 'successful' but contrasted this with his 'final failure' and the fact that 'he was no longer capable of fulfilling his duties' (*Neus Deutschland* 21 November 1964). None of this appears in the CPSU's condemnation of Khrushchev.

The SED was very aware of the fact that socialism in the GDR had been built on a solid industrial foundation. This dinstinguished the GDR from the other socialist states which had constructed socialism on an agrarian base and the consequences of this were spelt out. 'The developed socialist society has been achieved in a country which was already a highly developed industrial state under capitalism. This in itself is an objective reason for the increasing attractiveness of the GDR in the eyes of the progressive forces in West European capitalist countries.'

The stress placed on science and technology in the economy had an effect on SED thinking about its own role. It saw its goal as the 'scientific management of society'. In order to achieve this it was necessary to define precisely the responsibilities of each official so as to increase efficiency. The SED was not abdicating its leading role but was trying to master new methods and techniques so as to make its dominance even more effective. Public opinion research, psychology and cybernetics were only some of the disciplines pressed into service. Since the party claimed that it could comprehend the laws of human development it sought consciously to influence social processes. It maintained that it could do this more successfully than in the past due to the new insights being provided by science. Since such a premium was placed on scientific and technical knowledge, older functionaries who possessed little were gradually replaced by younger cadres who claimed the necessary expertise. Decision-making was gradually to be based on scientific or objective criteria and less and less on ideological or subjective criteria. The SED hoped that this would make the economy more efficient and thereby make it easier for the party to manage society. It soon transpired, however, that the problems involved in running the GDR from the centre were vastly more complex than had been imagined.

The concept of a developed socialist society involved changes in the laws and the constitution. A new criminal code was introduced on 12 January 1968 and it stated that the purpose of law was not to punish but to prevent crimes being committed. However political offences were to be severely dealt with. Law, it was made clear, was an 'instrument of the state management of society'. The 'struggle against all crime, especially against the criminal attacks on peace, on the sovereignty of the GDR and on the worker and peasant state is the common responsibility of socialist society' (*Gesetzblatt der DDR* 1968: 7). The rights of citizens were also spelled out but the penalties for political opposition remained severe. These rights were to be exercised in a socialist manner and the SED was the final arbiter of socialist behaviour.

A draft constitution was published in February 1968 and was presented for public comment. It replaced the 1949 constitution, as amended in 1955, which allowed for voluntary national service, in 1958 when the Länderkammer or land parliaments were abolished and in 1960 when the Council of State was established and the post of president of the republic was abolished. Many improvements were suggested by the public and a few of them found their way into the final text. This meant that freedom of conscience, the right to hold religious views and the immunity from prosecution of Volkskammer deputies when they criticised the state and the party were written in. A referendum was held on 6 April 1968 and 94.5 per cent of those entitled to vote accepted the constitution. Interestingly enough, in East Berlin only 90.9 per cent were willing to endorse it (Weber 1980: 132). The leading role of the SED was underlined in the first article. 'The GDR is a socialist state of the German nation. It is the political organisation of workers and employees in city and countryside who together, under the leadership of the working class and its Marxist—Leninist party, are building socialism.' Other articles guaranteed personal freedom, freedom from oppression and economic exploitation and freedom of conscience and belief, but these freedoms were intended to be exercised by socialist citizens in a socialist society. It was also stated that the Volkskammer was the supreme organ of state in the GDR. These provisions were closely related to those of the 1936 Soviet constitution. The USSR Supreme Soviet and the Volkskammer were held to be the supreme organs of the state since neither the CPSU nor the SED is supposed to rule or govern but to guide the state in its development. The communist party does not order state institutions to do anything but only proffers advice. Since its advice cannot be ignored it means, in reality, that the communist party is the centre of power in the state. The right to strike was included in the 1949 constitution but was omitted from the new one since under socialism it was held that workers had no one to strike against, the means of production belonged to society. On the whole, the new constitution corresponds much more closely to the realities of life in the GDR than the 1949 variant.

The First Secretary Goes

Walter Ulbricht's decision to retire as First Secretary of the SED was not taken willingly: in fact, he was pushed out of office. In formally retiring at the sixteenth plenum of the CC on 3 May 1971 he admitted that the decision to vacate the top office in the GDR had been a very difficult one to take. Although he only stepped down as First Secretary, his days of major political influence were over. He held on to the chairmanship of the Council of State and the chairmanship of the Defence Council but he soon lost the latter post. Under Erich Honecker, the new First Secretary, the Council of State rapidly diminished in significance and by Ulbricht's death on 1 August 1973 the job was almost entirely ceremonial. Although he remained in the Politburo he was kicked upstairs by being named chairman of the SED, a post which is not to be found in the party statutes. Ulbricht was approaching his seventy-eighth birthday when he departed the political stage and his age had begun to show increasingly during his last years in office. His legendary flexibility *vis-à-vis* the Soviet Union began to disappear and the negotiations over the Berlin Agreement exasperated some Soviet diplomats, including Pyotr Abrasimov, the ambassador to the GDR. Ulbricht wanted a settlement which was much more beneficial to the GDR but the Soviets wanted *détente*. The clash of interests resulted in the Soviet view prevailing, after Ulbricht had stepped down. Displeasure was evident from the telegram which the CPSU sent the SED on the occasion of its twenty-fifth birthday, on 21 April 1971. Instead of Brezhnev, as Secretary General of the CPSU, sending greetings to Ulbricht as First Secretary of the SED, it was unsigned and was from the CC of the CPSU to the CC of the SED. It lauded the role played by Pieck and Grotewohl in the development of the party: Ulbricht's name was not mentioned (*Pravda* 21 April 1971).

Although the Soviets had their reasons for wanting to see the back of the incumbent First Secretary his economic record was probably of key importance in his fall. The disproportions which had surfaced in the GDR economy, resulting from over-emphasis on some sectors and neglect of the consumer goods industries, were potentially dangerous as events in Poland in 1970 demonstrated. The GDR, with 17 million inhabitants, could boast, in 1969, of having passed the industrial output of the German Reich with 60 million citizens in 1936 but this did not impress the average person if it was not accompanied by an increase in the consumer goods available in the shops. The need to concentrate more on raising living standards was recognised and a much more expansive social policy was launched by Honecker. The impressive advances in education during the period 1966–70 only increased expectations. In 1970 85 per cent of schoolchildren were involved in ten-year high school courses. The number of university and technical college graduates per 1000 workers and employees rose from 86 in 1965 to 113 in 1970. Although industrial production rose 6.5 per cent annually between 1966 and 1970,

> some important goals of the Five Year Plan could not be attained. This especially affected energy, iron and steel and building . . . The non-fulfilment of key plan targets complicated the economic situation. This had negative socio-political consequences, affected the provisioning of the population and hindered the activities of the working population. This gave rise to serious problems in the further all-round strengthening of the GDR and in fulfilling the country's international obligations. (*DDR* 1975: 510–11)

This last phrase underlines the fact that the GDR could not meet her export commitments, first and foremost to the Soviet Union and other Comecon states. One reason for this was the lack of coordination between enterprises producing intermediate and final goods. Often the intermediate product was not available when needed. The party came to the conclusion that 'in the last few years there had been in many respects a certain overestimation of the potential of the GDR' (*Geschichte* 1978: 545).

The scene was set for Ulbricht to deliver his last major political speech at the eighth congress of the SED on 15 June 1971, but the main actor refused to attend. His speech had been written for him and handed to him the night before but it was Erich Honecker's speech, which he also saw, which raised his ire. It contained many overt criticisms of his style of leadership – unreceptiveness to criticism, a lack of concern for collective leadership and overweening self-confidence. In the end Ulbricht's speech, which opened the congress, was read for him but an abrasive account of his resignation which contradicted the smooth vocabulary of the official version was leaked to the *New York Times* and appeared on 22 June 1971.

Culture

The building of the Berlin Wall added a physical dimension to the claim that a common German culture no longer existed. In December 1961, Alexander Abusch, Minister of Culture, claimed that as the GDR was the only 'legal and humanist German state, the German republic of peace and freedom' one could no longer speak of a common German culture. The 'socialist German national culture' of the GDR had nothing in common with developments in the FRG. Since this new culture was only coming into being and since the Wall had confirmed the victory of socialism in the GDR there was room for experimentation; so reasoned some writers and artists. They wanted an end to taboos and to bring problems out into the open. Previously the cultural bureaucrats could claim that such behaviour could help the 'class enemies' in the West but this was no longer the case. Throughout the decade the struggle continued but by 1970 conservative opinions still prevailed.

Until 1962 it was quite common to print Western, mainly West German, writers in GDR periodicals such as *Sinn und Form*. This served to argue the case for modern writers such as Proust and Kafka. When the editor, Peter Huchel, was dismissed at the end of 1962 this practice stopped for a while. Also in 1962 there was a very frank poetry evening in the German Academy of Arts at which Sarah Kirsch, Volker Braun and Wolf Biermann, among others, read their work. An international conference on Kafka was held at Liblice, near Prague, in May 1963 and one of the speakers was Ernst Fischer, the Austrian writer, who went so far as to draw parallels between the strange, alienated world of Kafka and real, existing socialism. This helped to sting the SED into action and it condemned the whole trend towards 'modernism'.

The second Bitterfeld conference met in April 1964 and took stock of achievements. About 400 groups of worker writers and over 1000 groups of amateur artists had come into being and had some good work to their credit. The main theme of the conference, however, was technology and the future. Ulbricht spoke on the development of a socialist national culture which identified with the people but warned that the scientific—technical revolution was going to affect fundamentally the lives of every one in socialist society. GDR culture was to develop as part of socialist world culture. The socialist human community which was in the process of coming into being required a new relationship between artists and the public. What was needed was an 'open, creative work atmosphere' but this was not to be contaminated by a 'revisionistic softening up process'.

One of the writers to cross swords with the cultural bureaucracy was Stefan Heym. His piece *Die Langeweile von Minsk* (1965) was turned down flat by the censor as being totally opposed to the prevailing cultural—political norms. Heym was being provocative in calling it *The Boredom of Minsk* since this alluded to Brecht's claim that literature would reappear in the Soviet Union when a novel was published which began: 'Minsk is one of the most boring cities in the world' (Gransow 1975: 97).

The eleventh plenum of the CC in December 1965 saw a violent attack launched against some of the trends in GDR literature. Erich Honecker spoke of 'thinly disguised philistine—anarchic socialism . . . with strongly pornographic aspects'. He also reminded everyone that the GDR was a 'clean state' with certain standards of 'decency and good manners'. This strongly conservative reaction went hand in hand with Abgrenzung, the attempt to cut the GDR population off from West German contact and influence. No West German writing was published in *Neue Deutsche Literatur* after 1966. At a time when the socialist human community was developing, culture was treated with a heavy hand by the SED.

Literature in the 1960s mainly concerned the GDR but the pre-1945 period was a favourite theme. Germany under fascism appeared time and again and even some younger writers were attracted to the subject. The most popular writer was Johannes Bobrowski whose *Levins Mühle* appeared in 1964, followed a year later by *Boehlendorff und Mäusefest*. Two more novels were published posthumously. Bobrowski's theme is the clash of German and Baltic cultures. The most successful of the novels about the Nazi era was *Jakob der Lügner* by Jurek Becker which appeared in 1968. The author himself had spent part of his childhood in concentration camps. The demands of the NES required literature to be still 'production based', as in the 1950s. But whereas many novels were indeed set in an industrial landscape it is the struggles of the subjects with the milieu in which they find themselves which form the real essence. Whereas previously the subject was often the worker, in the 1960s economists, engineers and managers step forward. A trend towards subjectivity developed, in which the characters are uncertain and question their own motives. The four main writers who broached subjects which had as yet not been officially sanctioned were Erwin Strittmacher, Erik Neutsch, Hermann Kant and Christa Wolf. They did not feel obliged to provide the obligatory happy ending. They are the first to claim that not only society may demand something of the individual but that the individual may also ask something of society (Emmerich 1981: 146). Strittmacher's *Ole Bienkopp* (1963) is probably the most successful novel about a peasant in the GDR working out his own salvation. Along the same lines, Neutsch's novel *Spur der Steine* (1964) deals with the construction industry with engineers and production workers playing the key roles. Kant's *Die Aula* (1964) is one of the best known of GDR novels and deals with young workers taking a crash course in a Workers' and Peasants' Faculty in order to go to university. Christa Wolf's *Der geteilte Himmel* (1963) was an overnight success and was translated into many foreign languages and filmed. It is about a young woman who gives up her boy friend since he has decided to move to West Berlin. She attempts to commit suicide but then rebuilds her life. *Nachdenken über Christa T.* (1968) aroused even more interest. Christa T. is a friend who has recently died and the book is a series of reflections about her.

Theatre freed itself from the spell of Brecht in the 1960s and more and more plays on contemporary subjects were staged. The picture they gave of GDR society was sometimes quite realistic. Peter Hacks chose to retreat into history and mythology in order to put across his views. An important work concerned with the NES was Heiner Müller's *Der Bau* in which the party secretary is successful in raising labour productivity at the price of his own integrity. The play was written in 1963—4 but the revised version fell victim to the strictures uttered at the eleventh plenum of the CC in 1965 and had to wait to 1980 for its première. Another notable play which deals with the raw realities of the new relations of production is Volker Braun's *Die Kipper* (1967).

5 Real, Existing Socialism

The removal of Walter Ulbricht in May 1971 meant an end to experimentation in state and society. The new First Secretary (Secretary General as of 1976), Erich Honecker, plotted a course which coincided with that of the Soviet Union. The GDR became Moscow's most reliable ally, out of choice. The riots in Poland in 1970 were a clear signal that working-class aspirations could not be ignored and this led to a greater emphasis on social policy.

In the realm of German policy the conviction struck home that closer relations with West Germany after the conclusion of the Four Power Agreement on Berlin and the Basic Treaty between the two German states were not in the interests of the GDR and by extension of the USSR. Abgrenzung was therefore practised and all talk of the unity of the German nation ridiculed. Concomitantly with this went a desire for closer integration in the socialist bloc. A new treaty of friendship was signed with the Soviet Union in 1975, tying the two countries closer together. Treaties with the other socialist countries soon followed. Diplomatically the GDR gained from *détente*. She enjoyed diplomatic relations with almost all states, she entered the United Nations in 1973 and Erich Honecker signed the Helsinki Final Act in 1975.

If the first half of the 1970s saw considerable economic success, the years since then have seen living standards stagnate. The explosion in oil and raw material prices which followed the Arab—Israeli War of 1973 cost the GDR dear. Anxieties about the performance of the economy spilled over into cultural policy. The expatriation of Wolf Biermann in 1976 signalled the end of the liberal cultural phase of the Honecker era. Writers, artists and painters who protested against this action were arrested, fined or expelled from the country as party policy hardened. The instruments of coercion, the military and the police, increased in significance in the state as the difficulties of the party mounted. The Soviet invasion of Afghanistan in December 1979 and the troubles in Poland which culminated in military rule in December 1981 found the GDR side by side with the Soviet Union. However an awareness of the cost of international tension caused the GDR to try to maintain her contacts with the FRG. On a personal level the SED has stemmed the flow of West Germans and West Berliners to East Berlin and the GDR by making it more expensive to pay a visit. At the same time the SED has sought to make plain to the GDR population that there is no alternative to real, existing socialism (the term dates from 1973) and that the GDR is an integral part of the socialist bloc. It has stressed the fact that the power of the SED is unassailable.

Honecker Becomes First Secretary

The dropping of Walter Ulbricht as First Secretary of the SED at the sixteenth plenum of the CC on 3 May 1971 was a watershed in the development of the GDR. Ulbricht admitted that he had found it difficult to step down but proposed that 'comrade Erich Honecker be elected First Secretary of the CC'. He assured the CC that his request had been 'thoroughly debated in the Politburo'. In 'honour of his services' to the party he was elected 'chairman of the SED', an office not to be found in the party statutes. The only other chairmen the SED has ever had were Otto Grotewohl and Wilhelm Pieck who had been co-chairmen between April 1946 and April 1954. Although he stayed in the Politburo, Ulbricht's days of political influence were over. It was decided to remove him before the eighth party congress in June 1971 since he was planning to make a major policy speech entitled 'The Developed Social System of Socialism in the 1970s' at the congress.

Honecker had long been regarded as the *Kronprinz*, as the local wits put it. His experience, however, was restricted to two main areas: security and youth. He had never held a top government post and had limited experience of economic and technical questions. Nevertheless he had been able to build up a 'tail' of appointees in the party apparatus due to his influence over the appointment of cadres. This was particularly so in the instruments of coercion.

Although Honecker inherited Ulbricht's mantle he did not inherit his authority. The incumbent Prime Minister, Willi Stoph, was a seasoned politician and skilled administrator who had also had extensive experience in security affairs. The situation in the GDR paralleled that of the USSR where Leonid Brezhnev and Aleksei Kosygin vied for supremacy. Just as Brezhnev, using the party as his base, had clearly outmanoeuvred Kosygin by the late 1960s, so Honecker, the party leader, was able to secure precedence over Stoph. This became clear to all on 3 October 1973 when Stoph was made chairman of the GDR Council of State, succeeding Ulbricht who had died on 1 August 1973. The Council of State had been increasing in significance as the main forum for the formation and implementation of policy during the late Ulbricht era but under Honecker its impact began to decline. Could Stoph emulate Nikolai Podgorny, who as President of the USSR, had upgraded that post? Günter Mittag, the most able economic administrator in the GDR and a key figure in the evolution of the economic policies of the 1960s, also saw his star wane. In October 1973, he lost his post as CC secretary for the economy and became first deputy to the new Prime Minister, Horst Sindermann. Werner Krolikowski took over Mittag's duties in the Secretariat. Hence within a few years Honecker had proved himself an able politician and had silenced all talk of a collective leadership in the GDR. His authority had so increased that by late 1976 he headed three of the key institutions in the GDR: the party, the National Defence Council — he had become its chairman on 24 June 1971 — and the GDR Council of State — he was elected its chairman by the Volkskammer on 29 October 1976. The chairmanship of the GDR Council of State had become vacant when Willi Stoph returned to his post of Prime Minister. Horst Sindermann was demoted to the relatively unimportant post of president of the Volkskammer whose previous president Gerald Götting, the CDU leader, in turn was demoted to president of the GDR League of International Friendship. Günter Mittag stepped back into his old position as CC secretary for the economy with Werner Krolikowski taking Mittag's old post as first deputy Prime Minister. All these changes took place on

29 October 1976 with the exception of the one affecting Götting, which took effect on 1 November 1976. The key reason for these events was the increasing economic difficulties of the GDR and the evident inability of Sindermann and Krolikowski to deal effectively with them. Honecker could evidently not do without the 'reformers' of the 1960s.

The Eighth Party Congress

Honecker grasped the opportunity afforded by the congress to present himself to the party and the country. The image he sought to impart was that of a sober, serious, reasonable but optimistic leader. Banished were the bombastic phrases and overoptimistic goals of the Ulbricht era. The new First Secretary realised that industry and agriculture were not capable of coping with a host of 'above plan economic miracles'.

Continuity was the watchword at the congress as far as the membership of the top party bodies was concerned. All full Politburo members were reelected and two new full members were added: Werner Lamberz and Werner Krolikowski. Harry Tisch, first secretary of Bezirk Rostock, and Erich Mielke, Minister of State Security, were made candidate members. All CC secretaries except Horst Dohlus, who only became a member of the Secretariat at the congress, were in the Politburo. Lamberz, CC secretary for agitation since 1966, was clearly identifiable as a close collaborator of Honecker. Krolikowski's promotion must have surprised many. He rose from CC membership to full membership of the Politburo without first going through the candidate stage. Mielke and Honecker had had close connections since the latter's days as CC secretary for security.

Changes in the Ideology

In seeking to become the national leader the head of the party strives towards four objectives: command of the instruments of control and coercion; to be acknowledged as successful in the pursuit of political, economic and social goals; to be an innovator in ideology; and to set in train a cult of his own personality.

As regards the first aim, Honecker recorded success quite quickly. In the field of ideology Honecker made his mark as a conservative, by rejecting the legacy of the Ulbricht era.

Strictly speaking the new ideological route had been mapped out on 15 April 1971 when the Politburo stated that the directives of the twenty-fourth congress of the CPSU, which had met in Moscow in March—April 1971, were of 'general theoretical and political importance' and as such were 'binding' on the SED in solving the 'basic questions in the creation of the developed socialist society in the GDR (*Einheit* no. 5/1971: 499—500). This brought to an end the independent line, adopted by the SED in the early 1960s, as regards the interpretation of Marxism—Leninism. Socialism as a 'relatively independent socio-economic formation' which was to develop on its own base, the 'developed social system of socialism' and the 'socialist human community' — concepts which had originated with Ulbricht — were quickly dropped. Hence the 'developed social system of socialism' gave way to 'developed socialist society'. The term 'real, existing socialism' made its first appearance in 1973 and quickly became the standard expression for the present stage of maturity of GDR society.

Describing society as a system — adopted at the seventh party congress in 1967 — has thus been openly rejected. The harmonious concept of the 'socialist human community' in which class differences were smudged has been superseded by viewing society as a 'class society of a special type' while the state retains the 'birthmarks of the old society', although of course to a decreasing extent. In stressing class distinction in GDR society the SED was underlining the leading role of the working class and by extension of its vanguard, the SED. This had never been formally given up under Ulbricht but the adoption of a systems theory approach to social processes raised the significance of the government and the GDR Council of State as regulators of economic and social life and thereby relegated the party increasingly to a supervisory role. The Honecker era has seen the relationship between the government and the party neatly reversed. This was formalised by the new party statute, adopted in 1976. Whereas under the previous statute, adopted in 1963, party organisations in ministries and other state organs due to the 'special conditions of work in the state apparatus cannot exercise controlling functions', the position now is that party organisations in the ministries and the other central and local state organs have the 'right to control the activities of the apparatus in the implementation of party and government resolutions and the observance of socialist legal norms' (Fricke 1976: 134).

The Economic System of Socialism had seen the rise of disciplines which had put the leading role of the SED in doubt. Kurt Hager, at the congress, gave vent to his frustration. The 'clear meaning and content of the policy of the SED was lost in a jumble of concepts borrowed from systems theory'. It had been claimed that the socialist human community produced a 'completely new class structure'. One way this was coming about was the very generous definition of who belonged to the working class. Indeed the concept had become very elastic. Hager, again at the congress, was very critical. 'When an attempt is made to define the content of society using the systemic contents of cybernetics, the result is that the socio-economic and class content of socialism is positively undermined.' The father of cybernetics in the GDR, Georg Klaus, went so far as to attempt to elaborate a cybernetics of society which would have rendered historical materialism obsolete. Hager, once more, revealed how threatened the ideologists had felt during the late Ulbricht years. 'The function of historical and dialectical materialism is seriously endangered when Marxist—Leninist philosophy is robbed of its Weltanschauung and partly deideologised by the uncritical acceptance of views and concepts drawn from various disciplines' (*Einheit* no. 11/1971: 1207).

The concepts associated with systems theory, organisation theory and cybernetics were fought over, principally by Lenin and A. A. Bogdanov, during the first two decades of this century. The latter, influenced by philosophers such as Ernst Mach, attempted to develop a science of the automatic regulation of society. Bukharin took up some of the ideas and sought to evolve a theory of dynamic equilibrium. These theories relied on feedback or information flow from the periphery to the centre in order to allow the latter to refine increasingly its decisions in the light of popular aspirations and achievement. Lenin's main objection, later taken up by Stalin, was that such theories robbed the party of its right to intervene in society. As society came more and more to resemble a dynamic self-regulating mechanism, so the role of the party diminished.

Stalin's revolution from above from 1929 onwards directly contradicted such theories. Hence when cybernetics, systems management and the other disciplines connected with work regulations were legitimised by Khrushchev, the ideas of Bogdanov and Bukharin again gained currency, although neither has been rehabilitated in the Soviet Union. By this token, the debate about the scientific management of society, using these concepts, has a long Marxist pedigree. Klaus and others in the GDR were quite aware of this. It is instructive that a man such as Ulbricht, usually seen as a Stalinist, a conservative dogmatist, should have encouraged such un-Stalinist disciplines as systems theory and cybernetics, which were plainly undermining the leading role of the party by placing influence over social processes in the hands of mathematicians and applied scientists.

Another way in which Honecker was able to project his persona was through the written word. To distinguish his era sharply from that of his predecessor, the eighth party congress was presented as a decisive turning point in the evolution of the GDR, indeed a new 'social phase' had begun. Ulbricht's name appeared less and less frequently: in the first edition of *Politisches Grundwissen*, a widely used text in ideology, published in 1970, Ulbricht is mentioned on about 100 occasions, but in the second edition, which appeared in 1972, he is not mentioned at all (Weber 1980: 147). This distorted the historical perspective since Ulbricht influenced the development of the GDR as much as Stalin that of the Soviet Union. Until the leadership role of individuals is integrated into the ideology, successive leaders will seek to increase their own legitimacy by denigrating the record of their predecessors.

The Chief Task

To give the new era a sense of purpose and direction, Honecker, at the eighth congress, enunciated the chief task facing the party: to raise further the material and cultural level of the people. This was to be achieved 'by a high tempo of development of socialist production, increasing efficiency, scientific–technical progress and the growth of labour productivity'. (The term scientific–technical progress replaced that of the scientific–technical revolution, so typical of the 1960s.) Honecker also spelled out the point of reference for all party policy. 'We recognise only one goal which penetrates all the policies of our party: to do everything to achieve the well-being of men and women and the happiness of the people in the interests of the working class and of all employees. This is what socialism means.' Raising labour productivity was the key to the expansion of the socialist economy and this involved disposing of 'old practices and habits'.

Honecker was signalling that the hopes and aspirations of the average person were to be accorded greater priority and this involved more investment in social policy goals. The late Ulbricht era had led to a sharp differentiation in incomes as those with the requisite technical skills saw their living standards rise while the rest lagged badly behind. The worst off were the pensioners. In a way the SED was a victim of its own propaganda since it continually promised higher living standards for all and this had created an air of expectancy. There are two strands which run through SED policy. One is the aim of creating an egalitarian society, and this desire is deeply entrenched in the GDR; the other is to use economic incentives to stimulate people to achieve the results necessary for growth. The latter inevitably produces inequality.

The wild optimism of the 1960s, when it had been assumed that a scientific—technical revolution would produce a rapid increase in output, had to give way to the sober realisation that growth would be relatively slow. There was not going to be a revolution, only steady progress. Since there had been neither a quantitive nor a qualitative expansion of the economic base, the same was true *a fortiori* of social development. Improving living and working conditions would have to be closely linked to labour productivity.

The Party and the State

The Honecker era has been characterised by the great emphasis placed on the leading role of the SED. Marxism—Leninism has been accorded great significance as have the political economy of socialism and scientific communism. This has permitted the party to recapture the ground lost to the empirical sciences during the 1960s. However this does not mean that ideological categories are imposed on scientific and technical research. This might be rather difficult to achieve since there is no agreement on the precise definition of concepts such as forces of production, the relations of production, base and superstructure, for example. What the party has done is to establish a system of scientific councils attached to the GDR Academy of Sciences, the Academy of Social Sciences of the CC, SED and other central and party organisations which permits the SED to plan, co-ordinate and supervise the subject matter and results of research more competently. The key integrative force thereby becomes the party (Zimmermann 1978: 20—1).

The SED has made clear that under real, existing socialism the leading role of the party increases. No problem of any significance can be resolved without the 'political, ideological and organisational work' of the party. There is 'no alternative' to the rising influence of the SED (*Neuer Weg* no. 5/1974: 199; Weber 1980: 148). The replacement of the concept of a 'socialist human community' by that of a 'class society of a new type' allowed the SED to stress the leading role of the working class. The latter guided society, mainly through the agency of its 'Marxist—Leninist party'.

Strict adherence to the norms of democratic centralism and 'iron' party discipline were emphasised early on by Honecker. His personnel policy reflected his predilections. Shortly after the eighth congress, five of the fifteen first secretaries at the Bezirk level were replaced. Four of the five new appointees had played significant roles in the FDJ and three of them had been closely connected with the new First Secretary during his FDJ days: Konrad Naumann (East Berlin); Werner Felfe (Halle) and Hans-Joachim Hertwig (Frankfurt/Oder). Horst Schumann (Leipzig) should be added to this list although he had become first secretary in November 1970.

The tenth plenum of the CC in October 1973 saw decisive changes in personnel. It was at this plenum that Mittag lost his position in the CC Secretariat and Stoph ceased to be Prime Minister. Walter Halbritter, responsible for price reform during the 1960s, lost his position as a candidate member of the Politburo. This confirmed a trend of the Honecker era that technocrats, especially economists, gradually give way to func-tionaries in the upper echelons of the SED. At the same plenum Heinz Hoffmann, Minister of National Defence, became a full member and Werner Felfe, Joachim Herrmann (chief editor of *Neues Deutschland*), Ingeborg Lange (who also became CC secretary for women), Konrad Naumann and Gerhard Schürer (chairman of the State Planning Commission) became candidate members of the Politburo.

The election of the new Bezirk and Kreis party executives, in early 1974, produced a few changes. Of the 95 Bezirk secretaries, 24 were dropped and of the remaining 124 members, 39 were replaced. At the Kreis, city and city Bezirk level, about one-third of the executive committee members were changed. Of the 263 Kreis first secretaries only nine were women, of whom three were in Bezirk Leipzig. At a time when the leading role of the SED was being emphasised, this puts the political power of women in the GDR in perspective.

The social composition of the SED is of some interest. At the ninth party congress, in 1976, Honecker put the number of workers among party members at 56.1 per cent but stated that 74.9 per cent of full and candidate members were of working-class origin. Interestingly enough both figures were lower than those quoted in 1971. Then 56.6 per cent were workers and 76.8 per cent of working-class origin. Collective farm peasants made up 5.2 per cent in 1976 (5.9 per cent in 1971), the intelligentsia amounted to 20 per cent (17.1 per cent in 1971), and employees constituted 11.5 per cent (13 per cent in 1971); 7.2 per cent of members went unclassified in 1976. These figures are quite instructive. At a time when the SED was emphasising its working-class credentials, the proportion of women members actually declined compared with the heyday of the Ulbricht era. On the other hand, the intelligentsia, which had gained most during the 1960s, increased its representation in the SED. This at a time when technocrats were losing their positions in the CC, Secretariat and the Politburo. The explanation appears to be that the party leadership had taken the decision to coopt the intelligentsia so as to exercise greater control over it. This is chiefly reflected in the educational qualifications of party members in 1976. Then 27.4 per cent of full and candidate members were graduates. This was a startling rise on the 1973 figure of 22.5 per cent. Moreover, all secretaries of Bezirk and Kreis committees and 93.7 per cent of party secretaries in Kombinate and large enterprises were graduates in 1976. Officials who completed courses at higher party schools are here classified as graduates (McCauley 1979: 215). Thus party functionaries acquired more academic expertise and in so doing they made it easier for the centre, through democratic centralism, to impose its will on developments in the GDR. The emphasis placed on economic and social goals meant that the primary party organisations, especially in factories, assumed considerable significance. Here party activists had the task of convincing the workforce that party directives and goals corresponded with their own aspirations. A good party activist was not only someone who was convincing when putting across the latest party instructions but someone who was also a first-class worker. Party activists and members do not have to decide party policy for themselves or how it should be implemented. They receive instructions, often in the minutest detail, from full-time members of the apparatus. Since instructions have to be followed to the letter, any sidestepping or opposition immediately becomes evident. Democratic centralism classifies all such behaviour as anti-party. The party control commissions deal with such cases. The strength of democratic centralism is that it works on the principle that the immediately superior body always knows best. Hence there is little leeway for anyone to diverge from the line which in the last resort comes from the centre. Party control is exercised through the full-time, paid officials who make up the apparatus or party bureaucracy. The apparatus is organised along strictly hierarchical lines with democratic centralism also applying to it. The various levels of the apparatus, the Bezirk, Kreis, city and so on, issue detailed instructions and advice to their subordinate bodies. Since the kernel of the apparatus, only needs to take the key decisions, it delegates all others to the lower echelons. Policy is decided at the top, the task of the rest of the apparatus is to ensure that it is implemented. In order to ensure that the leadership is acquainted with opinion at each level there is a constant flow of information to the centre. However it is filtered through the apparatus and this circumscribes it. All party posts are elective and the apparatus supervises the elections. Just who should be elected to the various committees and who should become a full-time functionary are matters of primary concern to the SED. The party is constantly seeking new recruits for its apparatus and selects men and women according to certain criteria. Preferably they should be from the working class, should possess political and technical expertise, have shown themselves as willing activists — these party members are unpaid — possess leadership qualities, be dedicated Marxist—Leninists, lead a good, moral life and be devoted to the cause of proletarian and socialist internationalism. This means, in practice, accepting the hegemony of the Soviet Union in the world socialist movement. The party arrogates to itself the right to decide who fills all the top posts in government, the mass organisations, the police, the military and the like. A list of all these positions and the men and women capable of filling them together make up the nomenklatura. By means of the nomenklatura, the central party apparatus controls all important appointments.

Hence by reason of the central party apparatus, the nomenklatura and the discipline imposed on each member, the party leadership exercises power in the GDR. Its command over the instruments of control and coercion makes its position almost unassailable. There can be no loyal opposition. Only crass incompetence *à la polonaise* or loss of willpower can threaten its hold on power.

The new emphasis on the leading role of the SED involved more pressure being applied on non-socialist parties. All the members of these parties must acknowledge the leading role of the working class and of the SED and be positive in their reaction to the Soviet Union. These parties serve as 'transmission belts' for SED influence in strata of the population not normally reached by the party. The CDU, for example, purports to demonstrate that Christianity and socialism go hand in hand and actively encourages its members to participate in the building of socialism. At its fifteenth congress in October 1982 the CDU stated that it had 125 103 members, an increase of about 10 000 since its last congress in October 1977. But this is still far short of the 218 000 members the party had in December 1947 — the largest total ever recorded by the CDU. It may appear to speak for believers but in reality does not since most believers are wary of it. Church opposition to SED policies, such as the monopoly of education and the creeping militarisation of GDR youth, tend to be channelled through church organisations.

The liberal democrats (LDPD) have seen their numbers rise since 1971. At the twelfth party congress in 1977, the party had 75 000 members but at the thirteenth congress, in 1982, this had risen to 'over 82 000'. At the congress it was stated that 20 000 new members had joined since 1977. Since the net increase was only 7000, the other 13 000, one presumes, died during these years, reflecting the age structure of party membership. The fortunes of the party declined during the first half of the 1970s due to the decision to nationalise the semi-private enterprises. However the increased emphasis placed on the private sector afterwards saw a rise in interest. This remains the main party of the self-employed. Its political position was succinctly summed up at the thirteenth congress. 'The general line of the 10th Congress of the SED is also the general line of our activity.'

The NDPD had 85 000 members in 1977 but this rose to 91 000 in 1982 and the DBD also saw its membership rise, from 92 000 in 1977 to 103 000 in 1982. None the less, these parties saw their room for manoeuvre diminish.

In 1982 it became clear that the non-socialist parties no longer recruit any workers — the SED has a monopoly in this regard. Members of the police and the military, with very few exceptions, are not recruited either. Again they join the SED. When someone applies to join the NDPD, for example, the local secretary immediately establishes contact with the SED. If the SED judges that the NDPD is well enough represented in the locality then the applicant is passed on to one of the other non-socialist parties.

The growth in membership of the non-socialist parties is striking. This has only been achieved by recruiting considerable numbers of young people to compensate for rising mortality among older members. At a time when these parties have lost their room for political manoeuvre, even stressing that their policies are those of the SED, why should party membership grow? One reason is that parties are a valuable extra source of information. Simply being a member makes one better informed politically. It would appear that advancement in the state bureaucracy requires membership of a political party. In the LDPD, for example, 40 per cent of members in 1982 were state functionaries. The expansion of these parties testifies to their usefulness as 'transmission belts' for SED policies.

In an era when raising labour productivity was seen as the key to economic success, the mass organisations most closely involved, the trade unions (FDGB) and the youth movement

(FDJ), assumed heightened relevance. With a declining population a greater and greater proportion of the able bodied had to be attracted to productive labour. In 1976 the FDGB had 8.9 million members which represented about 95 per cent of the employed population. This climbed to 9.1 million members in 1982, accounting for 97 per cent of the employed population. In 1976 the largest organisation was I. G. Metall with 1.6 million members, accounting for 97.7 per cent of metalworkers. The lowest level of unionisation was recorded by farm, food and forestry workers, 91 per cent (*DDR-Handbuch* 1979: 353).

The party does not intend the FDGB to represent the interests of workers but rather to secure the implementation of the SED's economic policy more effectively. This was underlined in 1975 when Harry Tisch became head of the FDGB in succession to Herbert Warnke who had died. Tisch was first secretary of Bezirk Rostock and as such was a leading party functionary with little union experience. In fact the party 'delegated' him to work in the trade union organisation. He soon promised that the unions would raise their economic performance and were to be regarded as 'true comrades-in-arms of the party'.

More attention is being paid to the women's mass organisation, the DFD. At its eleventh congress, in 1982, membership was put at 1.5 million, an increase of over 300 000 since the previous congress in 1975, with two-thirds of the members being under 35 years of age. Among the new tasks of the DFD is involvement in civil defence.

The oncoming of *détente*, the signing of the Berlin Agreement, the Basic Treaty between the GDR and the FRG and the resultant flow of visitors from West Berlin and West Germany compounded the party's youth problem. Margot Honecker, Minister of Education and wife of the First Secretary, in a speech to head teachers in May 1973, appealed for greater attention to be paid to cultivating a more resolute class view. She proposed that political and ideological instruction be stepped up and that the 'whole military—political, military—sporting and pre-military training and education at school level be conducted with more rigour and at a higher level' (*Deutsche Lehrerzeitung* 3 May 1973).

New directives about socialist military training for classes 8—10 were announced in May 1972. Further regulations came into effect on 1 September 1973, affecting classes 9 and 10.

Most of the instruction consists of firing practice and field training. Four hours one afternoon per week was recommended. Obligatory pre-military training for boys and medical training for girls in class 11 were imposed in February 1973. Apprentices were also to receive pre-military training. Even the five- to eight-year-olds were not forgotten. They were to collect photographs of soldiers and to develop friendly relations with them.

Sport is of great importance in preparing young men for military service. The Society for Sport and Technology plays a leading role in this respect. Hence sport serves two functions in the GDR: it helps to raise the international prestige of the country and it prepares youth for military service. Most young men, however, regard military service as a necessary evil. Conscientious objectors serve in a construction batallion (but must wear uniform) while others go to gaol since they will not even agree to do this. The SED laments the fact that most young men do not perceive West Germany as the enemy. This is due in part to the fact that 'West German imperialism is not conducting a visible war'. The image conjured up by watching West German television and meeting relatives from the FRG evidently conflicts sharply with that projected by the SED.

A draft youth law was published just before the Tenth World Youth Festival which took place in East Berlin during July and August 1973. One reason for making it available at that time was to provide GDR youth with material for discussion when they met foreigners at the festival. It placed great emphasis on the young person's obligations towards the state and the community. In return the state promised improvements in the living and working conditions of young people. Military duty was not forgotten. 'The defence of the socialist fatherland and the socialist state community are the honourable duty of all young persons.' The new youth law was finally passed by the Volkskammer on 28 January 1974.

In October 1972 a law spelling out the responsibilities of the GDR Council of Ministers was passed by the Volkskammer. It widened its powers at the expense of the GDR Council of State which thereby ceased to be the leading state political institution. The GDR Council of Ministers, previously responsible for economic and cultural policy, now took over domestic and foreign policy. The locally elected assemblies and organs were given more to do by a Volkskammer decree of July 1973 as the central organs sought to divest themselves of essentially regional problems.

The twenty-fifth anniversary of the founding of the GDR, in October 1974, was marked by a revision of the 1968 constitution. Whereas article 1 of the 1968 constitution stated: 'The GDR is a socialist state of the German nation' it became: 'The GDR is a socialist state of workers and peasants', in the revised formulation. All other references to Germany's re-unification and the German nation were excised. A range of institutions lost the word German in their title. For example, the German Academy of Sciences became the Academy of Sciences of the GDR and the National Front of Democratic Germany became the GDR National Front. However the name of the party remained the SED, the 'D' standing for Germany; its organ *Neues Deutschland* (New Germany) retained its name; the trade union organisation, the FDGB, and the youth movement, the FDJ, remained as they were and the country continued to be referred to as the GDR. The non-socialist parties, all of whom have the word Germany in their name, retained it. It is difficult to understand why, for instance, the *Deutschland Sender* (The Radio of Germany) was renamed whereas *Neues Deutschland* was not. On the other hand the railways still bore their pre-1945 name, *Deutsche Reichsbahn*, even though the Reich has passed away and the GDR has few kind things to say about it. The reason is not difficult to divine. The *Deutsche Reichsbahn* has right of access to West Berlin.

The main purpose behind the renaming appears to have been the desire to convince the GDR population that a united Germany was inconceivable in the near future. The changes in the constitution strengthened the bond between the GDR and the USSR. Also the legislative period of the Volkskammer and the GDR Council of State was extended from four to five years. The accretion of power by the GDR Council of Ministers at the expense of the GDR Council of State was confirmed in the constitution.

The quality of the weapons and equipment provided the NVA increased sharply during the 1970s. Enterprise workers' detachments also saw their equipment improve. The NVA began to play a more active role in the Warsaw Pact and in Africa where NVA personnel provided instruction in the use of weapons and signalling equipment. More budgetary resources were also directed to the political police.

Participation by citizens in state and social affairs is one way of increasing the commitment of the average person to the GDR. In the mid-1970s there were about 200 000 elected members in parliaments and assemblies and about half a million citizens were involved in local representative institutions. Then there were about 100 000 jurors or members of committees of arbitration, 200 000 in commissions and committees of the Workers' and Peasants' Inspectorate and another 700 000 in parent—teacher associations (Weber 1980: 152). Hence approximately one adult in five was involved in some activity which influenced the way the state functioned. The SED, of course, did not devolve any of its power to any of these state institutions but expected, not without reason, that participation on such a scale would raise the commitment of these citizens to the state.

The Ninth Party Congress

The congress took place in East Berlin between 18 and 22 May 1976 in the impressive new glass and concrete structure, the Palace of the Republic. The Secretary General, for such he became at the congress, exuded self-confidence during the proceedings which saw a new party programme and statute and the directives for the Five Year Plan 1976—80 adopted unanimously. Just like the twenty-fifth congress of the CPSU, which had taken place in March—April 1976, the SED congress produced no surprises with no new departures in economic or social policy. The whole show was superbly stage managed and the exemplary facilities afforded foreign journalists multiplied the plaudits the grateful party received. The GDR had arrived internationally; she was a member of the United Nations and enjoyed diplomatic relations with most states. Living standards had noticeably improved. Well could Honecker exclaim: 'We have chosen the right road' and 'it has all been worth while'. Never had the Secretary General's authority been so great.

Expectations among the population that the congress would announce improvements in living and working conditions by, for instance, reducing the working week from 43¾ to 40 hours, by raising pensions and by lengthening the holiday period were very high. The party, during the run up to the congress, invited citizens to write in and express their opinions. Over 1.2 million requests flowed in and two days before the congress convened *Neues Deutschland* took the unprecedented step of publishing some of the aspirations. It was a source of great disappointment, therefore, when the expected improvements did not materialise. The Five Year Plan directives did contain the hope that the 40-hour week would be introduced but it would appear that the leadership took a more sombre view of the economy's prospects due to the swing of the terms of trade away from the GDR. Productivity would have to precede higher living standards. Nevertheless five days after the conclusion of the congress it was announced that old age pensions would rise on 1 December 1976 and the minimum wage was also increased, as from 1 October 1976. Longer holidays and other improvements followed. It would appear that these concessions were forced out of the SED by a disappointed population. Had the leadership been planning to introduce them much political capital would have been gained by trumpeting them from the platform of the Palace of the Republic. They underlined the importance placed on social policy by the Secretary General and his awareness of the danger of allowing resentment to well up. These concessions benefited the less well off members of society most.

The new Central Committee elected was the largest ever with 145 full and 57 candidate members. The dominance of the party and state apparatuses continued and the educational level of members rose; 63 per cent of full members and 91 per cent of candidate members were graduates.

The Politburo elected was again the largest ever, with 19 full and 9 candidate members. One reason for this was Honecker's desire to underline continuity. No full member of the Politburo was removed between 1971 and 1982 except in a hearse. The new full members were Werner Felfe, first secretary of Bezirk Halle; Erich Mielke, Minister of State Security and Konrad Naumann, first secretary of Bezirk Berlin. New candidate members were Horst Dohlus, a CC secretary; Joachim Herrmann, who became a CC secretary after the congress; Egon Krenz, first secretary of the FDJ and Werner Walde, first secretary of Bezirk Cottbus.

The milieu from which these promoted men came mirrored the Secretary General's own career; youth work and security. Nine of the 29 full and candidate members have been FDJ functionaries.

The New Programme and Statute

Real, existing socialism required its own party programme and statute. The previous ones dated from 1963 when the language of the day had been full of the flavour of systems theory and cybernetics. A new draft programme was published in *Neues Deutschland* on 14 January 1976 and 'presented for discussion'. Two days later the new draft statute appeared. They produced much lively debate at party meetings and the proposed amendments to the programme resulted in 125 changes or additions. The leading role of the Soviet Union is unequivocally stated. It is the 'leading force of the socialist community' and the SED is guided by the 'valid laws of the socialist revolution' in the USSR. The impact of the Brezhnev doctrine is clear from the statement that the socialist states are closely united with the Soviet Union whereas the 1963 programme spoke of the principles of 'equality, mutual respect, independence and sovereignty' of these states.

The goal of the GDR is a 'developed socialist society' and the SED promises to strive to 'improve continuously the living standards of the population'. This is to be achieved through the 'unity of economic and social policy'. A developed socialist society is based on the principle of achievement and in this way social differences can be reduced. In the 1963 programme 'social need' came before 'personal interest'. The programme makes clear that the chief task of the party is economic, hence raising labour productivity takes preference.

In foreign policy preserving peace through peaceful coexistence is the main goal. However the desire to restrict contact between the populations of the GDR and the FRG, Abrenzung, leads to the statement that the flowering of the socialist nation in the GDR is linked to the 'development of closer links with the other countries of the socialist community'. A goal of the party is no longer 'national unity' or a 'confederation', all that the GDR desires is peaceful coexistence with the FRG. The provisions of the GDR—Soviet friendship treaty of October 1975 are also worked into the text.

The new statute was also the subject of some debate and 51 changes were made as a result of proposals submitted. Conditions of entry remained as before. A newcomer, who must be at least 18 years old, remains a candidate member for one year. Two testimonials are required from persons with at least two years' full membership of the SED. A primary party organisation can accept a candidate or full member but his registration is only effective when it has been endorsed by the relevant Kreis executive. Between 1950 and 1976 a party member could not resign, he had to be struck off or expelled to quit the SED while alive. The new statute allows him to resign.

The supreme party organ is the congress, which is to meet every five years. The CC is to meet at least once every six months and its sessions are private. It is the supreme organ between congresses. The CC elects the Politburo which 'guides politically the work of the CC between congresses'. The CC also elects the Secretariat, which is responsible for 'day-to-day business, chiefly the fulfilment and control of party decrees and the selection of cadres'. The SED is organised at Bezirk, city, Kreis and city Bezirk level, depending on the territorial location. These bodies 'provide the political leadership of social development in their area, basing themselves on the party statutes'.

A primary party organisation may have as few as three or as many as 150 members. Honecker said at the congress that there were 74 306 primary organisations.

A fierce attack on real, existing socialism, *Die Alternative*, by Rudolf Bahro, an SED member, was published in West Germany in 1977. Bahro's thesis was that the SED, in its present form, is a hindrance to the development of socialism and that a 'politbureaucracy' runs the country very inefficiently. The whole planning system, with its attendant bureaucracy, is quite unnecessary. Bahro advocated a return to Marxist fundamentals in the form of free economic associations. The SED chose not to enter into a debate with him and instead sent him to prison. After a short while he was then deported to West Germany.

Another critic of the regime, Robert Havemann, continued his assaults on SED policies. He was placed under house arrest and between 19 April and 20 June 1979 he was submitted to 24-hour daily surveillance. Eventually Havemann was fined 10 000 marks for currency offences.

Critics such as Bahro and Havemann are Marxist fundamentalists who reject the Leninist accretions to the master's doctrines. Since Marxism—Leninism has led to bureaucratic rather than democratic socialism, ruling parties such as the SED have no effective reply. The party avoids debate with its critics and prefers to imprison, expel or wait for them to die. Robert Havemann died on 8 March 1982. The reason why he was never imprisoned or expelled to West Germany under Honecker may have been connected with the fact that the Secretary General and he shared the same prison during part of the Nazi era.

The Honecker era has been marked by a more relaxed attitude towards the Christian churches. A high water mark was reached on 6 March 1978 when the Secretary General received the executive committee of the Association of Evangelical Churches — at a time when church membership was falling. The party does not perceive the churches as a threat to its power and as such they can perform very useful functions in society. The developing relationship was affected by events in Poland after August 1980. Mindful of the role of the Roman Catholic Church there, the GDR had no desire to allow a similar situation to develop. During the first half of 1980 there had been many contacts between East and West German churches to discuss peace and disarmament and East German church leaders had had talks with West German politicians. However the SED would not allow the churches to publish anything which contradicted official policy. In November 1980, at the end of a ten-day action programme on peace and disarmament, it was planned to ring church bells throughout the land but the party decided to test the nation's sirens at precisely the same moment. In Poland the ringing of church bells sometimes signalled the beginning of a strike. Although conscientious objectors can serve in military building units many believers would prefer to do social work, as in the FRG. The authorities have refused to permit this. Relations have been further strained by the beginnings of a peace movement, centred on the churches. The SED slogan: 'There is no peace without weapons' was countered by 'peace without weapons'. When young people took to wearing patches depicting the Old Testament message 'swords into ploughshares' the People's Police were instructed to oblige wearers to remove them. The rather lame official reason given was that such activity could be misused by opponents of socialism.

The Tenth Party Congress

The congress, held in April 1981, was designed to demonstrate to the GDR population that there was no need for a free trade union, such as Solidarity, at home. The SED was determined to portray itself as a united party with a successful economic policy. The party had 2.2 million members on the eve of the congress, with the number of primary organisations rising to 80 000. Workers now constitute 57.6 per cent of the membership, compared to 56.1 per cent in 1976. However the intelligentsia grew even faster, from 20 per cent in 1976 to 22 per cent in 1981. Albert Norden was dropped from the Politburo and CC without a word of thanks for all his years of service. He died on 30 May 1982. The only new candidate member was Günter Schabowski, chief editor of *Neues Deutschland*. Before the congress he had not even been a member of the CC. However it has always been the tradition that the chief editor of *Neues Deutschland* sits in the Politburo. The new CC is larger than ever with the military increasing its representation from eight to thirteen. General Heinz Hoffmann, Minister of National Defence, is a member of the Politburo and six of his eight deputies are members (three full, three candidate). Colonel General Erich Mielke, Minister of State Security, is a member of the Politburo and two of his four deputies are candidate members of the CC. Colonel General Friedrich Dickel, Minister of the Interior, is a member of the CC and two of his six deputies are candidate members. Whereas Ulbricht kept the military and security apparatus at a distance, since some of its members had plotted against him, Honecker, himself a former CC secretary for security, appears to have no such reservation. The CC department of security affairs is now headed by a general, the first time this sensitive post has been occupied by a non-civilian.

If the CC has grown in size, the proportion of women has not. Now only 12 per cent of members, compared to 13 per cent in 1976, are female. Since about one-third of SED members are women and the avowed policy of the party is to promote more women to responsible posts, the underrepresentation of women in the CC is very striking.

The Economy

In the first half of the 1972 the GDR leadership nationalised all semi-private enterprises, privately-owned industrial and construction concerns and artisan cooperatives producing industrial goods. This created more than 11 000 new VEB. The proportion of the industrial workforce employed in the VEB thereby rose from 87.1 per cent in 1971 to 99.4 per cent in mid-1972. In all 585 000 workers and employees moved into the state sector. The former owners of the concerns were paid some compensation and over 85 per cent chose to stay on in some capacity. As an official source expressed it, these changes represented 'one of the most significant changes in the socio-economic base of the GDR. It led to the further strengthening of the socialist relations of production which were now complete in industry and enhanced the leading role of the working class in the economy and society (*DDR* 1975: 534).

During the early years of the Honecker era the GDR gradually developed all the trappings of a modern industrial state. In 1975, of the labour force of 7.9 million, 3 million, or 38 per cent, were employed in industry, 99.7 per cent of whose output came from the state sector. There were in addition about half a million involved in cooperative, artisan and private concerns, as follows: 300 000 employees in 105 000 private artisan workshops; 130 000 members of cooperatives; and 55 000 private retailers. Agriculture was almost entirely socialist in 1975. Collective farms (LPG) of types I and II were gradually transformed into type III (full collectivisation of production). Whereas in 1970 there had been 3485 type I and type II farms working 870 000 hectares, in 1975 there were only 306, farming 95 000 hectares. Whereas the number of type III farms declined by a quarter between 1970 and 1975, the area worked rose slightly to almost 5.1 million hectares. Hence the average collective increased in size and in turn those involved in grain production were gradually merged to form KAP (cooperative section, grain production). These huge concerns farmed two-thirds of the agricultural land by 1975. As socialist agriculture was concentrated in fewer but larger farms, so the number of farm operatives declined: from 2.2 million in 1950 to 840 000, or 10.6 per cent of the labour force, in 1975. The GDR has the lowest proportion of her labour force in agriculture of any socialist country.

The number of university and technical college graduates rose to 1 019 000 or 12.9 per cent of the labour force in 1975. University graduates increased from 4.3 per cent in 1971 to 5.5 per cent in 1975, with about half of these employed in social and cultural institutions. The proportion of skilled workers in the labour force rose from 44.9 per cent in 1970 to 53 per cent in 1975; also 42 per cent of the women were classified as skilled in 1975. The percentage of unskilled dropped from 43.7 per cent in 1970 to 32.9 per cent in 1975 (*Statistisches Jahrbuch* 1976: 15–16, 62, 180; Weber 1980: 153).

The level of skill is closely related to age. Whereas only about 45 per cent of the age group 55–60 are skilled, this rises to over 80 per cent among the 25–30 year-olds.

The economy has not kept pace with the supply of skilled labour. About 25 per cent of workers in industry and on collective farms are engaged in heavy physical work and about 40 per cent of industrial workers perform predominantly manual tasks even though over half the labour force is classified as skilled. An estimated 20 per cent of skilled workers are not employed on tasks commensurate with their level of skill; this affects women more than men. The situation is unlikely to improve in the short term as every young person capable of becoming a skilled worker is accepted for training. The most adversely affected will increasingly belong to the older generation.

By the mid-1970s the GDR was a modern, industrial society. The dominance of industry, the rise in the level of skill and expertise of the labour force, especially the growth in the number of university and technical college graduates, heralded a future in which more and more could be expected from scientific—technical progress. The social structure of the population had been radically altered in the late 1940s and 1950s by the widespread changes in the ownership of the means of production and the nationalisation of semi-private and many private enterprises in 1972 completed the process. Then the state became the employer of almost all GDR labour. Social changes since then have not been related to the ownership of the means of production but to the acquisition of technical, scientific and managerial skills. The expansion of the intelligentsia, especially of the technical intelligentsia, has been very marked.

The imbalance in the GDR economy, caused by concentrating on 'structurally-determining' sectors of the economy such as electronics and chemicals, was not entirely overcome during the plan period 1971—5. In the official parlance, planning and management gave way to management and planning, once more underlining the point that planning was to be a managerial tool. The plan period recorded some excellent results with national income rising by over 4 per cent annually. However a cloud on the horizon began to cast a larger and larger shadow over economic performance: that of foreign trade. Due to the poor resource base of the GDR, many essential raw materials and energy have to be imported. This led to the situation where foreign trade turnover grew faster than national income. Over the period 1960—75, foreign trade grew on average by 9.7 per cent annually while national income rose by only 4.7 per cent annually. By 1975 the GDR's exports were equivalent to 25 per cent of the gross social product or as high as that of the Federal Republic. The rapid increase in the price of hydrocarbons and raw materials after the Arab—Israeli War of 1973 were a severe blow to the GDR. Her terms of trade rapidly worsened. If world market prices over the years 1952—6 are put at 100, by 1975 food prices had risen to 218.1 but industrial raw materials had soared to 294.6 and energy prices to 470.9. This led to the prices of GDR imports jumping 34 per cent over the years 1972—5 whereas export prices only rose by 17 per cent. This represented a deterioration of 13 per cent in the GDR's terms of trade. As a concession the Soviet Union did not immediately charge world prices for its energy and raw materials exports to the GDR and other socialist states. Rolling five-year averages meant that Soviet prices were always behind world prices. Price increases became significant only in 1975 (Cornelsen *et al.* 1977: 247, 251–2).

The difficulties of the GDR were compounded by the fact that the regional structure of her trade changed. Whereas during 1961–5, 76 per cent of GDR imports were from the socialist bloc, this dropped to 72.2 per cent over the years 1966–70 and to 65 per cent during 1971–5. Imports from the Western world, during the same periods, rose from 20.1 per cent to 23.9 per cent and to 30.9 per cent of total imports. There was a parallel drop in exports to socialist countries during the same periods; from 76.9 per cent to 74.6 per cent and to 72.7 per cent of total exports. Western countries took 19 per cent, 20.8 per cent and 23.3 per cent of GDR exports over the same periods. Again it must be borne in mind that the price rises for energy and raw materials from the socialist bloc only came into operation in 1975 (Cornelsen *et al.* 1977: 354).

The deterioration of the terms of trade led to the GDR incurring a considerable foreign debt, especially with Western countries. Since 1973 GDR foreign trade has been in deficit. Before that GDR trade with the socialist bloc and the Third World was always in surplus whereas trade with the West has been in the red since 1969. Over the years 1960–72 the GDR recorded a surplus of 6800 million Valuta marks (VM) (1VM = 0.72 DM in 1976) on her world trade. The deficit in 1973 was 1200 million VM but it climbed to 4200 million VM in 1975, the worst ever recorded. Hence the 1960–72 surplus of 6800 million VM turned into a 1960–75 deficit of 1700 million VM. 1975 was a particularly poor year, with trade with the socialist bloc, the Third World and the West all in the red. Intra-German trade almost doubled between 1970 and 1975 with the GDR piling up an accumulated debt of DM 2,600 million by 1976. Debts to other Western countries amounted to US$3500 million by mid-1976 (McCauley 1979: 197; Zimmermann 1978: 23–4).

The GDR exports mainly industrial products, especially machinery, equipment and means of transport, while half of her imports are taken up by energy and raw materials. This trade structure means that the GDR has been at a considerable disadvantage since the price of finished products has increased much more slowly than that of energy and raw materials. The

recession in the West since 1974 has made it increasingly difficult to boost exports to Western markets. The result is that
trade deficits have become normal.

The need to export a larger quantity of goods in order to
import the same quantity means that the domestic market
has had to put up with shortages. Saving energy and cutting
down on the amount of materials needed to fulfil the plan have
become a way of life. There is considerable scope for improve-
mement. In 1977, 7.1 tonnes of hard coal equivalent per capita
were consumed compared with only 6.1 tonnes in the FRG.
If the social product in the East is taken at about 20 per cent
below that of the West, the East German figure should be
lower, not higher, than the West German.

Waste of energy and raw materials is partly due to the pricing
system which until recently put little pressure on enterprises
to economise. The reforms which would have led to prices
reflecting average costs were never completed under Ulbricht.
The problems facing GDR industry were compounded by the
deficiencies of the management and planning systems. The
recentralisation of the Honecker era has increased the pressure
on the centre. There is simply not enough time or personnel
to analyse the mass of data and information in such a way as
to allow the centre to arrive at real alternatives to the present
policies. The management structure also lacks a clear definition
of lines of competence. This has produced a system which is
too inflexible to cope competently with sudden changes in the
world market or domestic demand. An important goal is the
rapid application of research findings but this is being hampered
by the existing planning system. Hence innovation is slowed
down, products are not keeping pace with the outside world
and as time passes the GDR slips further and further behind.
Since only about 10 per cent of GDR research and development
is up to world standards, the country is faced with an uphill
task. Here political and economic goals conflict. Whereas the
GDR leadership wishes to disengage from the West and to inte-
grate with the East, economically it should be doing the reverse.

The pressure to raise labour productivity by economising on
materials, improving factory efficiency and by simply working
harder is now a fact of life. Since there are practically no labour
reserves, the existing labour force must produce more. One
method is to increase two- and three-shift working of expensive

machinery and equipment. In 1977, 14.3 per cent of all workers were engaged on two-shift working and 28.3 per cent on three-shift working. This was still short of the target. Erich Honecker stated that in the same year it had been planned to utilise highly productive machinery and equipment 15.6 hours per day but only 14.7 hours per day was actually achieved. Labour productivity in the GDR is still about one-third lower than in the FRG.

The GDR became, in the words of Peter Christian Ludz, a 'careerist' society with everyone trying to move upwards especially into those positions which enjoyed social prestige. Education and expertise were the chief qualifications. This led to some 'socially necessary jobs' enjoying less prestige. This affected, for example, 'skilled workers in tunnelling and road building and several types of services and trades' (*Einheit* no. 1/1976: 70; Weber 1980: 153).

The unfavourable structure of the GDR population exacerbated labour problems. Whereas in 1950, for every 100 persons of working age there were 56.1 who were not capable of working, this rose to the high figure of 72.8 in 1970 but by 1978 it had dropped to 60.7. The main reason for the rise was the rapid increase in the number of pensioners; the number dropped mainly due to the fall in the birth rate.

The permanent labour shortage in the GDR (there has been no unemployment since the late 1950s) has made it more important to get as many women as possible out to work. This has been one of the facets of the Honecker era and some success has been recorded. Whereas in 1971, 77.8 per cent of women were gainfully employed, in 1977 the figure had risen to over 82 per cent. However most of those who took up jobs in the 1970s only work part time. Indeed 29.5 per cent of all women worked part time in 1980 but this was an improvement on 1971 when the figure was 35 per cent.

The living standards of the GDR population rose during the first half of the 1970s with the vast majority better off than during the 1960s (see Table 5.1). The average monthly wage rose from 762 marks in 1970 to 897 marks in 1975. This improvement was a by-product of industrial expansion. Since its inception the high points in the growth of the GDR economy were recorded during the years 1962–8 and 1971–5. Industrial production grew sevenfold between 1950 and 1975, 71 per cent

Table 5.1: *Number of items per 100 households*

	1970	1975	1979
Television sets	69.4	82.0	103.5
Refrigerators	56.4	84.7	102.2
Electrical washing machines	53.6	73.0	79.9
Cars	15.6	26.2	36.3

Source: *Statistisches Jahrbuch* (1980) p. 33.

between 1961 and 1970 and 38 per cent between 1971 and 1975. As a result the output of consumer durables rose.

Living standards have stagnated since the late 1970s due mainly to the terms of trade turning against the GDR. Now about 3 per cent national income growth is needed to meet the increased price of imports.

In an attempt to make GDR industry more efficient, the nation's industrial enterprises were concentrated in Kombinate, beginning on 1 January 1980. There are now 160 Kombinate and they are run by a director general who normally also runs one of the key enterprises in the group. Kombinate embrace all enterprises in the industrial sector and have between 20 000 and 40 000 employees each. They account for 95 per cent of industrial output and employ 95 per cent of the labour force. Some have been great successes but others have so far failed to live up to expectations. One of the reasons for this is that since a Kombinat embraces all factories concerned with a certain sector of the industrial economy, for example glass-making, if that sector was efficient before 1980 the Kombinat started off with very good prospects. If the performance was poor before 1980 those Kombinate will need time to improve the situation.

Despite the fact that the 1976—80 plan was not fulfilled, only slightly lower goals have been set for the period 1981—5. Due to the level of her technology, the GDR would like to see faster economic integration in Comecon so as to make use of long production runs in, for example, computers. However the GDR has consistently complained that other states have been slow to provide marketing information and the events in Poland have further retarded integration. The recession in the West has made it more difficult to earn the hard currency needed to pay for increasing imports and to service debt repayments. In mid-1982 the GDR had an estimate hard currency debt of US$12 000 million.

Social Policy

Gesellschaftspolitik or societal policy is all embracing and is conducted primarily in the interests of the working class. Social structure is of key importance. *Sozialpolitik* or social policy, however, is only concerned with certain aspects of the development of society; anomalies in income distribution, health, welfare, etc., but is an integral part of *Gesellschaftspolitik*. Until the mid-1960s the SED avoided using the term *Sozialpolitik* since it was perceived as an attempt to correct the contradictions of capitalist society. Socialism, it was held, did not need a social policy since concern for human beings lay at its very core. Gradually the party came round to the idea that there could be a socialist social policy to take care of those who, through no fault of their own, are incapable of satisfying a basic minimum of their needs. This is not to be taken as a basic minimum of subsistence but a basic satisfaction of needs: foodstuffs, housing, health and education, consonant with the level of social production. As the economy expands so the level rises. A goal of social policy is not to make people equal but to provide equality of opportunity.

Honecker, ever since 1971, has spoken of the unity of economic and social policy. The latter plays a decisive role in the 'establishment of harmony' in society and is viewed as an ongoing process. Since there is 'no complete identity of interests' of any group in developed socialist society, intervention by the political leadership is necessary to overcome contradictions.

During developed socialism class structure is expected to assume less and less significance but social structure will become increasingly more complex. This means in effect that differentials in living and working conditions and levels of education and expertise will grow. One goal of social policy has already been mentioned — caring for those who fall behind in the race for the better life. The other is the desire to influence the development of the social structure. This must remain a long-term goal since an enormous amount of research will have to be undertaken in order to provide the decision-makers with the requisite information which would permit them to plan consciously the evolution of the social structure.

Although the SED speaks of the unity of economic and social policy, the former takes precedence. One of its tasks is to remove the obstacles which stand in the way of a more effective economic policy, especially that of raising labour productivity. The first social policy programme was launched on 27 April 1972 when a joint party, trade union and government decree promised that pensions and social benefits for 3.4 million citizens would be raised, that measures to help working mothers, young married couples and to raise the birth rate would be adopted, and living conditions for workers and employees would be improved. In September 1973 measures to improve health care were announced.

The main element in social policy under Honecker is housing. From 1971 to 1975 some 400 000 new dwellings were built and 209 000 renovated. During the 1976—80 plan period over 550 000 new and 200 000 renovated dwellings were completed, one of the few sectors to overfulfil its plan. The long-term goal is to construct or renovate 2.8 million to 3 million dwellings between 1976 and 1990. About one-third of the housing stock in 1980 consisted of new or renovated accommodation, with over 6 million citizens, or about 40 per cent of the population, benefiting. In 1980 45 per cent of new dwellings were put up by workers' building cooperatives. Private house-building is now favoured and accounted for 11 per cent of new dwellings in 1980. However the stock of older, private dwellings has deteriorated since the very low rents paid by tenants are insufficient to pay for repairs. Inner-city decay will not be tackled until the beginning of the next century. Villages are to be left more or less to their own devices. About two-thirds of all new and renovated dwellings planned are in cities and towns containing half the GDR population.

In the GDR, just as in the FRG, the birth rate declined during the 1960s, due to the rising number of women who

worked, the increased burden on those women who had to combine the roles of wife, mother and worker without receiving
much help either from husbands or labour-saving devices in
the home, the decline of religious belief and the growing economic independence of women. In 1972 abortion was legalised
and contraceptives were provided free. The net result was that
live births per thousand of the population declined from 17.6
in 1963 to an all-time low of 10.6 in 1974. Since the population
was not reproducing itself a pro-natal policy was launched
which has seen the birth rate rise.

Maternity leave was increased from 18 to 26 weeks and
mothers now receive 1000 marks on the birth of each child. If
the mother so desires she may take a year's unpaid leave after
the birth of the child without any loss of social benefits and
she is guaranteed her job back. After the birth of a second child
the mother is entitled to a year's leave on sick pay. Full-time
working mothers with three children in their household only
work a 40-hour week (extended to mothers of two children in
1977) and are entitled to 21 days' holiday (instead of 18 days)
without any reduction in pay. Working mothers with children
under six years of age do not need to engage in shiftwork or
do overtime. Full-time employed women receive a day off
a month for housework, if they have children under 18 years
of age. Women over 40 and single fathers also receive a day off
a month.

The one-child family is still the norm in the GDR. In 1977
only 6.6 per cent of live births were to mothers having their
third child and 3.7 per cent to those having their fourth or
subsequent child. Indeed there were only 90 000 families in
1980 with four or more children.

The increase in the availability of consumer durables has
helped to take some of the drudgery out of housework but
the simplest solution would be for husbands to do more about
the house. However the literature makes it quite clear that
the average husband is quite unwilling to give up his role as the
Hauspascha. He only does 6 hours of housework per week, on
average, leaving the other 41 hours to the wife and children.
Not surprisingly, the incidence of illness among working women
is higher than among men.

In order to overcome the widespread resistance to three-
shift working, the length of the working week for three-shift

workers was reduced to 40 hours and to 42 hours for two-shift workers in 1977. These two groups were also granted an extra three days' holiday. Nevertheless the night shift is very unpopular and enterprises are obliged to employ some workers who drink on the job. There is simply no other labour available. A GDR quip has it that one should never buy anything produced on the night shift.

The minimum wage was raised from 350 to 400 marks on 1 October 1976 with smaller increases for those earning between 400 and 500 marks. About one million workers and employees benefited from these measures, revealing that about one in seven had been on these very low rates. This went some way towards raising the minimum standard of living. It was hoped that one of the by-products would be to lift labour productivity but it was not specifically tied to performance. A wage reform was then initiated and implemented during the plan period ending in 1980. Jobs were reclassified, and work norms were raised, as were wages. However this only affected about 1.5 million persons in key industrial sectors. The GDR leadership has always been hesitant about raising work norms, due to its traumatic experience in 1953, and has sought to reduce opposition by using the FDGB to articulate its policy.

Further social improvements were included in the new labour code which was introduced on 1 January 1978. Among the benefits were: payment for worktime spent in consulting a doctor; greater job security; and greater care to be taken to place a worker in a job with similar pay when rationalisation replaces the previous employment.

Pensioners have traditionally been low on the order of priorities in the GDR. Up to 1968 the maximum income for pension assessment was 600 marks, with the years before 1945 being treated very unfavourably. As of 1968 voluntary supplementary contributions could be made to boost one's pension. Pensions were increased in 1971 and again in 1972 when they rose by 20 per cent. The 1972 measures benefited about 4 million pensioners. Because of this the income of old age pensioners, over the years 1965–72, increased at an annual rate of 6.5 per cent, faster than any other group in society. The minimum pension was again raised on 1 December 1976 to 230–300 marks, depending on how many years the pensioner had worked. The average pension rose from 199 marks in 1970 to about 300 marks in

1976 and to 327 marks in 1979. Whereas in 1970 the average
pension was 26.1 per cent of the average wage of workers and
employees, this had risen to 32.3 per cent in 1979. Hence
pensions policy is designed to encourage as many pensioners to
work as possible, since the higher the income the greater the
drop on retirement. About one in five of GDR pensioners now
work. It should be pointed out that a privileged group of pensioners, accounting for about 20 per cent of the total, exists
in the GDR. Pensions paid to the police and certain officials
are up to 70 per cent of their last year's working wage; teachers,
doctors and other members of the intelligentsia receive about
60—80 per cent of their last salary and transport and post office
workers are also generously treated.

During the Honecker era general polytechnical education
has expanded. Whereas about 85 per cent of pupils passed into
the ninth class in 1970 this had risen to over 90 per cent in
1973, demonstrating that practically all children were receiving
some post-secondary education. Great emphasis was placed on
technical subjects but just as much effort went into turning
pupils into model GDR citizens. In line with the policy of
getting mothers out to work, crèche and kindergarten facilities
were extended. Whereas only 25.6 per cent of children up to
the age of 3 were looked after in crèches in 1970, this had
risen to 40.3 per cent in 1974 and to 60 per cent in 1980.
Those in kindergartens (3—6 years) increased from 59.7 per cent
in 1970 to 76.3 per cent in 1974 and to 92 per cent in 1980.
Also in 1980, 86 per cent of children aged between 7 and 11
were supervised after school hours until their parents returned
from work. The question of whether young children would not
be better off at home rather than in crèches has not been discussed in the literature since 1965. At that time there were
some who strongly favoured the mother staying at home.

Admissions to universities and technical colleges declined
during the 1970s. Since the high hopes entertained for the
scientific—technical revolution were not realised, it meant that
many students had embarked on courses which would not lead
to commensurate jobs. The high point of admissions was
reached in 1971 when the total student population reached
158 000 with 44 000 enrolled in universities. Total student
enrolment dropped to 137 000 in 1975 and to 129 000 in 1979.
University admissions fell to 34 000 in 1975 and to 32 000 in

1979. The worst affected were those who were trying to acquire the qualifications necessary for their post or to acquire the expertise for the job they desired. Correspondence course admissions were severly cut back. The social group most affected by the restrictions on further education during the 1970s was the working class, especially those men and women who had hoped to secure social mobility through part-time study. In socialist countries an educational policy based on merit always favours the intelligentsia and increasingly so as time passes. One reason is that the education their sons and daughters receive is superior — partly due to home help — and another is that expectations and motivation are higher. Since further education is largely in the hands of the intelligentsia, it is easier for their offspring to gain admission. In the GDR in 1971 around 50 per cent of the student population were from the intelligentsia. The country had reached the stage where a self-recruiting socialist intelligentsia had, to all intents and purposes, come into being. Greater emphasis has been paid to political criteria in selecting students under Honecker, with membership of the FDJ, involvement in paramilitary training and a good record in voluntary work being most highly regarded by the SED. This, of course, does not solve the problem of how to increase the proportion of students of working-class background. Along with their academic skills the intelligentsia should be the most capable of displaying the social and political behaviour necessary for admission.

Although it became much more difficult to obtain places in higher education after 1971, female students were markedly more successful than hitherto. Whereas only 37 per cent of the student population was female in 1971, this had risen to 48.1 per cent in 1979. Women were even more successful in securing university places. Female enrolment increased from 40.4 per cent in 1971 to 50.5 per cent in 1979. The situation in technical colleges is even more favourable; 70 per cent of the students in 1980 were female. Women have moved into technical disciplines to a significant degree. In 1980, 40 per cent of all places in these disciplines in universities and technical colleges were filled by women.

Under Honecker social policy has continuously been accorded high priority. Whereas social expenditure per capita rose by 90 per cent between 1971 and 1979, national income only increased by 46 per cent. Housing was afforded clear priority; outlay in 1979 was 3.2 times that of 1971. On the other hand, expenditure on health rose by only 20 per cent over the same period and remains the Cinderella of social policy. The government's decision to keep the price of essential foodstuffs and services stable has resulted in a larger and larger subvention each year. In 1979 it amounted to 94 marks per head of the population.

Since social expenditure growth under Honecker has been greater than national income growth there has been a redistribution, with investment suffering as a consequence. In 1970 investment amounted to 24.4 per cent of national income but this dropped to 22.9 per cent in 1975 and to 20.1 per cent in 1979. In the socialist bloc the GDR now invests the lowest proportion of her national income.

Subsidising essential foodstuffs and services benefits all sections of the population. However the money must be recouped and the method chosen is to impose higher taxes on non-essential goods. These goods, which account for 80 per cent of all sales, can also be increased in price from time to time. This pricing policy favours the better off. The less well off would be better served if these price subsidies were abolished and replaced by supplementary benefits. However there is a long tradition of keeping the prices of essential foodstuffs and services stable in socialist countries and the strikes in Poland in 1970, 1976 and 1980 would seem to underline the wisdom of keeping food prices as they are.

Cultural Policy

The beginning of the Honecker era was marked by considerable self-confidence on the part of the SED which felt that writers and artists were capable of contributing much to the development of socialism in the GDR. At the fourth plenum of the CC in December 1971 Honecker gave the signal for a more open attitude to culture. 'In my opinion there can be no taboos in the realm of culture and literature, provided one starts from a solidly socialist position. This refers to the question of content as well as to style; in other words, the questions which concern artistic mystery.' On the face of it this meant that convinced socialists could write about anything in the manner of their own choosing without needing to seek approval from the party's cultural bureaucrats. The only way to discover how broadly 'party-mindedness' would be interpreted was to experiment. The party was taken aback by the explosion of controversial writing and expression which followed. Ulrich Plenzdorf's *Die neuen Leiden des jungen W.* appeared in March 1972 in the journal *Sinn und Form* and was deliberately provocative. Bearing comparison with Goethe's work on the sufferings of the young Werther, Plenzdorf presents the thoughts of Edgar, a socialist drop-out, who has suffered the inflexible norms and pressure to conform in a society in which people live to work and are afraid of their freedom (Emmerich 1981: 183). Official critics panned the work but a poll in the FDJ journal *Forum* revealed that 40 per cent of young people questioned agreed with Edgar's criticisms and over 60 per cent could imagine having him as a friend. The work became very well known through a stage production. However, despite official discomfiture at the popularity of an 'anti-hero', the work was not banned.

Another breakthrough was the appearance in 1974 of three novels about women by female writers and the following year an anthology, *Blitz aus heiterem Himmel*, was published, which dealt for the first time in GDR literature with the emancipation of women. An attempt was made in it to break away from masculine form and style. Novels about the difficulties of women in GDR society have continued to appear and many are by women writing from experience.

The honeymoon with the cultural intelligentsia came to an end on 17 November 1976 when the folk singer Wolf Biermann was deprived of his GDR citizenship while on a tour of West Germany. Biermann, born in Hamburg, had chosen to live in the GDR. He was accused of 'hostile behaviour' and *Neues Deutschland* informed him that a 'feeling of loyalty towards the state' was part and parcel of citizenship. Thereby the regime signalled that the frontiers of the permissible had been crossed. Many GDR authors scented danger: such a view could also affect their work. Twelve writers immediately wrote an open letter protesting about Biermann's expatriation and the signatories included Christa Wolf, Volker Braun and Stefan Heym. They were soon followed by more than 70 other writers and artists, including Ulrich Plenzdorf. On the other hand established writers such as Anna Seghers and Hermann Kant supported the move against Biermann.

It is now clear that the Biermann episode was a turning point in GDR cultural policy. The party, literary and state organs immediately launched a well-prepared campaign against the signatories. Imprisonment, house arrest, expulsion from the Writers' Union and from the GDR were all practised. Until 1976 there had been a net inflow of writers and artists into the GDR but after that date it became an exodus. Besides the many writers, artists, producers, actors, musicians and composers who left the GDR for good, there were others who were encouraged by the authorities to apply for long-term visas. Jurek Becker and Günter Kunert, for instance, took up this option. Leaving the GDR marked the end of a chain of restrictions placed on those affected. It was a conscious policy practised, apparently, in the belief that the security authorities could not cope with the problems which these creative citizens posed. Since the vast majority of the exiles belonged to the 'loyal opposition', in that they were dedicated socialists but were not satisfied with Marxism–Leninism as interpreted by the SED, 'real, existing socialism' assumed a more precise meaning. It was what the SED leadership – and only that leadership – said it was.

For those who remained, the restrictions increased. A long-standing problem for the GDR cultural authorities had been the ability of authors to have those works, rejected by GDR publishing houses, published in West Germany. In May 1979 Robert Havemann was fined 10 000 marks for having contravened the currency offences and Stefan Heym 9000 marks for having published his novel *Collin* in the FRG without first having received permission. The criminal code was amended so that any author who published a work abroad which 'damaged the interests of the GDR' could be arrested and imprisoned.

After writing a letter to Erich Honecker in which they protested against the practice of 'defaming critical writers', 'silencing others' and arraigning others before the courts, all signatories were expelled, on 7 June 1979, from the Writers' Union, with the exception of those who were no longer members. The Berlin branch which expelled them was not unanimous in its condemnation: about 50 of the 300 members voted against the motion. Since 1976 the Writers' Union has lost about 30 authors, out of a membership of 700, either through expulsion or resignation (Emmerich 1981: 193).

Foreign Policy

Since the removal of Ulbricht the SED has constantly reiterated its belief that the Soviet Union plays the 'leading role' in the world socialist community and is the model developed socialist state. Erich Honecker has stated that the close relationship between the SED and the CPSU is the 'cornerstone' of his party's policy and that friendship with the USSR is one of the 'necessities of life'.

Some of the tangible results of this fraternal relationship have been evident in the field of foreign policy. When, on 18 September 1973, the GDR became the 133rd member of the United Nations she achieved a long-sought-after goal, recognition of her statehood in international law. Enjoying diplomatic relations with over 100 states the GDR could feel satisfied that she had at long last mounted the world stage. However a price had to be paid for such progress. The Four Power Agreement on Berlin, signed on 3 August 1971, demonstrated to the world that since the Soviet Union was willing to make limited concessions this obliged the GDR to accept them even though she viewed them as against her own national interest. The Soviet Union, in the agreement, guaranteed the transit of non-military persons and goods between West Berlin and the FRG and acknowledged that the links between West Berlin and West Germany would 'remain and be expanded'. In the light of this a transit agreement was signed on 17 December 1971 by the GDR and the FRG, followed by one facilitating travel, signed by the West Berlin senate and the GDR. All these agreements came into effect on 6 June 1972 as a result of the final protocol of the Four Powers.

The next step was to negotiate a Basic Treaty with the FRG. The Americans feared that if the GDR was accorded UN membership she could interpret this as a declaration of full sovereignty and ignore her obligations under the Berlin Agreement. Hence membership was made contingent on the signing of the Basic Treaty. The goals of the two German states were quite different. Bonn wanted to see East Berlin confirm its links with West

Berlin and to avoid anything which would make eventual reunification more difficult. East Berlin, on the other hand, wanted to achieve full sovereignty by ridding itself of the West Berlin connection and avoiding any recognition of Four Power responsibility for Germany, by denying the existence of one German nation and one German citizenship, by holding off the unification of Germany until it could dictate its own terms and by forcing the FRG to recognise the GDR as a foreign state, thereby obliging the FRG to amend her constitution.

The two sides had to compromise on most issues, especially on the national question. This was written into the preamble when the Basic Treaty was signed on 21 December 1972. The West German view that permanent representatives and not ambassadors should be exchanged, since the FRG and the GDR were not foreign countries, was also conceded. Neither German state achieved full sovereignty because of the consequences of the Second World War.

Speaking at the eighth congress of the SED, Erich Honecker referred to talk about the unity of the German nation as 'twaddle'. Instead a new type of nation, a socialist nation, had come into being in the GDR. The concept of class is all important. Since the SED felt threatened by Willy Brandt's concept of two German states in one German nation it had to produce a counter-proposal. This turned out to be two German states and two German nations with the unity of the nation having been shattered in 1945. The SED complicated the situation by asserting that the GDR was the legitimate heir of that nation. Furthermore, at a CC plenum on 12 December 1974, the Secretary General claimed that in comparison with the FRG, the GDR was an 'historical epoch ahead'. 'We represent', he stated, 'in comparison with West Germany, socialist Germany.' The population are 'GDR citizens' with the overwhelming majority of 'German nationality'. Hence, according to the SED, there is no German nation, no German citizenship but there is a German nationality. The aim of the SED is clear — the creation of a specific GDR national consciousness — but little progress has been made so far, partly because the arguments adduced in support of this concept are so unconvincing.

The constitution was amended accordingly on 7 October 1974. It is worthy of note that the SED did not publish draft amendments and offer them to the public for discussion. This is, after all, what article 65 (4) of the constitution requires. 'Fundamental changes . . . will be discussed by the population.' Since the SED could hardly argue that the emendations were so minor as not to constitute major changes, the only conclusion one can draw is that the party was not confident that citizens would accept them. The Volkskammer passed the changes into law without further ado.

The special GDR—Soviet relationship needed to be articulated anew in the light of all these changes. A treaty of friendship, cooperation and mutual aid was accordingly signed on 7 October 1975. The treaty's aim, as expressed by Leonid Brezhnev, was to secure a 'further rapprochement of both countries and peoples' and it spoke of eternal friendship and 'fraternal, mutual aid in all fields'. It also stated that it does not affect any of the provisions of the Berlin Agreement. Under the new treaty the military obligations of the GDR have been extended and her armed forces could be called upon to render assistance in any military theatre. The GDR and the USSR are duty bound to render aid if 'socialist achievements' in the 'socialist community' are 'under threat'.

The Basic Treaty made it incumbent on both sides to negotiate a whole series of agreements to improve relations. This has led to the signing of many accords and the constant need to be in contact to cope with the multitude of problems which have arisen during the implementation of these agreements. Other questions, not covered in any accord, have to be discussed and resolved. Since the GDR has constantly tried to interpret agreements in her own favour, intra-German relations have developed their own intensity.

Two further events enhanced the standing of the SED and the GDR. Soviet interest in a conference which would place a seal on the post-war frontiers in Europe led to the signing of the Helsinki Final Act in August 1975 with Erich Honecker representing the GDR. In order to obtain an agreement, however, the Soviet Union had to make concessions on human rights, contained in Basket Three. This aroused considerable interest in the GDR and led to an estimated 100 000 citizens requesting permission to leave the country. The other event was the convening of the conference of European communist and workers' parties in June 1976 in East Berlin. It was quite an achievement to get everyone, except the Albanians and the Icelanders, to the GDR capital. Brezhnev, Ceausescu, Tito, Berlinguer, Carrillo and Marchais sitting around the same table and willing to accept the final document constituted quite a feather in the cap of the SED. *Neues Deutschland* was required to publish all the set speeches and the welter of differing opinion about socialism and how it should develop must have aroused great interest among party members. The SED, predictably, proposed that the CPSU be afforded hegemony but such sentiments did not find their way into the final document.

The various agreements signed by the GDR with the FRG and West Berlin resulted in a rapid increase in the flow of visitors to the GDR. The number of West Germans visiting the GDR rose from 1.3 million in 1971 to 3.6 million in 1979. Besides this there were one-day visits by FRG citizens to East Berlin; these came to 1.4 million in 1977. On the other hand, the number of GDR citizens (almost all pensioners) visiting the FRG only rose from 1.1 million in 1971 to 1.4 million in 1979. Then there were the visits of West Berliners to East Berlin and the GDR. These came to 3.4 million in 1977 — the population of West Berlin then was 1.9 million.

The influx of Western visitors saw much needed hard currency flowing into the GDR State Bank but it also allowed Germans from both states to make contact with one another and decide on what united and separated them. The West Germans have proved willing, so far, to foot most of the bill to improve road, rail and water communications to West Berlin. The GDR's desire to negotiate agreements which are beneficial to herself has led the USSR to warn against developing relations with Bonn too rapidly.

The Soviet intervention in Afghanistan in December 1979 and the unrest in Poland, which began in August 1980, upset the tenor of East–West German relations. The GDR became alarmed at the implications of the Polish situation and ended visa-free travel between the two countries. She also quadrupled in East Berlin and doubled in the GDR in October 1980 the amount of money which must be exchanged daily by visitors. This had the expected effect on the number of visits, which were down 50 per cent by the summer of 1981.

The emergence of the Polish free trade union, Solidarity, resulted in the SED becoming increasingly critical of the Polish

United Workers' Party. It favoured military intervention by the Warsaw Pact, so little faith did it have in the ability of Poland's communists to reestablish their authority. The trouble in Poland affected the GDR economy, since the Poles were quite incapable of meeting their export obligations to the GDR. The imposition of military rule on 13 December 1981 was warmly welcomed by the GDR but it came at a time when Chancellor Helmut Schmidt was on the point of leaving the GDR after having met Erich Honecker. So nervous were the GDR security forces that they placed all citizens in Güstrow under house arrest during the Chancellor's short visit there. Only the officially approved were allowed on the streets on 13 December 1981. The GDR has repeatedly stated that she seeks better relations with the FRG but this now means at state level. Human contact, as perceived by the GDR, can only benefit the FRG.

The foreign currency law of December 1973 permits GDR citizens to accept up to DM500 from visitors but since most party and government functionaries are forbidden to cultivate foreign contacts they are excluded. The state allows the hard currency to be expended in Intershops which are full of Western goods. Not all the money flows directly into the Intershops since it is also used to pay artisans to effect much needed repairs and other skilled work. This has led to two currencies circulating in the GDR, with the local mark the weaker currency of the two. Those GDR citizens who have a ready supply of GDR marks can purchase GDR goods, unobtainable elsewhere, in Exquisit and Delikat shops at about four times the normal price. Thus there are haves and have-nots in GDR society. Those with manual skills and Western relations enjoy a good living while those lacking both are considerably worse off. Probably the most aggrieved are the lower-level bureaucrats whose position does not afford them access to the perquisites of office.

The Third World

The GDR's active involvement in Africa dates from 1959 when the SED attended the fifth congress of the ruling party in Guinea and seized the opportunity to express its solidarity not only with Guinea but also with the rest of Africa. It gradually developed links with 'revolutionary democratic' parties but the harvest came in the mid-1970s when countries such as Ethiopia, Angola, Mozambique and Guinea Bissau decided on the Marxist— Leninist path of development. An SED delegation, headed by Werner Lamberz, attended the third Frelimo congress, in Maputo, and Lamberz assured President Samora Machel that the 'SED and the socialist German state would also in the future be found on the side of Frelimo to assist in carrying through the people's revolution and to vitiate all imperialist attacks against the young people's republic' (*Neues Deutschland* 10 February 1977). The GDR provides skilled labour, especially in mining, in return for hard coal, media specialists to aid the information organs, instructors to train troops and it is involved in security. In Angola and Ethiopia the GDR plays a somewhat similar role. One estimate puts the number of military personnel in Africa at 2720 (*Der Spiegel* no. 10/1980). There is a division of labour among socialist military personnel in Africa. The Soviets provide high-ranking officers who command, the GDR junior officers, NCOs and skilled men to train indigenous troops and the Cubans get involved in the fighting.

Economically the GDR needs the Third World. Since the USSR is unable to provide all the necessary energy and raw material imports, the GDR must look elsewhere and so far has shown a keen business sense in Africa and in other parts of the Third World. Another advantage is that the conflict with the FRG can be extended outside Europe and the West Germans have found on several occasions that African countries have adopted the GDR interpretation of the Berlin question.

Such is the reputation which East Germans have earned for themselves by dint of hard work and endeavour that when President Kenneth Kaunda of Zambia visited East Berlin in August 1980 he praised GDR agriculture as the most successful in the socialist world and went on: 'The resources of our country are almost untouched ... we need managerial cadres, we need equipment, we need technology and generous financial support.' Despite this plea, GDR—Zambian cooperation in agriculture and industry is limited.

Vietnam is the most important country in Asia as far as the GDR is concerned. It is now that country's second closest ally, after the Soviet Union, and has sent medical equipment, food and technical equipment to Hanoi. Vietnam adopted the GDR position on Berlin and Germany in a treaty of friendship signed in December 1977.

GDR geologists are active in Mongolia and have discovered zinc ore. The mines will be collectively exploited by Mongolia, the USSR and the GDR. These countries will also operate a combine for the processing of copper and molybdenum which 'will help to meet some of the raw material needs of the GDR'.

In Afghanistan the GDR sides unequivocally with the USSR and has set up field hospitals and treatment centres and has provided ambulances as well as establishing news and information services and training security police.

The Contemporary Situation

In mid-1982 the SED now finds itself in a situation comparable to that of the late 1950s. The good years, the early 1970s, are over and there is little likelihood that the terms of trade will significantly improve during the 1980s. As a resource-poor country the GDR must export more to import the same quantity. Growth rates on paper are commendable but most of the increased wealth is immediately exported. Even so GDR trade is not in balance with the Soviet Union or the West. The hard currency debt has made it very difficult to borrow from Western banks.

The SED's command of the instruments of control (the government, the mass organisations, etc.) and coercion (the military and police) has never been so complete. However the dimming of self-confidence in a bright future has led to a rise in the influence of the military—security complex. Defence expenditure is now rising at about double the rate of national income growth and the bill for security is also mounting. Along with this has gone a militarisation of society, especially of youth. The events in Poland caused acute anxiety, reflected in the harsh reports and commentaries in *Neues Deutschland*. They have also cost the GDR money through providing aid and having to import from the West to make up for the short-fall in Polish exports.

Economic success is the foundation of stability in the GDR and the source of the legitimacy of the party. On paper the economy is growing but living standards are stagnating. A leading party political economist, Otto Reinhold, has spoken of the possibility of social conflict if the population perceives that the economy is running into difficulties. The 1980s will be a difficult decade.

Chronology

1945

End of April/ beginning of May	Three KPD groups arrive in Germany and commence work in Soviet occupied areas: Ulbricht group in Berlin; Ackermann group in Saxony and the Sobottka group in Mecklenburg—Vorpommern.
7—8 May	Unconditional surrender of the Wehrmacht at Rheims and Berlin Karlshorst.
9 May	Stalin declares that Germany is not to be broken up or annihilated; A. I. Mikoyan arrives in Berlin to assess the situation in Germany.
17 May	Soviet city commandant appoints Dr A. Werner head of a Berlin city government.
23 May	Reich government, formed on 2 May at Mürwik—Flensburg, under Admiral Dönitz, arrested by British troops.
5 June	Declaration of the defeat of Germany and the assumption of supreme power in Germany by the USSR, the USA, Great Britain and France. Allied Control Council for Germany established in Berlin.
9 June	Soviet Military Administration in Germany (SMAD) established in Berlin.
10 June	Order no. 2 by SMAD: anti-fascist democratic parties and trade unions permitted in Soviet zone.
11 June	KPD refounded; KPD proclamation.

15 June	Committee for the formation of anti-fascist democratic trade unions set up in Berlin.
15–17 June	SPD refounded; central executive committee constituted.
19 June	KPD and SPD agree on joint action.
26 June	CDU founded in Berlin.
1–3 July	American and British troops leave western parts of Soviet zone; Western allies take over their sectors of Berlin.
4–16 July	SMAD confirms in office Land or provincial administration in Mecklenburg, Saxony, Thuringia, Mark Brandenburg and Saxony–Anhalt.
5 July	LDPD founded in Berlin.
11 July	The Interallied Military Kommandatura takes over power in Berlin and by order no. 1 divides the city into four sectors.
14 July	Bloc of anti-fascist democratic parties established; joint committee composed of five representatives from each of KPD, SPD, CDU and LDPD set up in Berlin (Anti-fa bloc).
17 July–2 August	Potsdam Conference attended by USSR, USA and Great Britain and chaired by Stalin, Truman and Churchill/Attlee.
27 July	Order no. 17 by SMAD establishes 11 central administrations in the Soviet zone.
31 July	Central youth committee founded; Erich Honecker elected chairman on 10 September in Berlin.
4 August	France accedes to the Potsdam Agreement of 2 August.
5 September	Anti-fa bloc decides in favour of an immediate land reform.

1 October	Schools reopen; KPD and SPD in favour of the democratisation of education on 18 October.
3 October	Order no. 49 by SMAD removes all NSDAP members from administration of justice.
22 October	SMAD empowers Land and provincial administrations to promulgate laws and ordinances.
30–31 October	Orders no. 124 and 126 by SMAD permit the sequestration and confiscation of the property of the German Reich, the NSDAP, the Wehrmacht and large industrial, mining and trading concerns.
20 November– 30 September 1946	International Military Tribunal meets in Nuremberg.
8–21 December	Conflict within the Anti-fa bloc over the land reform; CDU leaders Hermes and Schreiber refuse to agree to confiscation without compensation and are forced to resign; Jakob Kaiser becomes chairman.
20–21 December	Joint conference of KPD and SPD (the conference of the sixty) in Berlin; rapid fusion of both parties decided.

1946

Beginning of February	Article by Anton Ackermann 'Is there a special German way to socialism?' appears in *Einheit*.
9–11 February	Founding congress of Free German Trades Union Association (FDGB) in Berlin; Hans Jendretzky (KPD), Bernhard Göring (SPD) and Ernst Lemmer (CDU) elected co-chairman.

7 March	Free German Youth organisation (FDJ) founded in Berlin; chairman is Erich Honecker.
31 March	SPD in West Berlin votes on fusion with KPD; 82 per cent against immediate fusion but 62 per cent for cooperation with KPD.
21–22 April	Socialist Unity Party (SED) founded at the unification party congress in Berlin; parity principle leads to Wilhelm Pieck (KPD) and Otto Grotewohl (SPD) being elected co-chairmen.
23 April	First meeting of central committee (Vorstand) of SED; a central Secretariat elected; *Neues Deutschland*, central organ of SED, appears for the first time.
25 April–15 May, 15 June–12 July	Conference of Foreign Ministers of Four Powers meets in Paris; no binding decisions taken.
31 May	SPD and SED permitted in all of Berlin by the Allied Kommandatura.
8–10 June	First FDJ parliament in Brandenburg (Havel).
15–17 June	First CDU congress in Berlin; J. Kaiser and E. Lemmer elected co-chairmen.
30 June	Referendum in Saxony on nationalisation of concerns of war and Nazi criminals; 77 per cent for; between 24 July and 16 August these concerns are nationalised elsewhere in the Soviet zone.
6–8 July	First LDPD congress in Erfurt; Dr Wilhelm Külz elected chairman.
1 August	German Academy of Sciences reopened in Berlin.
17 August	Order no. 253 of SMAD enacts 'equal pay for equal work' for all workers, employees, men, women and young people.

1—15 September	Local (Gemeinde) elections in the Soviet zone.
20 October	Land and Kreistag elections in the Soviet zone and to the Berlin city parliament.
14 November	A draft constitution of a German democratic republic is published by the executive committee of the SED.
3—12 December	Land and provincial governments formed in the Soviet zone; constitutions adopted between December and February 1947.

1947

1 January	Bizonia formed; merging of economic administrations of American and British zones.
22 February	Union of the Persecuted during the Nazi Regime (VVN) founded in Berlin.
25 February	Prussia ceases to exist, according to law no. 46 of the Allied Control Council; during summer 1947 the provinces Saxony—Anhalt and Mark Brandenburg are each made a Land.
1 March	The executive committee of the SED calls for a referendum on establishment of a united German state with autonomous democratic administration for Länder and communities (Gemeinden).
7—9 March	Women's Democratic Association of Germany (DFD) founded in Berlin.
10 March—24 April	Conference of Allied Foreign Ministers in Moscow; no agreement is reached except to confirm the dissolution of Prussia and that all prisoners-of-war are to be released by the end of 1948.
17—19 April	Second FDGB congress in Berlin.
20—21 May	First congress of the German cultural association (Kulturbund) in Berlin.
23—26 May	Second FDJ Parliament in Meissen.

29 May	Agreement by American and British military governments on economic council for Bizonia; on 25 June it becomes the supreme German economic administration in the Western zones; sits in Frankfurt-am-Main.
4 June	German Economic Commission (DWK) founded by SMAD order no. 138; becomes supreme economic administration in Soviet zone on 14 June; sits in Berlin.
6–9 June	Munich conference of the prime ministers of all Länder in four occupation zones; a failure.
30 June	Society for the Study of Soviet Culture founded; later renamed the Society for German–Soviet Friendship.
4–7 July	Second LDPD congress in Eisenbach.
23 July	Central Secretariat of SED rejects Marshall Plan.
6–8 September	Second CDU congress in Berlin.
20–24 September	Second SED congress in Berlin.
9 October	SMAD order no. 234 lays down measures to raise labour productivity and to improve the provisioning of the population. Trade unions are made responsible for its implementation.
22–23 November	First German Peasant Congress in Berlin; central organisation of the Association for Mutual Peasant Aid (VdgB) formed.
25 November–15 December	Conference of Allied Foreign Ministers in London; no agreement reached on German question.
6–7 December	First German People's Congress for Unity and a Just Peace meets in Berlin, on the initiative of the SED; a People's Congress movement results from it; standing committee elected; resolution passed on German unity and submitted to London Conference of Foreign Ministers; a dele-

gation is elected but not received by Western powers.

20 December | Jakob Kaiser and Ernst Lemmer, co-chairmen of the CDU, are removed by SMAD for refusing to participate in the People's Congress movement.

1948

23 February—
6 March,
20 April—3 June | Conference of the three Western Powers and the Benelux states in London; 'London recommendations' include the fusion of the three Western zones into a separate German state with the possibility of eventual German reunification.

26 February | SMAD order no. 35 winds up the activities of the denazification commissions in the Soviet zone.

9 March | The German Economic Commission takes over the central management of the economy of the Soviet zone; its chairman is Heinrich Rau (SED).

17—18 March | Second German People's Congress in Berlin; election of a German People's Council with Wilhelm Pieck (SED), Otto Nuschke (CDU) and Wilhelm Külz (LDPD) as co-chairmen of its presidium.

20 March | Allied Control Council ceases to function as a result of differences between the USSR and the Western Allies over the London Conference; on 16 June the Soviets quit the Kommandatura in Berlin.

17 April | SMAD order no. 64 ends the activities of the sequestration commissions; the nationalisation of the concerns belonging to war criminals is regarded as over; order no. 76 of 23 April sees the formation of associations of people's enterprises (VVB).

29 April	Democratic Peasants Party of Germany (DBD) founded in Berlin.
23 May—13 June	Proposal for a referendum on German unity voted on in the Soviet zone and in parts of the Western zones.
25 May	National Democratic Party of Germany (NDPD) founded in Berlin.
18—20 June	Currency reforms in the Western zones.
23—24 June	Soviet troops block access routes to Berlin; air lift begins on 26 June.
23—24 June	The Soviet Union and the East European people's democracies convene a conference in Warsaw and condemn the London recommendations and propose the formation of an all-German government, a peace treaty, the demilitarisation of Germany and reparations from the Western zones.
24—28 June	Currency reform in the Soviet zone.
1 July	Military governors of the three Western zones meeting in Frankfurt-am-Main instruct the eleven West German prime ministers to convene a Parliamentary Council by 1 September 1948 in order to draft a constitution.
16—17 July	First DBD party conference in Schwerin; Ernst Goldenbaum elected chairman.
21 July	Adoption of two-year plan for 1949—50.
28—29 July	As a result of the expulsion of Yugoslavia from the Cominform the twelfth plenum of the SED alters the party line and stresses the leading role of the Soviet Union, the struggle against nationalism, recognises the Oder—Neisse line and decides to transform the SED into a 'party of a new type'.
5 August	Bloc of anti-fascist democratic parties widened to include the DBD and the FDGB and, on 7 September, the NDPD.

2–3 September	First NDPD party conference in Potsdam; Dr Lothar Bolz elected chairman.
15–16 September	Thirteenth plenum of the CC, SED sets up the Central Party Control Commission.
18–20 September	Third CDU Congress in Erfurt; Dr Otto Nuschke elected chairman.
14 November	Publication of a draft constitution for a German democratic republic; drawn up by the German People's Council.
15 November	The first state trade organisation (HO) shops opened.
25–26 November	FDGB conference in Bitterfeld; tasks of trade unions in a planned economy laid down; works' councils abolished by being merged with enterprise trade union organisations.
26–27 November	German Economic Commission extended by including elected representatives from Landtage, political parties, the FDGB and the VdgB as a result of SMAD order no. 183.
30 November	The establishment of a provisional city government for East Berlin, headed by Friedrich Ebert, effectively brings the administration of Berlin as a whole to an end; on 6 September, as a result of communist demonstrations, the Berlin city government had met for the first time in West Berlin; the SED was not present.
13 December	The children's organisation Young Pioneers is founded in Berlin. It is now called the Ernst Thälmann pioneer organisation.

1949

25 January	Council for Mutual Economic Aid (Comecon) founded in Warsaw.
25–28 January	First SED party conference in Berlin.

17 February	CC, SED decides to expand Machine Tractor Stations (MTS) in agriculture.
18—19 March	Sixth session of German People's Council; adoption of the draft constitution; elections to be held to third German People's Congress with unified lists.
29 March	Central Secretariat decides to establish a Marx, Engels, Lenin Institute of the CC, SED; when it opens on 1 September 1949 the research institute for scientific socialism, founded on 29 December 1947, is merged with it.
4 April	North Atlantic Treaty Organisation established in Washington.
12 May	Berlin Blockade ends; 30 September airlift ends.
15—16 May	Elections to third German People's Congress in Soviet zone.
23 May	Basic Law of the Federal Republic of Germany takes effect.
23 May—20 June	Conference of Allied Foreign Ministers in Paris ends without agreement on German question; Western Allies refuse to receive delegation from third German People's Congress.
29—30 May	Third German People's Congress in Berlin; adopts draft constitution for the German Democratic Republic.
1—5 June	Third FDJ Parliament in Leipzig.
23—25 June	First NDPD congress in Halle.
14 August	Elections to Bundestag in Western zones.
7 September	Bundestag and Bundesrat meet in Bonn; 12 September, Theodor Heuss elected Federal President; 15 September, Konrad Adenauer elected Federal Chancellor; 20 September, government formed.
4 October	Twenty-second plenum of CC, SED; decision to form a provisional GDR government.

5 October	Presidium of the German People's Council and Democratic Bloc, in joint session, call on German People's Council, by 7 October, to transform itself into a provisional GDR Volkskammer and to elect a government.
7 October	GDR founded; provisional Volkskammer declares constitution in effect.
8 October	Agreement on intra-German trade by FRG and GDR in Frankfurt-am-Main.
10 October	SMAD dissolved; Soviet Control Commission formed; all administrative functions transferred to provisional GDR government.
11 October	Wilhelm Pieck elected President of the GDR by the provisional Volkskammer and the provisional Länderkammer.
12 October	Provisional GDR government, headed by Prime Minister Otto Grotewohl, confirmed in office by provisional Volkskammer.
15 October	GDR and USSR enter into diplomatic relations.
17 October–2 December	GDR establishes diplomatic relations with Bulgaria, Czechoslovakia, Poland, Hungary, Romania, the People's Republic of China, North Korea and Albania.
8 December	Provisional Volkskammer sets up supreme court and state lawyers association.

1950

7 January	Secretariat of National Front of Democratic Germany established; 3 February, National Council of National Front formed from former presidium of German People's Council; 15 February, programme of National Front adopted by National Council.

20 January	Provisional Volkskammer passes law on 1950 economic plan.
8 February	Provisional Volkskammer passes a youth law and sets up Ministry of State Security.
24 March	German Academy of Arts founded in Berlin; Arnold Zweig elected president.
13 April	Diplomatic relations between GDR and Mongolia established.
24—29 April	Trial of economic functionaries accused of 'economic crimes' results in Willi Brundert (SED), Leo Herwegen (CDU) and others being sentenced to long periods of imprisonment.
17 May	Coming of age in the GDR dropped from 21 to 18 years.
5—6 June	First GDR government delegation, headed by Walter Ulbricht visits Poland; 21—23 June visits Czechoslovakia and on 24 June visits Hungary.
4—6 July	German Writers' Union formed in East Berlin; Bodo Uhse elected chairman.
6 July	Agreement on Oder—Neisse Line signed by GDR and Poland in Zgorzelec.
6 July	FDJ joins Democratic Bloc of parties and mass organisations.
20—24 July	Third SED congress in East Berlin.
25 July	First plenum of CC, SED; new CC, Secretariat and Politburo elected; Walter Ulbricht secretary general of CC.
24 August	Second plenum of CC, SED; party purge committees set up.
25—26 August	First National Congress of the National Front of Democratic Germany in East Berlin.
12—19 September	Conference of Foreign Ministers of three Western Powers in New York; declares

FRG government only legal German government until reunification; to represent German people in international affairs; 22 September, GDR Council of Ministers protests; 20—21 October, USSR, GDR and other people's democracies reject New York declarations in Prague.

29 September	GDR becomes member of Comecon.
15 October	Elections to Volkskammer, Landtage, Kreistage and local assemblies.
22 October	German High School of Physical Culture opens in Leipzig.
26—27 October	Third plenum of CC, SED; all full and candidate members to be checked during first half of 1951.
4—5 November	First German Peace Congress in East Berlin.
15 November	Government changes announced by Prime Minister Otto Grotewohl; after Volkskammer convened for its first session on 8 November, word 'provisional' dropped from government and Volkskammer.
30 November	Letter from Otto Grotewohl to Konrad Adenauer proposing the formation of an all-German council to prepare all-German elections.
22 December	Management changes announced in nationalised industry (VEB and VVB).

1951

30 January	Otto Grotewohl, in the name of the GDR government, proposes to Bundstag the setting up of an all-German council.

5 March	Presidium of Volkskammer calls on Four Powers to negotiate German peace treaty in 1951; calls for 'Germans at one table' to solve German problem.
15—17 March	Fifth plenum of CC, SED; decree on struggle against formalism in art and literature and for adoption of socialist realism.
13—15 June	Sixth plenum of CC, SED, decree on new methods to raise labour productivity and economic accounting to be adopted by VEB.
5—19 August	Third World Youth and Student Games in East Berlin.
20 September	Berlin Agreement on intra-German trade signed by FRG and GDR.
27 September	Federal German government proposes all-German free elections; to be supervised by UN.
27 September	Trade aggreement (1952—5) and agreement on scientific—technical cooperation signed by GDR and USSR; long-term trade agreements signed with East European people's democracies 1951—2.
1 November	Volkskammer passes law on five-year plan 1951—5.
2 November	Letter from Wilhelm Pieck to Theodor Heuss proposing a meeting to discuss all-German problems; Heuss declines on 7 November.
25 November	SED announces national reconstruction plan for Berlin.
27 November	CC, SED instructs local party bodies to provide members of the intelligentsia, when engaged in scientific work, with material privileges.
11 December	GDR government delegation, in Paris, rejects UN commission to supervise all-German elections.

21 December	Institute of Social Sciences of the CC, SED founded in East Berlin.

1952

29 April	Further 66 sequestered enterprises handed back to the GDR by the USSR; transformed into VEB.
26—27 May	GDR Council of Ministers and Ministry of State Security decide to establish a no-go area along the demarcation line with West Germany.
26 May	German Treaty signed by FRG and Western Powers; 27 May, European Defence Community Treaty signed in Paris.
13 June	DFD becomes permanent member of Democratic Bloc.
9—12 July	Second SED conference in East Berlin decides to establish the foundations of a socialist society in the GDR.
23 July	GDR divided into 14 Bezirks; five Länder remain but gradually lose authority to centre.
7 August	Mass organisation Society for Sport and Technology founded.
19 September	Hermann Ehlers, president of the Bundestag, receives Volkskammer delegation in Bonn but contacts not developed.
5—10 October	Soviet government delegation in GDR on occasion of third anniversary of founding of GDR.
7 October	People's Police in Barracks (KVP) receive new uniforms and new military ranks introduced; 16 May, border police placed under Ministry of State Security.
28—29 November	German Congress for Understanding and Peace meets in East Berlin; German peace committee, headed by Professor W. Friedrich, formed.

1953

15 January	Georg Dertinger, Foreign Minister and deputy chairman of CDU, arrested on suspicion of espionage.
21 February	Committee of anti-fascist resistance fighters formed; union of the Persecuted during the Nazi Regime (VVN) dissolved.
6 March	Twelfth plenum of CC, SED; death of Stalin mourned; township of Eisenhüttenkombinat Ost renamed Stalinstadt on 7 May.
9 April	Rationing of textiles and shoes ended; from 1 May no more ration cards issued to about 2 million self-employed; 20 April, prices of rationed food raised.
15 April	CPSU Politburo recommends CC, SED to soften policies.
21 April	Protestant bishops protest against restrictions of church work, especially state action against *Junge Gemeinde*, young people's groups.
5 May	On the occasion of the 135th anniversary of Marx's birth, CC, SED renames Chemnitz, Karl-Marx-Stadt.
28 May	Soviet Control Commission in Germany disbanded by Soviet government; V. Semenov appointed Soviet High Commissioner in Germany.
28 May	GDR Council of Ministers raises work norms.
28–31 May	Fifth LDPD congress in Dresden.
9 June	SED Politburo announces introduction of New Course; state power to be strengthened; closer linking of party, state and people and raising of living standards.

11 June	The New Course results in changes concerning ration cards of 9 April being rescinded.
16 June	Meeting of SED Berlin aktiv at which Ulbricht and Grotewohl comment on mistakes committed by party and government; decree on raising of work norms of 28 May rescinded.
16 June	Building workers in the Stalinallee in East Berlin strike and there are protests against increased work norms.
17 June	Uprising in East Berlin and the GDR; state of emergency lifted on 11 July.
21 June	Fourteenth plenum of CC, SED; decree on the 'situation and the immediate tasks of the party'; uprising denounced as a 'counterrevolutionary fascist putsch' initiated by West.
16 July	Former Minister of Justice Max Fechner (SED) arrested; Fechner had defended the right to strike on 29 June.
24—26 July	Fifteenth plenum of CC, SED; despite uprising, party line held to be correct; New Course to be continued; new Secretariat and Politburo elected; Walter Ulbricht becomes First Secretary; Zaisser and Herrnstadt expelled from the CC for factionalism; Fechner expelled from CC and party.
4 August	Bundestag declares 17 June to be 'Day of German Unity'.
20—22 August	Negotiations between Soviet and GDR government delegations in Moscow; all reparations to cease from 1 January 1954 and diplomatic missions to become embassies.
1 November	Arrest of 'agents' in several GDR cities.

21 November	GDR Ministry of Interior abolishes interzonal passes after the Western Allies and the FRG had done the same on 14 November.
10 December	GDR Council of Ministers decrees improvements in working and living conditions of workers and extension of the rights of trade unions.

1954

1 January	USSR hands back last SAG enterprises to the GDR.
7 January	GDR Council of Ministers sets up a committee for German unity and a Ministry of Culture; the office of reparations is disbanded.
22–23 January	Seventeenth plenum of CC, SED; Zaisser and Herrnstadt expelled from party; Ackermann, Jendretzky and Elli Schmidt removed from CC.
25 January– 18 February	Conference of Foreign Ministers of USSR, USA, Great Britain and France in Berlin but no agreement on German question.
15 February	CC, SED sends letter to executive committee and all members of SPD calling on them to join the KPD, DGB and FDGB in supporting the Soviet proposals for the solution of the German question; rejected by Erich Ollenhauer on 17 February.
25 March	Soviet government recognises the sovereignty of the GDR.
30 March–6 April	Fourth SED congress in East Berlin.
15–16 May	Second national congress of the National Front in East Berlin; proposes a referendum on an alternative to EDC treaty or an all-German peace treaty.

9 June	Former Foreign Minister Georg Dertinger and others sentenced to long periods of imprisonment; many other trials; 14 July former Minister for Trade and Supply Dr Hamann (LDPD) (under arrest since 15 December 1952) and four others receive long prison sentences.
10 September	First German Workers' conference in Leipzig; aim is to restart interzonal trade union conferences which had ceased during the summer of 1948; resolves to recreate the 'unity of action of the working class' in Germany.
13 September	Prices of food, drink and consumer goods cut by state trade organisation (HO); postal charges lowered.
17 October	Elections to Volkskammer and the Bezirkstage; unity list of the National Front receives over 99 per cent of votes.
23 October	Paris Treaties signed; FRG enters the West European Union and NATO (5 May 1955); occupation ends.
16 December	Diplomatic relations established between GDR and Democratic Republic of Vietnam (North Vietnam).
29–31 December	GDR, Poland and Czechoslovakia meet in Prague; decide on common defence of existing frontiers.

1955

25 January	State of war between USSR and Germany declared to be at an end by Moscow; Western Allies had taken this step in 1951.
18 February	Volkskammer proposes all-German elections under international supervision to Bundestag.

2 March	Volkskammer opposes ratification of Paris Treaties by Bundestag and proposes a referendum on reunification.
27 March	First youth consecration ceremony (Jugendweihe) in East Berlin; central committee for this ceremony had been set up on 13 November 1954.
30 April	First award of Banner of Work (created on 10 December 1953) to 'leading employees' and 'socialist collectives'.
1 May	First appearance of defence units of the working class (Kampfgruppen) at a May Day demonstration.
5 May	FRG receives its sovereignty as Paris Treaties take effect; however Western Powers retain all-German responsibility and right to act if a state of emergency is called in FRG.
11—14 May	Warsaw Pact formed.
1—2 June	Twenty-fourth plenum of CC, SED; ten-point programme for reunification of Germany adopted; demand for closer cooperation with social democrats and trade unionists in the FRG.
18 June	National Olympic Committee of the GDR becomes a provisional member of the International Olympic Committee.
17—23 July	Geneva summit conference of heads of government of USSR, USA, Great Britain and France; no agreement on German question.
24—27 July	Soviet delegation, headed by Khrushchev and Bulganin, in GDR; Khrushchev states that reunification is above all a matter for the German people; the political and social achievements of the GDR must not be put in jeopardy.

18 August	Model statutes for collective farms (LPG) types I and II passed by GDR Council of Ministers.
27 August	National Olympic Committees of GDR and FRG decide to send joint team to Melbourne Olympics in 1956.
9—13 September	FRG delegation, headed by Konrad Adenauer, in Moscow for negotiations with Soviet government; diplomatic relations established.
17—20 September	Soviet—GDR negotiations in Moscow: treaty on mutual relations agreed; Soviet High Commission in Germany disbanded; orders and instructions of the SMAD and Soviet control commission already void on 7 August 1954.
26 September	Law passed by Volkskammer amending constitution to make creation of armed forces constitutional.
27 October— 16 November	Conference of Foreign Ministers of Four Powers in Geneva; no agreement on German question; GDR delegation, with observer status, declares that all-German elections are only possible after the democratisation and demilitarisation of the FRG.
24 November	Presidium of the GDR Council of Ministers restructures government apparatus; Walter Ulbricht becomes first deputy Prime Minister.

1956

9—14 January	Congress of German Writers in East Berlin; demands for implementation of socialist realism; statute adopted; Anna Seghers, Hans Marchwitza and Erwin Strittmatter elected co-chairmen.

18 January	Volkskammer adopts law creating the National People's Army (NVA) and the Ministry for National Defence.
14–25 February	Twentieth CPSU congress in Moscow; SED delegation led by Walter Ulbricht and Otto Grotewohl.
15–16 February	Social security becomes the responsibility of the FDGB.
24–30 March	Third SED party conference in East Berlin.
1 May	May Day parade begun by NVA military display for first time.
15–18 May	Fifth Pedagogical Congress in Leipzig proposes introduction of polytechnical education and expansion of the ten-class middle school.
30 May	Government declaration by Otto Grotewohl including eight proposals to bring both German states closer together; including non-introduction of national service and a limit on the size of the armed forces.
30 June	CC, SED proposes to SPD Vorstand joint opposition to introduction of national service in the FRG.
16–17 July	Negotiations between government delegation, headed by Otto Grotewohl, with Soviet government in Moscow; support costs for Soviet troops in GDR reduced by 50 per cent; credits granted and trade turnover to increase.
27–29 July	Twenty-eighth SED plenum; Franz Dahlem, Anton Ackermann, Hans Jendretzky, Elli Schmidt and others rehabilitated.
17 August	KPD banned in West Germany.
14–16 September	First congress of the Society for Sport and Technology in Karl-Marx-Stadt.

4—6 October	LDPD and West German sister party FDP discuss reunification of Germany and possible cooperation.

1957

3—8 January	GDR-Soviet agreement on increasing trade flows and granting of credits.
17 January	Volkskammer passes law on local organs of state power and law on rights and duties of Volkskammer *vis-à-vis* local representative assemblies.
18 January	Volkskammer adopts law on gradual introduction of 45-hour week in socialist industry, transport and communications; also applies to private industry.
31 January— 1 February	Thirtieth SED plenum; due to lengthy coexistence of two German states with opposing social systems, unification only possible through a confederation and an All-German Council with equal numbers from GDR and FRG.
26—28 February	Fifth conference of chairmen and activists of LPG in Rostock; there are 6200 LPG with 220 000 members farming 23 per cent of agricultural land.
7—9 March	Trial of Wolfgang Harich and others; accused of incitement to boycott (article 6 of constitution); sentenced to long terms of imprisonment. Another group of Harich supporters sentenced on 26 July.
12 March	Agreement on the temporary stationing of Soviet forces in the GDR concluded by GDR and USSR.
12 April	GDR Council of Ministers sets up Economic Council to improve planning and management of the economy.

25 April	Sixteenth plenum of the FDJ; FDJ declared socialist youth organisation of GDR.
27—28 April	German Gymnastics and Sports Association (DTSB) founded as central sports organisation of GDR in East Berlin.
10—12 July	Thirty-second SED plenum; 'theses' on simplification of organisation of state apparatus and changes in methods of work; formation of associations of nationalised enterprises (VVB) announced.
24 August	GDR Research Council set up.
2 October	Polish Foreign Minister, Adam Rapacki, proposes formation of nuclear-free zone in Central Europe at UN; Rapacki Plan temporarily becomes part of foreign policy of all Warsaw Pact states.
16—19 October	Thirty-third SED plenum; preferential development of raw materials industries; socialist transformation of agriculture (collectivisation); most industrial industries to be dissolved and VVB to be main economic organ; formation of commission of culture in Politburo under Alfred Kurella.
19 October	Diplomatic relations between the FRG and Yugoslavia broken (Hallstein Doctrine) after GDR and Yugoslavia entered into diplomatic relations on 10 October.
23—24 October	CC, SED organises cultural conference in East Berlin; decree on immediate tasks involved in realising a socialist cultural policy.
14—16 November	Meeting of 12 European and Asian communist and workers' parties in Moscow; 16—19 November meeting of 64 communist and worker' parties in Moscow; peace manifesto adopted.

11 December

Volkskammer changes law on passports; extension of controls on intra-German travel; Volkskammer appeal to Bundestag to create nuclear- and missile-free zone in Central Europe; 30 April GDR government had proposed to FRG government that both should renounce nuclear armaments.

16 December

First atomic reactor in GDR, at Rossendorf, near Dresden, on stream.

1958

10 January

LDPD calls on handicraft concerns to form production cooperatives (PGH) and to contribute to socialist construction; 16—17 December 1957 CDU had called on private entrepreneurs to accept state participation in their concerns and retailers to sign commission contracts with the state.

3—6 February

Thirty-fifth SED plenum; Karl Schirdewan and Fred Oelssner expelled from Politburo; Schirdewan and the Minister of State Security, Ernst Wollweber, expelled from CC; Erich Honecker becomes member of Secretariat; FRG to be overtaken in per capita production.

7—9 February

Fifth congress of the Cultural Association for the Renewal of Germany; is renamed German Cultural Association (Kulturbund); Max Burghardt elected chairman.

10—11 February

Volkskammer adopts law on simplification of work of state apparatus; VVB formed and industrial ministries dissolved.

24–25 April   SED School Conference in East Berlin;
                   discussions on introduction of poly-
                   technical education and the promotion
                   of the ten-class middle school; 1 Sep-
                   tember introduction of school day spent
                   in factory or on farm as part of poly-
                   technical education.

16 May   CC, SED sends letter to delegates to SPD
                   congress in Stuttgart proposing joint
                   action in struggle to secure withdrawal
                   of troops and neutrality of Germany.

28 May   Volkskammer decree on abolition of
                   rationing and introduction of unified
                   prices for food; salaries, wages and
                   pensions raised.

12 June   GDR Council of Ministers decree on
                   socialist transformation of agriculture;
                   expansion of LPG and MTS.

7 July   Decision by USSR not to seek support
                   costs for Soviet troops, from 1 January
                   1959.

10–16 July   Fifth SED congress in East Berlin; during
                   July and August all parties and mass
                   organisations take up the main task, as
                   adopted at the congress, to secure the
                   victory of the socialist relations of
                   production.

4 September   GDR government proposes in notes to
                   four great powers and the FRG the
                   formation of a Four-Power commission
                   to prepare a German peace treaty; the
                   Soviet Union accepts on 18 September;
                   Western Allies reject proposal on 30
                   September; the FRG on 17 November.

3–4 November   SED conference on the chemical in-
                   dustry; chemical industry to be rapidly
                   expanded.

10 November   N. S. Khrushchev expresses Soviet in-
                   tention of ending Four Power respon-

	sibility for Berlin; 27 November in notes to other three powers Soviet government annuls occupation agreement on Berlin and demands a 'demilitarised Free City of Berlin (West)'; 31 December Allied Powers reject Soviet moves.
16 November	Elections to Volkskammer, Bezirkstage and city parliament in East Berlin; 99.87 per cent of votes for candidates of National Front in Volkskammer election.
8 December	New government headed by Otto Grotewohl with Walter Ulbricht as first deputy chairman of the Council of Ministers; laws on Council of Ministers and on dissolution of Länderkammer passed.

1959

5 January	Friedrich Engels Military Academy opens in Dresden.
10 January	Soviet Union publishes note containing proposal for a German peace treaty; 8 April Otto Grotewohl proposes to Federal Chancellor Konrad Adenauer preliminary discussions on peace treaty.
15–17 January	Fourth SED plenum; decree on restructuring of educational system and introduction of ten-class polytechnical education; draft law on LPG.
4–12 March	Soviet delegation, headed by Khrushchev, in the GDR; Khrushchev challenges view that note of 27 November was an ultimatum and underlines Soviet determination to conclude peace treaties with both German states; 9 March Khrushchev meets the SPD chairman, Walter Ollenhauer, in the Soviet embassy in East Berlin.
18 March	SPD Vorstand publishes a plan for Germany.

2 April	CC, SED sends letter to Vorstand, all social democratic organisations and all SPD members about SPD plan for Germany; again proposes joint action by both parties and trade unions.
24 April	First Bitterfeld cultural conference convenes under slogan: 'Take up your pens, coal miners; the socialist national culture needs you!' Basic questions of cultural policy decided — referred to as the Bitterfeld Way.
11 May– 20 June, 13 July–5 August	Conference of Foreign Ministers of USA, Great Britain, France and the USSR in Geneva ends without any agreement on the German question; FRG and GDR delegations participate on equal footing.
12–15 May	Sixth parliament of FDJ in Rostock; 'Younger generation's plan for the victory of socialism' adopted; statutes revised and Horst Schumann elected first secretary.
22–23 May	Fifth SED plenum; proposal to conclude a non-aggression pact between the two German states; 19 June Lothar Bolz, GDR Foreign Minister, hands a similar proposal to those attending Geneva conference.
3 June	Volkskammer adopts law on LPG.
1 September	Introduction of curriculum of ten-class general polytechnical high school adopted at Fourth SED plenum; 2 December Volkskammer law on socialist development of education decrees that new school system to be introduced in the whole of the GDR by 1964.
1 October	Volkskammer passes law on the Seven Year Plan for the Development of the Economy (1959–65) and law on GDR state flag — black, red, gold flag with state coat of arms.

10–13 December	Seventh SED plenum; agricultural questions dominate; Landkreis Eilenburg first in GDR to declare full collectivisation, on 12 December; end 1959 over 43 per cent of agricultural land collectivised in GDR with 10 132 LPG and 435 365 members.
18 December	Signing of agreement on building of oil pipe line from Belorussia to Schwedt an der Oder by USSR, Poland and the GDR in Moscow.

1960

6 January	National Olympic Committees of FRG and GDR agree on all-German team to winter and summer games.
23 January	Letter from Walter Ulbricht to Federal Chancellor Konrad Adenauer proposing disarmament and the negotiation of a peace treaty is returned unopened on 27 January.
10 February	Volkskammer passes law on formation of National Defence Council (chairman: Walter Ulbricht) and the creation of a permanent committee for national defence.
30 March–2 April	Eighth SED plenum, decree on increasing agricultural production and development of LPG; between 4 March and 14 April collectivisation of agriculture completed.
17 April	CC, SED publishes open letter to 'workers of West Germany' and proposes 'plan for the German people'; non-use of force; setting up of all-German committee with equal numbers from GDR and FRG; renunciation of nuclear armaments and missile bases; agreement on conclusion of peace treaty.

27–29 April	CC, SED organises cultural conference together with Ministry of Culture and Kulturbund; decrees of Bitterfeld conference (24 April 1959) discussed; decisions on cultural work in Seven Year Plan reached.
28 April	Council of Ministers issues guidelines for the work of the new conflict commissions set up in enterprises.
23–25 June	Second congress of the GST in Magdeburg; turn towards pre-military training and recruitment for NVA and other armed organs.
24 June	Meeting of 12 ruling communist and workers' parties in Bucharest; in November–December 81 communist and workers' parties in Moscow end their deliberations with an appeal to all the peoples of the world.
22 July	GDR Committee for Solidarity with the Peoples of Africa founded in East Berlin with representatives from 14 African countries attending.
29 August	GDR Ministry of Internal Affairs bans West Germans attending a reunion in West Berlin from entering East Berlin between 31 August and 4 September except those with valid visas; becomes permanent from 8 September.
8 September	Council of Ministers forwards aide memoire on total disarmament of both German states to UN.
12 September	After the death of President Wilhelm Pieck on 7 September a GDR Council of State is formed to provide collective leadership; chairman is Walter Ulbricht.
15 November	Draft labour law published.
1 December 1960– 31 January 1961	Exchange of party documents in SED.

29 December	FRG annulment of agreement on intra-German trade (30 September—31 December) cancelled.

1961

7 February	Politburo communiqué on role of youth during construction of socialism.
16—19 March	Twelfth SED plenum; economic problems discussed by party and government officials, economists and scientists; preference given to raw materials industries and machine-building; plan for 1961 adopted as well as a plan for new technology.
28—29 March	Meeting of Political Consultative Committee of Warsaw Pact in Moscow; measures adopted to improve defence capacity of forces, including more modern equipment for NVA.
12 April	Volkskammer passes labour law which takes effect on 1 July.
25—27 May	Fifth German Writers' Congress in East Berlin; decrees of fifth SED congress and Bitterfeld conference discussed; Anna Seghers reelected chairman.
30 May	Negotiations between USSR and GDR in Moscow on expanding economic relations between 1962 and 1965 concluded; USSR grants GDR credits worth over 2000 million marks.
3—4 July	Thirteenth SED plenum; draft 'German peace plan' confirmed; recommends setting up of State Planning Commission and an Economic Council; 5 July Council of Ministers sets up Economic Council; 6 July Volkskammer adopts German peace plan.

12–13 July	CC, SED conference on propaganda; 'dogmatic tendencies' and 'ignorance of new social phenomena' to be overcome.
3–5 August	Meeting of first secretaries of communist and workers' parties of Warsaw Pact states in Moscow; discussion of peace treaty with Germany and a 'solution of the West Berlin question'.
4 August	City government in East Berlin decrees that East Berliners who work in West Berlin will be required to pay rent, rates etc. partly in DM West as from 1 August; all these workers to be registered.
11 August	Volkskammer instructs Council of Ministers to 'prepare and take all measures' decided on at Warsaw Pact meeting on 5 August.
13 August	Berlin Wall erected; 16 August border with FRG and West Berlin closed to all inhabitants of GDR and East Berlin.
23 August	Berlin SPD closes its bureaux in East Berlin after encountering great difficulties; West Berlin SED bureaux temporarily closed.
20 September	Volkskammer passes law on the defence of GDR, military and civic service and call up in case of emergency.
10–11 October	Economic conference organised by CC, SED; discussions on how to fulfil 1961 plan and on becoming economically independent of the FRG.
13 November	De-Stalinisation measures in the GDR; Stalinstadt, for example, becomes Eisenhüttenstadt, Stalin-Allee in East Berlin becomes the Karl-Marx-Allee and the Frankfurter Allee.
23–26 November	Fourteenth SED plenum; economic problems dominate; closer cooperation in Comecon; recommendation to govern-

ment to take steps to normalise gradually relations with FRG; Otto Grotewohl sends a letter to Chancellor Konrad Adenauer on 30 November proposing mutual respect for sovereignty, recognition of passports and so on.

15 December   League for International Friendship founded in East Berlin; all friendship societies fused in it.

1962

5–6 January   Conference on women organised by CC, SED; role of women in socialist society discussed; in 1961 46 per cent of labour force was female with over 70 per cent of all women and girls between 15 and 60 years employed; in enterprises and administration there were over 20 000 women's committees involving over 130 000 women.

24 January   Volkskammer passes law on national service; it also applies to East Berlin.

21–23 March   Fifteenth SED plenum; discussion of 'national document'.

24 May   CC, SED sends letter to all SPD members just before SPD congress in Cologne urging a political alternative in the SPD and in the FRG.

24 May   Council of Ministers publishes instructions about statutes of Economic Council and the State Planning Commission and passes decree on further development of socialist law involving increased significance of conflict commissions.

30 May   German Academy of Arts in East Berlin after receiving new statutes regards itself as GDR socialist academy; writer Willi Bredel president.

16—17 June	National Congress of National Front adopts National Document on historical mission of the GDR and future of Germany; demands for peace treaty along lines of 1959 Soviet draft, coexistence and confederation of both German states.
26—28 June	Sixteenth SED plenum; decree on measures to improve working of Council of Ministers.
4 July	Management of economy and expertise of state officials of primary concern to Council of Ministers; Willi Stoph elected first deputy chairman of Council of Ministers.
12 July	Worker and peasant faculties in universities to be disbanded by 1963.
23 August	NVA general named city commandant in East Berlin after Soviet city Kommandatura dissolved on 22 August.
3—5 October	Seventeenth SED plenum; sixth SED congress called for 15—19 January 1963; new draft party programme and party statute.
23 November	New SED draft programme published.

1963

12 January	GDR and Cuba raise their missions to embassies; GDR now has diplomatic relations with 13 states.
15—21 January	Sixth SED congress in East Berlin.
30 January	Scientific councils set up in all institutes of German Academy of Agricultural Sciences in East Berlin to speed up introduction of fruits of scientific research.
4 February	Presidium of national council of National Front declares new SED programme basis of all activities of all parties and mass organisations.

7 February	Agricultural councils set up in Bezirks and Kreise with production management in Council of Ministers; state committee for procurement of agricultural produce, and agricultural machinery and material—technical supply established; Ministry of Agriculture dissolved.
26 February	Politburo decree on organisation of party work according to production principle.
14 May	CC, SED and Council of Ministers decide to establish Workers and Peasants Inspectorate as a 'social supervisory organ'.
28 May–1 June	Seventh FDJ Parliament; discussion of role of youth in construction of socialism; Horst Schumann reelected first secretary.
20 June	GDR government publishes appeal to the West German population for workmanlike, normal relations between the two German states.
21 June	Council of Ministers publishes order on measures to be taken to protect 'state frontier' between GDR and West Berlin and creation of special border area along frontier.
24–25 June	Economic conference organised by CC, SED and Council of Ministers on New Economic System of Planning and Management of Economy (NES); NES guidelines confirmed by Council of State on 15 July.
28 June– 4 July	Khrushchev in GDR on occasion of seventieth birthday of Walter Ulbricht (30 June).
3 July	Joint decree of Politburo and Council of Ministers on expansion of polytechnical and general political education and the creation of special schools and classes.

25 July	Agreement on banning of nuclear tests in atmosphere, under water and in space initialled by USSR, USA and Great Britain in Moscow; GDR joins 8 August in Moscow.
20 September	Politburo publishes communiqué on youth question; 19 September Council of State had debated a draft youth law and recommended publication to Council of Ministers.
29 October	Politburo decree on tasks and methods of work of VEB production committees.
13–14 November	Volkskammer meets after elections of 20 October; Johannes Dieckmann reelected president.
8 December	Walter Ulbricht announces on radio his willingness to negotiate with government headed by Ludwig Erhard.
17 December	Signing of first pass agreement between GDR government and West Berlin Senate permitting West Berliners to visit relatives in East Berlin between 19 December 1963 and 5 January 1964.
18 December	Friendship oil pipeline bringing Soviet oil to chemical Kombinat in Schwedt an Oder in operation.

1964

2 January	New internal passports state bearer 'citizen of GDR'.
6 January	Walter Ulbricht sends a letter to Federal Chancellor Erhard including a draft treaty between the FRG and the GDR and renunciation of atomic weapons; letter returned unopened; 26 May second letter from Ulbricht to Erhard proposing that production, testing and

stationing of nuclear weapons in both German states be prohibited.

3–7 February	Fifth SED plenum; special attention to be paid in 1964 plan year to chemical industry; NES to apply to trade.
28 February–1 March	Eighth German Peasants Congress in Schwerin; discussion about application of NES to agriculture and introduction of industrial-type production methods in agriculture.
13 March	Professor Robert Havemann loses his Chair for Physical Chemistry at Humboldt University in East Berlin.
1 April	First stage of industrial price reform in effect.
24–25 April	Second Bitterfeld conference organised by CC, SED and Ministry of Culture discusses development of a 'socialist national culture' in the GDR.
4 May	Volkskammer passes new youth law.
29 May–13 June	Walter Ulbricht heads government delegation to USSR; 12 June treaty of friendship, mutual aid and cooperation signed in Moscow.
25–27 June	Congress on role of women in GDR during all-round building of socialism; statutes of DFD amended and executive committee elected.
2 July	Politburo and Council of Ministers discuss perspective plan 1964–70.
1 August	New bank notes carrying the new designation 'Mark of the German Currency Bank' issued.
9 September	Council of Ministers decree on permission for visits by GDR pensioners to the FRG and West Berlin.

19 September	Meeting of Walter Ulbricht and Josip Broz Tito in Belgrade.
24 September	Volkskammer confirms Willi Stoph as chairman of Council of Ministers and deputy chairman of Council of State following death of Otto Grotewohl on 21 September.
24 September	New pass agreement signed by Council of Ministers and West Berlin Senate.
6 October	Amnesty for 10 000 prisoners on occasion of fifteenth anniversary of founding of GDR.
10—24 October	All-German team participates in Tokyo Olympics.
14—15 October	Leonid Brezhnev elected First Secretary of CC, CPSU and Aleksei Kosygin, Chairman of USSR Council of Ministers. Khrushchev loses all his party and government posts.
25 November	GDR government requires all visitors from FRG and West Berlin to change a minimum amount of DM West daily into GDR marks.
2—5 December	Seventh SED plenum; decree on 1965 plan and budget and on party elections in 1965.
18 December	Wolfgang Harich released as part of amnesty of 6 October; he had been sentenced to 10 years in March 1957.
28—31 December	Census in GDR; on 31 December population is 17 003 632; compared to 18 388 172 at last census in 1950.

1965

14 January	Society for International Law in the GDR founded in East Berlin. Professor Rudolf Arzinger elected president.
5 February	Dates for West Berlin visitors to East

	Berlin during Easter and Whitsun 1965 agreed under pass agreement of 24 September 1964.
19 February	GDR general consulate opens in Tanzania; this raises number of general consulates in African and Asian countries to nine.
24 February–2 March	GDR delegation, headed by Walter Ulbricht, pays state visit to Egypt.
25 February	Volkskammer passes law on unified socialist educational system and law on contract in a socialist economy.
26 March	Foreign Minister Lothar Bolz (NDPD) resigns for reasons of health and is succeeded on 24 June by Otto Winzer (SED).
5 May	Council of State, Council of Ministers and National Council of National Front issue Manifesto to the German People and the Peoples and Governments of the World; Walter Ulbricht makes statement on National Mission of GDR and peace forces in West Germany; repeats views expressed at eighth SED plenum that a reunited Germany can only be a socialist Germany.
14 July	Agreement on cooperation between GDR and USSR on construction of atomic power stations in GDR signed.
1 August	Ulbricht declares on TV and radio that he is prepared to discuss reunification with a new Federal Chancellor and proposes the formation of a joint economic commission.
17–28 September	Party and government delegation, led by Walter Ulbricht, in USSR, communiqué on formation of joint government committee on economic and scientific–technical cooperation.

8 October	International Olympic Committee decides to admit two German teams to 1968 Olympics; GDR National Olympic Committee becomes full member of IOC.
30 October	German Sports Association (DSB) reverses its decision of 16 August 1961 to terminate sports contacts with the GDR at executive meeting in Cologne.
3—6 November	Conference on 'technical revolution and the trade unions' at the FDGB Fritz Heckert High School in Bernau.
27—29 November	Leonid Brezhnev, First Secretary of the CC, CPSU visits GDR.
3 December	Trade agreement (1966—70) between GDR and USSR signed in East Berlin.
15—18 December	Eleventh SED plenum; discussion about second stage of NES; sharp criticisms of Stefan Heym, Wolf Biermann and cultural officials.
18 December	Council of Ministers sets up State Secretariat for All-German Questions headed by Joachim Herrmann.
20 December	Family law code passed by Volkskammer.
22 December	Council of Ministers decides to set up nine new industrial ministries and to dissolve Economic Council; five-day week every other week and shortening of working week for further 3 million from April 1966.

1966

12 January	Klaus Gysi becomes new Minister of Culture replacing Hans Bentzien.
13 January	Council for All-German Questions set up in East Berlin; Joachim Herrmann, State Secretary for All-German Questions,

	declares willingness of GDR government to negotiate with FRG government on basis of complete equality.
11 February	CC, SED sends 'Open letter to the delegates to SPD congress in Dortmund and to all members and friends of social democracy in West Germany' inviting discussion on German question; 19 March SPD Vorstand puts seven questions and states preconditions for dialogue between two parties.
28 February	Council of State in letter to UN Secretary General requests membership of UN.
7 March	Pass agreement covering Easter and Whitsun 1966 agreed.
25 March	CC, SED answers SPD Vorstand's letter of 19 March by proposing exchange of speakers; 14 April SPD Vorstand puts forward concrete proposals for speakers, places and dates.
1 April	German Academy of Sciences in East Berlin announces expulsion of Professor Robert Havemann.
21 April	Celebrations on the occasion of Twentieth anniversary of founding of SED; Walter Ulbricht speaks on 'Way forward to the German Fatherland'.
27–28 April	Twelfth SED plenum; Ulbricht proposes that speaker exchange be postponed until July (SPD had proposed May on 14 April).
29 April	SED and SPD representatives discuss exchange of speakers in East Berlin; 2 May SPD not agreeable to postponement of exchange.
9 May	First atomic power station at Rheinsberg on stream.

26 May	SED and SPD representatives agree in East Berlin on meetings in Karl-Marx-Stadt on 14 July and in Hanover on 21 July.
22 June	Letter from Walter Ulbricht to Willy Brandt proposing discussions before exchange of speakers.
23 June	West German Bundestag passes law guaranteeing safe conduct to SED officials in Hanover; 29 June Albert Norden, referring to this law, cancels exchange of speakers at international press conference in East Berlin.
2 July	CC, SED addresses an 'open word' to members and friends of the SPD, the trade unions and to all FRG citizens whose concern is peace in Germany.
4–6 July	Meeting of Political Consultative Committee of Warsaw Pact in Bucharest; declaration on European security proposing reduction of troop levels in both German states after holding of European security conference.
26 September–2 October	State visit by GDR delegation, headed by Walter Ulbricht, in Yugoslavia; GDR and Yugoslavia raise their missions to embassies.
22 October	*Neues Deutschland* publishes six questions on German question about which the SED would like to talk to the SPD leadership; on same day Herbert Wehner (SPD) at a meeting in West Berlin puts four questions to the SED.
2–4 November	First annual conference of the German Writers' Union of the GDR in East Berlin.
23 November	Volkskammer amends and adds to labour law.

1967

31 January	Diplomatic relations established between FRG and Romania as first Warsaw Pact state; this produces sharp exchanges between the SED and the Romanian Communist Party.
2 February	State Secretariat for All-German Questions renamed State Secretariat for West German Questions; Council for All-German Questions also renamed.
20 February	Volkskammer passes law on GDR citizenship.
15 March	GDR and Poland sign treaty of friendship, cooperation and mutual assistance in Warsaw.
17 March	GDR and Czechoslovakia sign treaty of friendship, cooperation and mutual assistance in Prague.
31 March	Council of State adopts document on 'youth and socialism' containing ten principles of socialist youth policy.
12 April	Federal Chancellor Kurt-Georg Kiesinger lists 16 possible ways of reducing tension in intra-German relations; 20 April presidium of seventh SED congress declares that GDR government is prepared to negotiate, on an equal footing, and for normalisation of relations.
17–22 April	Seventh SED congress in East Berlin.
24–26 April	Conference of 24 European and workers' parties on problems of European security in Karlovy Vary. GDR delegation led by Walter Ulbricht.
3 May	Council of Ministers decrees five-day week with 43¾ hours of work from 28 August 1967.

10—15 May	Eighth FDJ Parliament and Easter meeting of FDJ in Karl-Marx-Stadt; Günther Jahn elected first secretary.
10—11 May	Willi Stoph, chairman of Council of Ministers, sends letter to Federal Chancellor Kurt-Georg Kiesinger proposing discussions about normalisation of relations between both German states; 13 June Kiesinger in favour of discussion of factual questions by emissaries of both governments.
18 May	GDR and Hungary sign treaty of friendship, cooperation and mutual assistance in Budapest.
27 June	Open letter from CC, SED to members and supporters of CDU/CSU proposing discussions about intra-German questions without any preconditions and the establishment of normal relations between the two German states.
13—14 July	Volkskammer meets after elections of 2 July.
7 September	GDR and Bulgaria sign treaty of friendship, cooperation and mutual assistance in Sofia.
18 September	Willi Stoph sends another letter to Kiesinger proposing the establishment of normal relations; 29 September Kiesinger reminds Stoph of his proposals made on 12 April and 13 June 1967.
1 December	Volkskammer sets up a commission, headed by Walter Ulbricht, to elaborate a new socialist constitution.

1968

10 January	Council of German Cultural Association (Kulturbund) discusses cultural tasks during the development of the 'socialist

	human community' on the basis of the decrees of the Council of State of 30 November 1967.
12 January	Volkskammer passes five laws including new criminal code.
31 January	Volkskammer presents new draft constitution for discussion.
13 March	In a TV address Walter Ulbricht rejects the views of Federal Chancellor Kurt-Georg Kiesinger expressed on 11 March and repeats the views of the GDR on the normalisation of relations.
15 March	Council of State decrees increases in pensions from 1 July 1967.
23 March	Leading politicians from GDR, USSR, Czechoslovakia, Bulgaria and Hungary meet in Dresden to discuss internal developments in Czechoslovakia.
26 March	Volkskammer approves draft of new GDR constitution and chooses 6 April for referendum to approve it; over 94 per cent of eligible voters accept constitution which becomes effective on 8 April.
2–4 May	International conference to mark 150th anniversary of birth of Karl Marx in East Berlin.
10–11 June	Volkskammer decrees introduction of passports and visas for travel between the FRG and West Berlin.
13–15 June	Tenth German Peasants' Congress in Leipzig; discussions about problems involved in gradual introduction of industrial methods in agricultural production.
1 July	Foreign Minister Otto Winzer signs the treaty on the non-proliferation of atomic weapons in Moscow.

14—15 July	Meeting of leading party and government leaders from USSR, GDR, Poland, Hungary and Bulgaria in Warsaw to discuss the Prague Spring; letter sent to CC, CP of Czechoslovakia.
3 August	Discussions by party leaders from USSR, GDR, Poland, Hungary, Bulgaria and Czechoslovakia about Czechoslovak situation at Cierna and Tisou; joint communiqué published.
12 August	SED delegation, led by Walter Ulbricht, meets CP of Czechoslovakia delegation, led by Alexander Dubček, in Karlovy Vary.
20—21 August	Czechoslovakia occupied by five Warsaw Pact states, including GDR; CC, SED justifies presence of NVA units in Czechoslovakia in an 'appeal to all citizens of the GDR' on 21 August.
12 September	Mongolia and GDR sign treaty of friendship and cooperation in Ulan Bator.
26—27 September	Perspective plan commission of Politburo and Council of Ministers discuss tasks of perspective plan for 1971—5 to bring about the social system of socialism.
12 October	Walter Ulbricht delivers a major speech on the role of the socialist state during the creation of a developed social system of socialism.
12—27 October	Separate teams representing FRG and GDR participate in Mexico Olympics.
22—25 October	Ninth SED plenum; reaction to events in Czechoslovakia and review of economic development of GDR in 1968.
18—21 November	Conference of preparatory commission to convene meeting of communist and workers' parties in Budapest. SED delegation headed by Hermann Matern.

6 December	New agreement on interzonal trade foresees expansion of turnover between GDR and FRG.

1969

6 February	GDR government protests against proposed election of Federal President in West Berlin; protest notes also sent to three Western Powers.
21 February	Walter Ulbricht sends letter to Willy Brandt hinting that West Berliners will be able to visit relatives in East Berlin over Easter 1969 if election not held in West Berlin; 26 February Brandt rejects suggestion.
10 May	Establishment of full diplomatic relations between GDR and Iraq; 11 Third World countries recognise GDR by end of 1970.
12 May	Volkskammer elects Gerald Götting, deputy chairman of the Council of State and leader of the CDU, president in place of Johannes Dieckmann who had died.
28–30 May	Sixth German Writers' Congress in East Berlin; Anna Seghers reelected president; new statute adopted to correspond to demands of 'developed social system of socialism'; 22 May German Academy of Arts in East Berlin amended its statute along the same lines.
5–17 June	International conference of communist and workers' parties in Moscow; SED delegation led by Walter Ulbricht.
11–13 June	Second congress of GDR women in East Berlin.
29 June	Formation of a Scientific Council for Sociological Research in the Institute for Social Sciences of the CC, SED headed by Professor Rudi Weidig; 30 May in

June 29 (continued)	same institute Scientific Council for Marxist—Leninist Philosophy set up, headed by Erich Hahn and on 24 June Scientific Council for the Study of Imperialism set up under the direction of Professor Werner Paff.
10—14 September	First Synod of the Union of Protestant Churches in the GDR in Potsdam; eight Land churches formed union on 10 June 1969.
16 September	Negotiations by representatives of Ministries of Transport of FRG and GDR; 19 September negotiations between representatives of FRG Ministry of Posts and GDR Ministry of Posts and Communications.
29 September	Council of State ratifies treaty on non-proliferation of nuclear weapons.
30 September	Academy for Marxist—Leninist Organisational Science to train leading party, state and economic officials opens in East Berlin.
28 October	FRG government declaration by Chancellor Willy Brandt; liberal—socialist coalition government prepared to negotiate on equal terms with GDR; concept of two states in one German nation advanced.
18 December	Letter from chairman of Council of State Walter Ulbricht to FRG President Gustav Heinemann with draft treaty about establishment of relations on equal footing between GDR and FRG; 17 December Volkskammer passed resoluto this effect; 20 December President Heinemann replies by pointing out that letter and draft treaty should be addressed to FRG government.

1970

14 January

In report on the state of the nation Chancellor Brandt rejects proposals contained in Ulbricht's letter dated 18 December 1969 but suggests that both German states renounce use of force in international relations; 19 January Walter Ulbricht demands recognition of GDR in international law as precondition for agreement on renunciation of force.

22 January–
18 February

Exchange of letters between Federal Chancellor Willy Brandt and Chairman of Council of Ministers Willi Stoph on preparations for a meeting of both heads of government.

19 March

Meeting of Brandt and Stoph in Erfurt.

24 March

Formation of Committee for European Security headed by Professor Max Steinbeck in East Berlin.

26 March

Negotiations on Four Power agreement on Berlin begin in building of former Allied Control Council in West Berlin.

26 March

Closure of Allied Travel Bureau (it issued visas to GDR citizens travelling to NATO countries) in West Berlin.

17 April

CC, SED decree on exchange of party documents for all members and candidates of SED between 1 September 1970 and 31 October 1971.

7 May

GDR foreign trade centre opened in Paris.

21 May

Meeting of Brandt and Stoph in Kassel; FRG government submits 20-point plan to regulate relations between FRG and GDR.

1 July	GDR export goods marked Made in GDR or Hergestellt in der DDR instead of Made in Germany.
12 August	FRG and USSR sign treaty on renunciation of force and normalisation of relations in Moscow; 7 December a similar treaty signed by FRG and Poland in Warsaw.
13 August	Signing of protocol on coordination of plans for the development of the economies of the GDR and USSR over the years 1971–5 in Moscow.
16 September	Volkskammer passes law on civil defence.
1 October	Treaty of friendship, cooperation and mutual aid between GDR and Romania initialled in Bucharest.
12 November	Agreement on trade and payments between GDR and USSR covering the years 1971–5 signed in East Berlin.
27 November	Talks begin which last almost two years between state secretary Egon Bahr, the FRG government representative, and state secretary Michael Kohl, representing the GDR government, which lead to the drafting of the Basic Treaty, the transit agreement and the transport treaty between the two German states.
9–11 December	Fourteenth SED plenum; Economic System of Socialism radically altered.
17 December	Walter Ulbricht declares that the united bourgeois German nation no longer exists; instead a 'socialist German national state' has come into existence in the GDR in which a 'socialist nation' is being formed; the FRG is an imperialist state.

1971

1 January	There are 17 053 699 citizens in the

	GDR according to the third census since 1945.
29 January	Council of Ministers, CC, SED and FDGB adopt social political measures, including cuts in prices of certain textiles and industrial goods; pensions and social security payments raised.
31 January	Telephone links between both parts of Berlin partially restored after a break of 19 years.
24–25 February	Exchange of letters between chairman of Council of Ministers, Willi Stoph, and Klaus Schütz, governing mayor of West Berlin, about possible negotiations; 6 March discussions begin.
16 March	GDR and Chile enter into diplomatic relations; Chile is twenty-eighth state to recognise GDR.
30 March–9 April	Twenty-fourth CPSU congress in Moscow; SED delegation headed by Walter Ulbricht.
3 May	Sixteenth SED plenum; Erich Honecker elected First Secretary of CC, SED in place of Walter Ulbricht; Ulbricht becomes chairman of SED, post created for him.
12 May	Council of Ministers confirms Horst Sindermann, a Politburo member, as first deputy chairman of Council of Ministers.
15–19 June	Eighth SED congress in East Berlin.
24 June	Volkskammer elects Erich Honecker chairman of National Defence Council.
1 July	Mail and telephone calls from GDR to FRG and West Berlin charged at foreign rates.
7 July	Council of Ministers dissolves state secretariat for West German questions.

12 August	Politburo and Council of Ministers adopt complex programme drawn up by Comecon members at twenty-fifth meeting in Bucharest on 27–29 July 1971.
3 September	Signing of Four Power agreement on Berlin by three Western Powers and USSR.
21 October	Decree of Council of Ministers on promotion of private house building beginning in 1972.
15 November	Radio station 'Voice of the GDR' begins broadcasting; replaces station 'Germany (Deutschlandsender)' and the Berlin wave.
18 November	Politburo and Council of Ministers adopt price freeze for consumer goods and services until 1975.
26 November	Volkskammer meets after elections of 14 November; Walter Ulbricht reelected chairman of Council of State; Willi Stoph chairman of Council of Ministers; Erich Honecker chairman of National Defence Council; Gerald Götting president of Volkskammer.
17 December	Signing of transit agreement between FRG and GDR; becomes effective on 3 June 1972.
20 December	Signing of agreement between West Berlin Senate and GDR on travel arrangements; some land also exchanged.
22 December	Travel between GDR and Poland to be freed from passport and visa control from 1 January 1972; only identity card necessary.

1972

15 January	Travel between GDR and Czechoslovakia

	freed from passport and visa control; only identity card necessary.
11 February	German television renamed GDR Television.
23 February	CC, SED and Council of Ministers announce that during Easter and Whitsun travel between FRG and West Berlin will be according to transit agreement and that visits by West Berliners to East Berlin and GDR will be possible.
2 April	Visas no longer required for travel between GDR and Romania.
11 April	Otto Winzer, GDR Foreign Minister, signs international convention on banning of development, production and storage of bacteriological and toxic weapons and their destruction in Moscow.
27–28 April	Fifth SED plenum; pensions raised and some rents of new flats reduced; become operative between 1 July and 1 September 1972.
11–12 May	Party and government delegation, headed by Erich Honecker, visits Romania; treaty of friendship, cooperation and mutual aid signed.
26 May	Transport agreement signed by GDR and FRG.
3 June	Signing of final Four Power protocol to Berlin Agreement on 3 September 1971; Four Power agreement, transit agreement and agreements reached by West Berlin Senate and GDR thus become effective.
6 June	FRG citizens provided with visas when visiting East Berlin; previously they had received daily passes.
24 July	Automatic dialling between West Berlin and 32 telephone areas in GDR begins.

16 August	Negotiations between state secretaries Egon Bahr and Michael Kohl on a treaty on relations between the FRG and GDR begin.
6 October	Amnesty for political and other prisoners; many are sent to West Germany.
16 October	Volkskammer passes law on GDR Council of Ministers and law on citizenship which frees all those who fled the GDR before 1 January 1972 from prosecution.
26–28 October	Eighth congress of German Cultural Association; renamed GDR Cultural Association (Kulturbund); Professor Max Burghardt reelected president.
9 November	Four Power support for admission of both German states to UNO; until full membership on 18 September 1973 GDR is member of many UN organisations; from 4 December 1972 GDR is represented by a permanent observer at UN.
20 December	Switzerland becomes the fortieth state to recognise the GDR diplomatically.
21 December	Signing of Basic Treaty between GDR and FRG.

1973

26 January	Kurt Hager speaks of the evolution of socialist culture in the GDR and the continued existence of a bourgeois capitalist culture in the FRG and refutes view that there still exists a single German cultural nation.
2 February	GDR signs Vienna convention on diplomatic relations of 18 February 1961.
9 February	Great Britain becomes seventieth state to recognise the GDR diplomatically.

14 May	Council of Ministers announces increases of some pensions and social security benefits from 1 July 1973.
14 June	Central council of FDJ discusses new draft law on youth.
21 June	Basic Treaty becomes effective in both German states; regulations affecting travel between GDR and FRG, drawn up by GDR Ministry of Interior on 14 June come into effect.
3—7 July	Conference on Security and Cooperation in Europe begins in Helsinki; Walter Scheel, FRG Foreign Minister, and Otto Winzer, GDR Foreign Minister, meet twice for discussions.
23 July	Vatican elevates three of the four GDR commissars to rank of apostolic administrator who possess the rights and duties of a resident bishop and are directly subordinate to the Holy See; they are based on Erfurt, Magdeburg and Schwerin; previously these areas had belonged to the dioceses of Fulda, Paderborn and Osnabrück in the FRG.
28 July—5 August	Tenth World Festival of Youth and Students in East Berlin.
1 August	Walter Ulbricht dies.
18 September	GDR becomes the 133rd and the FRG the 134th member of UN.
21 September	GDR breaks diplomatic relations with Chile as a result of military coup.
2 October	Tenth SED plenum; decree on personnel changes in Politburo, CC, Council of State and Council of Ministers; building programme for 1976—90 discussed.
3 October	Volkskammer elects Willi Stoph chairman of Council of State and Horst Sindermann chairman of the Council of Ministers.

5 November	Ministry of Finance orders doubling, from 15 November of minimal amount which must be exchanged daily per person in the GDR and East Berlin by all citizens from non-socialist countries; in the GDR from DM10 to DM20; in East Berlin from DM5 to DM10.
14–16 November	Seventh German Writers' Congress in East Berlin; renamed GDR Writers' Union; Anna Seghers reelected president.

1974

1 January	An order of GDR Ministry of Interior instructs all goods vehicles when travelling abroad to carry the designation DDR instead of D (Germany).
28 January	Volkskammer passes third law on youth.
14 February	Council of Ministers decides on measures to make law on Council of Ministers more effective; government reshuffle takes place.
12 March	Formation of Scientific Council of research into youth, headed by Professor Walter Friedrich, in East Berlin.
26 April	Scientific Council for Ecology founded in the GDR Academy of Sciences in East Berlin headed by Professor Heinz Mottek.
30 April	Politburo, Council of Ministers and FDGB joint decree on social policy including raising of minimum annual holiday entitlement from 15 to 18 days.
2 May	Permanent missions in Bonn and East Berlin in operation according to protocol of 14 March 1974; 20 June, Günther Gaus, the FRG representative, and Michael Kohl, the GDR representative, present their letters of credence.

15—17 May	Second GDR congress of sociology discusses the contribution which Marxist—Leninist sociology can make to the management and planning of social processes during the formation of a developed socialist society in the GDR in East Berlin.
27—28 May	Meeting of the UN special anti-apartheid committee in East Berlin.
4 September	USA and GDR enter into diplomatic relations.
14 September	GDR State Bank begins to issue new bank notes with the inscription Mark der DDR (GDR Mark) instead of Mark der Deutschen Notenbank (Mark of German Currency Bank).
27 September	Volkskammer passes law supplementing and altering the GDR constitution of 7 October 1974; term German nation is removed; new law on legal procedure also adopted and reshuffle of Council of Ministers decided.
5—8 October	Twenty-fifth anniversary of GDR celebrated; Soviet party and government delegation, headed by Leonid Brezhnev, attends.
16 October	Council of Ministers publishes order on raising minimum holiday entitlement from 15 to 18 days and on payment of bonuses for shift work.
26 October	GDR Ministry of Finance reduces minimum amount which must be exchanged daily per person in GDR and East Berlin; from 15 November 1974 is DM13 for GDR and DM6.50 for East Berlin.
17 November	Pastoral letter from GDR bishops protesting against monopoly of education by state.

10 December	Pensioners and those under 16 years freed again from need to exchange minimum amount daily when visiting GDR and East Berlin.
12—13 December	Fourth congress of GDR philosophers discusses objective laws and conscious activity in a socialist society in East Berlin.

1975

20 January	Otto Fischer named Minister of Foreign Affairs in place of Otto Winzer.
20 March	Council of State proposes to Volkskammer that it increase the legislative period of the Bezirkstage from four to five years to correspond to that of the Volkskammer.
26 March	Consular agreement signed by GDR and Austria in East Berlin.
28 April	Harry Tisch, candidate member of the Politburo, elected chairman of FDGB in place of Herbert Warnke who had died on 26 March.
19 June	Volkskammer passes new civil code to come into effect on 1 January 1976; legislative period of Bezirkstage extended by one year.
28 July	Politburo and Council of Ministers provide Erich Honecker with power to sign Helsinki Final Act for GDR.
30 July—1 August	CSCE conference in Helsinki; Final Act signed by FRG and GDR; two meetings between Helmut Schmidt, FRG Chancellor, and Erich Honecker, Chairman of GDR Council of State.
3 October	GDR breaks diplomatic relations with Spain.

6—13 October	Official visit by party and state delegation, headed by Erich Honecker, to the USSR; Leonid Brezhnev and Erich Honecker sign new treaty of friendship, cooperation and mutual aid between USSR and GDR.
7 October	Twenty-sixth anniversary of founding of GDR celebrated as national holiday for first time.
20—25 October	World congress with about 2000 delegates from 135 states marks International Women's Year in East Berlin. Main themes are equality, development, peace.
26 October	Seventh congress of the International Federation of Democratic Women attended by over 500 delegates from 95 countries in East Berlin.
29 October	Politburo and Council of Ministers establish title Hero of the GDR, and medal for heroic deeds performed in the military defence of the state frontiers of the GDR and state security.

1976

1 January	New GDR civil code takes effect.
14—16 January	New draft programme, draft directives of ninth SED congress on development of GDR economy 1976—80 and new draft statute published by SED.
24 February—5 March	Twenty-fifth CPSU congress in Moscow; SED delegation led by Erich Honecker.
1 April	Egon Franke, Minister for Intra-German Relations, states that negotiations with the GDR in 1975 led to 5499 persons, including 1000 children, being allowed to leave the GDR for the FRG; 1200 political prisoners were freed and moved to the FRG as well.

15 April	Responsibilities of Council of Ministers extended at expense of Council of State; in operation since 1 April 1976.
23 April	Palace of the Republic opened; it is on Marx-Engels-Platz in East Berlin.
4 May	Consular agreement signed by GDR and Great Britain in East Berlin.
18–22 May	Ninth SED congress in East Berlin.
27 May	Joint decree of CC, SED, FDGB and Council of Ministers on social policy; improvement of working and living conditions during period 1976–80 promised; minimum wages and pensions to be raised and situation of working mothers to be improved.
24 June	Volkskammer passes new electoral law; Volkskammer and representative assemblies at Bezirk, Kreis, city Bezirk and village level to be elected in future for five years; age at which citizen can vote and be elected lowered from 21 to 18 years.
29–30 June	Conference of European communist and workers' parties in East Berlin with 29 delegations attending; some of speeches and final document published in full by *Neues Deutschland*.
1 October	Minimum wage raised from 350 to 400 marks, smaller increases for those earning between 400 and 500 marks take effect; 14 October Council of Ministers decree increases in holiday period for shift workers and working mothers with severely handicapped children from 1 January 1977.
29 October	Volkskammer meets after elections of 17 October; Horst Sindermann elected president of Volkskammer; Willi Stoph elected chairman of Council of Ministers;

Erich Honecker becomes chairman of Council of State and chairman of National Defence Council.

16 November | East Berlin poet and singer Wolf Biermann expatriated during a tour of the FRG; 3 November writer Reiner Kunze expelled from Writers' Union; 26 November Professor Robert Havemann placed under house arrest.

1977

1 January | Foreign visitors entering East Berlin from West Berlin now need visa; control posts between East Berlin and GDR removed; henceforth new GDR laws and regulations will apply automatically to East Berlin ending special status of city.

20 January | New draft labour law published.

25 February | GDR Ministry of Transport announces road taxes will have to be paid by lorries entering East Berlin from West Berlin.

2—4 March | Twelfth LDPD congress in Weimar.

4 April | GDR resumes diplomatic relations with Spain which had been broken off in late 1975.

14 April | The writer Reiner Kunze moves to the FRG; other writers and artists follow him during 1977.

19 April | Formation of Scientific Council for Social and Economic Questions of Agro-industrial Complexes in East Berlin.

3—7 May | Visit of Mongolian party and government delegation in the GDR; treaty of friendship and cooperation signed by GDR and Mongolia.

28—29 May	Visit of Polish party and government delegation, led by Edward Giereck, in the GDR; signing of new treaty on friendship, cooperation and mutual aid by GDR and Poland.
8—10 June	Visit by Romanian party and government delegation, led by Nicolae Ceausescu, in the GDR; declaration on deepening the friendship and cooperation between the GDR and Romania signed.
11—23 June	GDR party and government delegation, led by Werner Lamberz, to six Arab and African states.
16 June	Volkskammer passes new labour law which takes effect on 1 January 1978.
9 August	Politburo and Council of Ministers confirm new model statutes and management for crop and animal husbandry LPG.
23 August	Rudolf Bahro arrested after passages from his book *Die Alternative* appeared in *Der Spiegel*, the West German journal, on 22 August; 26 August six critics of GDR regime released from prison and expelled to West Berlin.
13—14 September	Visit of GDR party and government delegation, led by Erich Honecker, to Bulgaria; signing of new treaty of friendship, cooperation and mutual aid by GDR and Bulgaria.
22—24 September	GDR Cultural Association (Kulturbund) congress in East Berlin.
1—4 October	Visit of GDR party and government delegation, led by Hermann Axen, to Libya; signing of agreement on further development of friendly relations between the two states.
3—5 October	Visit of Czechoslovak party and government delegation, led by Gustav Husak,

to GDR; signing of new treaty of friendship, cooperation and mutual aid by GDR and Czechoslovakia.

7 October   GDR national day celebrated with gala in Palace of the Republic; during concert in Alexanderplatz in evening confrontation between police and young people.

1—6 December   Visit by GDR party and government delegation, led by Erich Honecker, to Vietnam; signing of treaty of friendship and cooperation by GDR and Vietnam; 6—8 December same delegation visits Philippines; economic agreement signed; 8—11 December same delegation visits People's Democratic Republic of Korea.

5—11 December   Werner Lamberz visits the People's Democratic Republic of Yemen, Ethiopia and Libya.

12—16 December   Otto Fischer, GDR Foreign Minister, visits Japan.

16—20 December   Visit of delegation of South West Africa People's Organisation (SWAPO) to GDR; agreement on cooperation between SED and SWAPO during 1978 and 1979 signed.

1978

5 January   Institute of Sociology and Social Policy to analyse the basic social processes of a socialist society set up in the GDR Academy of Sciences in East Berlin; Professor Gunnar Winkler nominated director.

9—15 February   Opening of the Brecht-Haus-Berlin as a research and memorial centre and an international Brecht dialogue on art and politics held to mark the eightieth anniversary of the birth of Bertolt Brecht in East Berlin.

6 March	GDR Protestant church leaders, led by Bishop Albrecht Schönherr, have discussions with party and government officials, led by Erich Honecker, on state—church relations.
7 March	Werner Lamberz killed in air crash in Libya.
30 March—1 April	Visit by Austrian government delegation, led by Chancellor Bruno Kreisky, to GDR; signing of agreement on scientific—technical cooperation, cultural agreement, a veterinary agreement and various other trade agreements.
3—4 May	Visit by Hungarian Foreign Minister, Frigyes Puja, to GDR; agreement on cultural and scientific cooperation signed.
11—12 May	Visit by Soviet Foreign Minister, Andrei Gromyko, to GDR; signing of new agreement on cultural and scientific cooperation.
29—31 May	Eighth GDR Writers' Union congress in East Berlin; main theme is the writer and the struggles of our time; Hermann Kant replaces Anna Seghers as president.
19 June	Willi Stoph, chairman of the Council of Ministers, receives a delegation of Protestant church leaders, headed by Bishop Albrecht Schönherr, for an exchange of views.
25 June	Pastoral letter read out in Protestant churches; it is critical of the planned military instruction in schools.
30 June	Rudolf Bahro sentenced to eight years' imprisonment.
26 August	NVA Lt Colonel Sigmund Jähn becomes first German in space on board Soviet spacecraft Soyuz 31.
28 September	Ewald Moldt, new head of permanent

GDR mission in Bonn, presents his letters of credence to Federal President Walter Scheel.

13 October	Volkskammer passes new law on national defence.
18–20 October	Eighth GDR Pedagogical Congress in East Berlin; chief speaker is Margot Honecker, Minister of Education.
8 December	Scientific Council for research into youth established in East Berlin; Professor Walter Friedrich named chairman; membership consists of academics, FDJ functionaries and officials from state and social organisations.
29 December	CC, SED celebrates sixtieth anniverary of founding of KPD.

1979

1 January	Regulation entitling all employees to at least three days extra holiday annually takes effect.
8 January	GDR party and government delegation, led by Erich Honecker, arrives in India.
10 January	Admiral Waldemar Verner retires as chief of political administration of NVA; replaced by Colonel General Heinz Kessler.
7 February	Fifth congress of GDR Psychology Society opens in East Berlin.
24 February	GDR Society for Space Research and Travel founded in East Berlin; Professor Hans-Joachim Fischer elected president.
5 April	GDR citizens no longer able to use Western currency in Intershops; must exchange money beforehand for special tokens.

9 May	House arrest of Professor Robert Havemann, in operation since November 1976, lifted.
14 May	Peter van Loyen, ZDF (TV) correspondent in East Berlin, becomes third West German journalist to be expelled.
20 May	Candidates of the National Front receive 99.83 per cent of votes cast at elections.
22 May	Stefan Heym fined 9000 marks for currency offences.
25 May	Professor Robert Havemann fined DM10 000 for currency offences.
31 May	Wolfgang Harich, on visit to Austria, decides not to return to GDR.
28 June	Volkskammer decides that in future its members representing East Berlin will be elected directly.
4 September	GDR and USA sign a consular agreement.
20 September	Council of Ministers decrees measures to save energy.
4 October	Soviet party and government delegation, headed by Leonid Brezhnev, arrives in East Berlin to take part in celebrations marking thirtieth anniversary of founding of GDR.
11 October	Rudolf Bahro freed from prison in amnesty marking thirtieth anniversary of GDR; 17 October moves to FRG.
19 October	GDR Attorney General declares that 20 000—25 000 prisoners were freed in amnesty.
4 December	Friedrich Ebert dies.

1980

1 January	GDR becomes non-permanent member of UN Security Council during 1980 and 1981.

13 March	GDR and PLO sign cultural agreement in East Berlin.
11 April	Gerhard Müller replaces Alois Bräutigam as SED first secretary in Bezirk Erfurt.
25 April	Dr Joachim Meisner named Roman Catholic Bishop of Berlin by Pope John Paul II in place of Cardinal Bengsch who had died in December 1979.
8 May	GDR party and government delegation, led by Erich Honecker, attends funeral of President Josip Broz Tito in Belgrade; Honecker meets Federal Chancellor Helmut Schmidt for discussions.
19 May	Gerhard Schaffran, Roman Catholic Bishop of Dresden–Meissen, named chairman of Berlin bishops' conference in place of late Cardinal Bengsch.
11 June	GDR and Cuba sign agreement on trade covering years 1981–5 which envisages increase of 45 per cent over previous five-year period.
3 July	Volkskammer confirms treaties of friendship signed by GDR with Ethiopia, People's Democratic Republic of Yemen, Kampuchea and Cuba.
3 August	Olympic Games end in Moscow; GDR team takes second place behind USSR; USA had boycotted Games.
14 August	Joachim Herrmann becomes head of chancery of Chairman of Council of Ministers and named state secretary. Veterinary agreement signed by GDR and FRG on 21 December 1979 takes effect.
9 October	GDR Ministry of Finance orders, as from 13 October 1980, raising of minimum amount exchanged daily for visitors to GDR and East Berlin to DM25.

21 November	GDR and Republic of Ireland enter into diplomatic relations.
17 December	GDR and India sign trade and payments agreement covering years 1981—5.
25 December	About 50 per cent fewer West Berliners than in 1979 visit GDR and East Berlin over Christmas due to increase in minimum amount to be exchanged daily.

1981

15 January	Erich Honecker receives the Roman Catholic Bishop Gerhard Schaffran, chairman of the Berlin bishops' conference, for discussions.
29 January	Erich Honecker takes leave of Günter Gaus, head of permanent FRG mission in East Berlin, on the occasion of his return to Bonn.
9 February	Klaus Bölling, new head of permanent FRG mission in East Berlin, presents his letters of credence to Erich Honecker.
1 March	NVA celebrates twenty-fifth anniversary of its foundation.
3 March	SED delegation, headed by Erich Honecker, returns to East Berlin after attending twenty-sixth CPSU congress in Moscow.
19 March	GDR and USSR sign trade agreement covering years 1981—5.
11 April	Tenth SED congress opens in East Berlin.
16 April	Albert Norden not reelected to Politburo.
2 May	GDR and Great Britain sign agreement on cooperation in cultural, education and science covering the years 1981—3.
4 May	Hans-Joachim Böhme becomes SED first secretary in Bezirk Halle succeeding Werner Felfe.

14 June	Elections to Volkskammer, Bezirkstage and East Berlin city parliament.
4 July	Michael Kohl, deputy GDR Foreign Minister, dies.
17 August	World Council of Churches meets in Dresden.
28 September	First congress of GDR mathematicians meets in East Berlin.
4 November	Gottfried Forck inducted as Bishop of Berlin—Brandenburg Protestant Church; succeeds Bishop Albrecht Schönherr.
11 December	Federal Chancellor Helmut Schmidt begins three-day visit to GDR; meets Erich Honecker on several occasions.

1982

1 February	Harry Ott, deputy GDR Foreign Minister, succeeds Peter Florin as permanent GDR representative at UN.
10 March	Hans-Joachim Hoffmann, GDR Minister of Culture, begins eight-day visit to India; 11 March signs agreement on cultural exchange between GDR and India during 1982—4.
26 March	Tenth Federal Congress of Domowina, Sorb parliament, opens in Cottbus.
29 March	General Wojciech Jaruzelski, Polish party and government leader, arrives in East Berlin on a one-day official friendship visit.
5 April	Thirteenth congress of LDPD opens in Weimar.
9 April	Professor Robert Havemann dies.
21 April	Tenth FDGB congress opens.
5 May	Eleventh DBD congress opens in Suhl; Ernst Mecklenburg succeeds Ernst Goldenbaum as chairman.

6 May	Erich Honecker takes leave of Klaus Bölling, head of permanent FRG mission in East Berlin, on his return to Bonn to become government spokesman.
13 May	Twelfth GDR Peasants' congress opens.
19 May	Afghan party and government delegation, led by Babrak Karmal, begins three-day visit to GDR; 21 May Erich Honecker and Karmal sign treaty of friendship; consular agreement, agreement on economic, industrial and scientific—technical co-operation; agreement on health and social policy signed; SED and Democratic People's Party of Afghanistan agreement on cooperation over years 1982—7 also signed.
24 May	Hans Otto Bräutigam, new head of permanent FRG mission in East Berlin, presents letters of credence to Erich Honecker.
30 May	Albert Norden dies.
18 June	Several GDR—FRG and GDR—West Berlin agreements signed in East Berlin; daily visits to GDR and East Berlin now end at 2 a.m. instead of midnight; persons who illegally left GDR up to end of 1980 will no longer be prosecuted by GDR courts.

Bibliography

Adler, H. (1959): *Berlin in jenen Tagen Berichte aus der Zeit von 1945–1948* (Berlin, DDR).

Agsten, R. and M. Bogisch (1970): *Bürgertum am Wendepunkt: Die Herausbildung der antifaschistisch-demokratischen und anti-imperialistischen Grundhaltung bei den Mitgliedern der LDPD 1945–1946* (Berlin, DDR).

Agsten, R. and M. Bogisch (1974): *LDPD auf dem Weg in die DDR Zur Geschichte der LDPD in den Jahren 1946–1949* (Berlin, DDR).

Auf dem Weg der sozialistischen Menschengemeinschaft: Eine Sammlung von Dokumenten zur Bündnispolitik und Kirchenpolitik 1967–1970 (1971) (Berlin, DDR).

Badstübner, R. and H. Heitzer (eds) (1979): *Die DDR in der Übergangsperiode Studien zur Vorgeschichte und Geschichte der DDR 1945 bis 1961* (Berlin, DDR).

Bahro, R. (1977): *Die Alternative: Zur Kritik des real existierenden Sozialismus* (Cologne).

Baring, A. (1972): *Uprising in East Germany June 17, 1953* (London).

Baylis, T. A. (1974): *The Technical Intelligentsia and the East German Elite* (London).

Belwe, K. (1979): *Mitwirkung im Industriebetrieb der DDR* (Opladen).

Benjamin, H., H. Anders and K. Görner (1976): *Zur Geschichte der Rechtspflege der DDR 1945–1949* (Berlin, DDR).

Benser, G. (1961): *Vereint sind wir unbesiegbar: Wie die SED entstand* (Berlin, DDR).

Berendt, A. (1968): *Wilhelm Külz* (Berlin, DDR).

Biermann, W. (1978): *Demokratisierung in der DDR: Ökonomische Notwendigkeiten, Herrschaftsstrukturen, Rolle der Gewerkschaften 1961–1977* (Cologne).

Binder, G. (1969): *Deutschland seit 1945* (Stuttgart).

Biskup, R. (1976): *Deutschlands offene Handelsgrenze: Die DDR als Nutzniesser des EGW- Protokolls über den innerdeutschen Handel* (Berlin).

Brandt, H. (1978): *Ein Traum der nicht entführbar ist: Mein Weg zwischen Ost und West*, 2nd edn (Munich).

Buch, G. (1979): *Namen und Daten wichtiger Personen der DDR* (Berlin).

Buhr, M. and A. Kosing (1975): *Kleines Wörterbuch der marxistisch—leninistischen Philosophie* (Berlin, DDR).

Childs, D. (1982): *The GDR: Moscow's German Ally* (London).

Cornelsen, D. *et al.* (1977): *Handbuch DDR-Wirtschaft* (Hamburg).

Cramer, D. (1973): *Deutschland nach dem Grundvertrag.* (Stuttgart).

Croan, M. (1962): 'Reality and Illusion in Soviet—German Relations', *Survey*, nos 44—5.

Croan, M. (1969): 'Czechoslovakia, Ulbricht and the German Problem', *Problems of Communism*, vol. xviii, no. 1.

Croan, M. (1976): *East Germany: The Soviet Connection* (London).

DDR-Handbuch (1979) 2nd edn (Cologne).

DDR Werden und Wachsen: Zur Geschichte der DDR (1975) (Berlin, DDR).

Deuerlein, E. (1974): *DDR 1945—1970: Geschichte und Bestandsaufnahme*, 5th edn (Munich).

Diepenthal, W. (1974): *Drei Volksdemokratien* (Cologne).

Djilas, M. (1969): *Conversations with Stalin* (Harmondsworth).

Doernberg, S. (1959): *Die Geburt eines neuen Deutschlands 1945—1949* (Berlin, DDR).

Doernberg, S. (1969): *Kurze Geschichte der DDR*, 4th edn (Berlin, DDR).

Dokumente der SED (1948—74) 13 vols (Berlin, DDR).

Dokumente zur Aussenpolitik der Regierung der DDR (1954): vol. I, *Von der Gründung der DDR am 7. Oktober 1949 bis zur Souveranitätserklärung am 25. Oktober 1954* (Berlin, DDR); vol. IV (1954): *Verträge und Abkommen von 7. Oktober 1949 bis 30. Juni 1956* (Berlin DDR).

Duhnke, H. (1955): *Stalinismus in Deutschland Die Geschichte der sowjetischen Besatzungszone* (Cologne and Berlin).

Duhnke, H. (1972): *Die KPD von 1933 bis 1945* (Cologne).

Ehlert, W. (ed) (1973): *Wörterbuch der Ökonomie Sozialismus* (Berlin, DDR).

Emmerich, W. (1981): *Kleine Literaturgeschichte der DDR* (Darmstadt).

End, H. (1973): *Zweimal deutsche Aussenpolitik Internationale Dimensionen des innerdeutschen Konflikts 1949—72* (Cologne).

Erbe, G. *et al.* (1979): *Politik, Wirtschaft und Gesellschaft* (Opladen).

Fischer, A. (1975): *Sowjetische Deutschlandpolitik im Zweiten Weltkrieg 1941—1945* (Stuttgart).

Fischer, P. (1978): *Kirche und Christen in der DDR* (Berlin).

Forster, T. M. (1980): *The East German Army* (London).

Förtsch, E. (1969): *Die SED* (Stuttgart).

Frank, H. (1965): *20 Jahre Zone* (Munich).

Fricke, K. W. (1976): *Programm und Statut der SED vom 22. Mai 1976* (Cologne).

Fricke, K. W. (1979): *Politik und Justiz in der DDR Zur Geschichte der politischen Verfolgung 1945—1968* (Cologne).

Gast, G. (1973): *Die politische Rolle der Frau in der DDR* (Düsseldorf).

Geschichte der SED Abriss (1978) (Berlin, DDR).

Gesetzblatt der DDR (Berlin, DDR) various years.

Glaessner, G.-J. (1977): *Herrschaft durch Kader Leitung der Gesellschaft und Kaderpolitik in der DDR* (Opladen).

Glaessner, G.-J. and I. Rudolf (1978): *Macht durch Wissen Zum Zusammenhang von Bildungspolitik, Bildungssystem und Kaderqualifizierung in der DDR* (Opladen).

Gniffke, E. W. (1966): *Jahre mit Ulbricht* (Cologne).

Goldman, M. I. (1967): *Soviet Foreign Aid* (New York).

Goroschkowa, G. N. (1963): *Die deutsche Volkskongressbewegung für Einheit und gerechten Frieden 1947–49* (Berlin, DDR).

Gradl, J. B. (1981): *Anfang unter dem Sowjetstern Die CDU 1945–1948 in der sowjetischen Besatzungszone Deutschlands* (Cologne).

Gransow, V. (1975): *Kulturpolitik in der DDR* (Berlin).

Grossner, A. (1977): *Geschichte Deutschlands seit 1945* (Munich).

Grotewohl, O. (1952): *Dreissig Jahre später*, 4th edn (Berlin, DDR).

Gruenewald, W. (1971): *Die Münchener Ministerpräsidentenkonferenz 1947: Anlass und Scheitern eines gesamtdeutschen Unternehmens* (Meisenheim/Glau).

Haase, H. E. (1978): *Grundzüge und Strukturen des Haushaltswesens der DDR* (Berlin).

Harnhardt, A. M., Jr (1968): *The German Democratic Republic* (Balitmore).

Hearnden, A. (1974): *Education in the Two Germanies* (Oxford).

Heitzer, H. (1979): *DDR-Geschichtlicher Überblick* (Berlin, DDR).

Helwig, G. (1974): *Zwischen Familie und Beruf Die Stellung der Frau in beiden deutschen Staaten* (Cologne).

Herspring, D. R. (1973): *East German Civil–Military Relations: The Impact of Technology 1949–1972* (New York).

Herz, H.-P. (1968): *Freie Deutsche Jugend* (Munich).

Hille, B. and B. Roeder (eds) (1979): *Beiträge zur Jugendforschung Sozialpsychologische Befunde zum Jugendalter in beiden deutschen Staaten* (Opladen).

Hillgruber, A. (1974): *Deutsche Geschichte 1945–1972: Die 'deutsche Frage' in der Weltpolitik* (Berlin, Vienna).

Hoffmann, U. (1971): *Die Veränderungen in der Sozialstruktur des Ministerrates der DDR bis 1969* (Düsseldorf).

Holmes, L. (1981): *The Policy Process in Communist States: Politics and Industrial Administration* (Beverly Hills and London).

Honecker, E. (1980): *Aus meinen Leben* (Frankfurt-am-Main).

Horn, W. (1960): *Der Kampf der SED um die Festigung der DDR und den Übergang zur zweiten Etappe der Revolution (1949–1952)* (Berlin, DDR).

Horn, W. *et al.* (1966): *20 Jahre Sozialistische Einheitspartei* (Berlin, DDR).

Hümmler, H. (1967): *Die Partei* (Berlin, DDR).

Immler, H. (1971): *Agrarpolitik in der DDR* (Cologne).

Introducing the GDR (1971) (Dresden).

Istoriya Germanskoi Demokraticheskoi Respubliki 1949–1979, 2nd edn (Moscow).

Jacobsen, H.-A. *et al.* (eds) (1980): *Drei Jahrzehnte Aussenpolitik der DDR*, 2nd edn (Munich).

Jaide, W. and B. Hille (eds) (1977): *Jugend im doppelten Deutschland* (Opladen).

Jänicke, M. (1964): *Der dritte Weg: Die antistalinistische Opposition gegen Ulbricht seit 1953* (Cologne).

Kaden, A. (1964): *Einheit oder Freiheit* (Hanover).

Keren, M. (1973): 'The New Economic System in the GDR: An Obituary', *Soviet Studies*, vol. xxiv.

Keren, M. (1974): *The Rise and Fall of the New Economic System in the GDR* (Jerusalem).

Knauft, W. (1980): *Katholische Kirche in der DDR Gemeinden in der Bewährung 1945–1980*, 2nd edn (Mainz).

Koch, H. G. (1975): *Staat und Kirche in der DDR Zur Entwicklung ihrer Beziehungen von 1945–1974* (Stuttgart).

Köhler, G. (ed) (1974): *Pontifex nicht Partisan Kirche und Staat in der DDR von 1949 bis 1958* (Stuttgart).

Köhler, H. (1965): *Economic Integration in the Soviet Bloc: With an East German Case Study* (New York).

Krieg, H. (1965): *LDP und NDP in der 'DDR' 1949–1958* (Cologne and Opladen).

Krippendorff, E. (n. d.): *Die Liberal-Demokratische Partei Deutschlands in der sowjetischen Besatzungszone 1945–1948* (Düsseldorf).

Krisch, H. (1974): *German Politics under Soviet Occupation* (New York and London).

Kulbach, R. and H. Weber (1969): *Parteien im Blocksystem der DDR* (Cologne).

Lamm, H. S. and S. Kupper (1976): *DDR und Dritte Welt* (Munich).

Lapp, P. J. (1972): *Der Staatsrat im politischen System der DDR (1960–1971)* (Opladen).

Lapp, P. J. (1975): *Die Volkskammer der DDR* (Opladen).

Laschitza, H. (1969): *Kämpferische Demokratie gegen Faschismus* (Berlin, DDR).

Lemke, C. (1980): *Persönlichkeit und Gesellschaft Zur Theorie der Persönlichkeit in der DDR* (Opladen).

Lenze, M. (1979): *Die Wirtschaftsbeziehungen DDR–Sowjetunion 1945–1961* (Opladen).

Leonhard, W. (1972): *Die Revolution entlässt ihre Kinder* (Frankfurt-am-Main).

Leptin, G. (1971): *Die deutsche Wirtschaft nach 1945: Ein Ost–West Vergleich* (Opladen).

Leptin, G. and M. Melzer (1978): *Economic Reforms in East German Industry*, transl. Roger A. Clarke (London).

Lindemann, H. and K. Müller (1974): *Auswärtige Kulturpolitik der DDR* (Bonn and Bad Godesberg).

Lippmann, H. (1971): *Honecker: Porträt eines Nachfolgers* (Cologne).

Ludz, P. C. (ed) (1970): *Studien und Materialien zur Soziologie in der DDR*, 2nd edn (Opladen).

Ludz, P. C. (ed) (1972a): *Soziologie und Marxismus in der Deutschen Demokratischen Republik*, 2 vols (Neuwied and Berlin).

Ludz, P. C. (1972b): *The Changing Party Elite in East Germany* (Cambridge, MA).

Ludz, P. C. (1977): *Die DDR zwischen Ost und West: Politische Analysen 1961 bis 1976* (Munich).

McCauley, M. (1979): *Marxism—Leninism in the German Democratic Republic: The Socialist Unity Party (SED)* (London).

McCauley, M. (1980): *East Germany: The Dilemmas of Division* (London).

McCauley, M. (1981a): *Power and Authority in East Germany: The Socialist Unity Party* (SED) (London).

McCauley, M. (1981b): 'Social Policy under Honecker' in I. Wallace (ed), *The GDR under Honecker 1971—1981* (Dundee).

McCauley, M. (1982a): 'The East German Response to Events in Poland', *Conflict Quarterly*, vol. II, no. 3.

McCauley, M. (1982b): 'The Rebirth of Democracy: Political Parties in Germany 1945—49' in H. Döring and G. Smith (eds), *Party Government and Political Culture in Western Germany* (London).

Mahncke, D. (1973): *Berlin im geteilten Deutschland* (Munich).

Mallinckrodt, A. D. (1971): *Propaganda hinter der Mauer* (Stuttgart).

Mampel, S. (1964): *Die Entwicklung der Verfassungsordnung in der sowjetischbesetzten Zone Deutschlands von 1945 bis 1963* (Tübingen).

Mattedi, N. (1966): *Gründung und Entwicklung der Parteien in der Sowjetischen Besatzungszone Deutschlands 1945—1949* (Bonn).

Messing, M. (1978): *Arbeitszufriedenheit im Systemvergleich Eine empirische Untersuchung an Bau- und Montagearbeitern in beiden Teilen Deutschlands* (Stuttgart).

Mitzscherling, P. *et al.* (1974): *DDR-Wirtschaft Eine Bestandsaufnahme* (Frankfurt-am-Main).

Moraw, F. (1973): *Die Parole der 'Einheit' und die Sozialdemokratie* (Bonn and Bad Godesberg).

Moreton, N. E. (1978): *East Germany in the Warsaw Alliance: The Politics of Détente* (Boulder, CO.).

Müller, W. (1979): *Die KPD und die 'Einheit der Arbeiterklasse'* (Frankfurt-am-Main).

Müller-Römer, D. (1974): *Die neue Verfassung der DDR* (Cologne).

von Münch, I. (1974–6): *Quellentexte zur Rechtslage des Deutschen Reiches, der BRD und der DDR*, 2 vols (Stuttgart).

Münzer, W. *et al.* (1975): *Dokumente und Materialien der Zusammenarbeit zwischen der SED und der Kommunistischen Partei der Sowjetunion 1971 bis 1974* (Berlin, DDR).

Nawrocki, J. (1979): *Bewaffnete Organe in der DDR Nationale Volksarmee und andere militärische sowie paramilitärische Verbände* (Berlin).

Neef, H. (1960): *Der Freiheit Morgenrot: Das deutsche Volk im Kampf um Einheit und Frieden 1945 bis 1947* (Berlin, DDR).

Nettl, J. P. (1951): *The Eastern Zone and Soviet Policy in Germany 1945–50* (London).

Neugebauer, G. (1978): *Partei und Staatsapparat in der DDR* (Opladen).

Niethammer, L. *et al.* (1976): *Arbeiterinitiative 1945* (Wuppertal).

Nolte, E. (1974): *Deutschland und der kalte Krieg* (Munich and Zürich).

Norden, A. (1963): *Ein freies Deutschland entsteht* (Berlin, DDR).

'Oberbürgermeister in Jena 1945/46: Aus den Erinnerungen von Dr Heinrich Troeger', (1977) *Vierteljahrshefte für Zeitgeschichte*, 4.

Otnosheniya SSSR s GDR 1945–1955gg: Dokumenty i Materialy (1974) (Moscow).

Politische Ökonomie des Sozialismus und ihre Anwendung in der DDR (Berlin, DDR).

Protokoll der 1. Parteikonferenz der Sozialistischen Einheitspartei Deutschlands, 25. bis 28. Januar 1949 im Hause der Deutschen Wirtschaftskommission zu Berlin, 2nd edn (1956) (Berlin, DDR).

Protokoll der Verhandlungen der 2. Parteikonferenz der Sozialistischen Einheitspartei Deutschlands, 9. bis 12. Juli 1952 in der Werner-Seelenbinder-Halle zu Berlin (1952) (Berlin, DDR).

Protokoll der Verhandlungen der 3. Parteikonferenz der Sozialistischen Einheitspartei Deutschlands, 24. März bis 30. März 1956 in der Werner-Seelenbinder-Halle zu Berlin (1956) (Berlin, DDR).

Protokoll des Vereinigungsparteitages der Sozialdemokratischen Partei Deutschlands (SPD) und der Kommunistischen Partei Deutschlands (KPD) am 21. und 22. April 1946 in der Staatsoper 'Admiralspalast' in Berlin (1946) (Berlin, DDR).

Protokoll der Verhandlungen des II. Parteitages der Sozialistischen Einheitspartei Deutschlands, 20. bis 24. September 1947 in der Deutschen Staatsoper zu Berlin (1947) (Berlin, DDR).

Protokoll der Verhandlungen des III. Parteitages der Sozialistischen Einheitspartei Deutschlands, 20, bis 24. Juli 1950 in der Werner-Seelenbinder-Halle zu Berlin, 2 vols (1951) (Berlin, DDR).

Protokoll der Verhandlungen des IV. Parteitages der Sozialistischen Einheitspartei Deutschlands, 30. März bis 6. April 1954 in der Werner-Seelenbinder-Halle zu Berlin, 2 vols (1954) (Berlin, DDR).

Protokoll der Verhandlungen des V. Parteitages der Sozialistischen Ein-

heitspartei Deutschlands, 10. bis 16 Juli 1958 in der Werner-Seelen-binder-Halle zu Berlin, 2 vols (1959) (Berlin, DDR).

Protokoll der Verhandlungen des VI. Parteitages der Sozialistischen Ein-heitspartei Deutschlands, 15. bis 21. Januar 1963 in der Werner-Seelen-binder-Halle zu Berlin, 4 vols (1963) (Berlin, DDR).

Protokoll der Verhandlungen des VII. Parteitages der Sozialistischen Ein-heitspartei Deutschlands, 17. bis 22 April 1967 in der Werner-Seelen-binder-Halle zu Berlin, 4 vols (1967) (Berlin, DDR).

Protokoll der Verhandlungen des VIII. Parteitages der Sozialistischen Ein-heitspartei Deutschlands, 15. bis 19. Juni 1971 in der Werner-Seelen-binder-Halle zu Berlin, 2 vols (1971) (Berlin, DDR).

Protokoll der Verhandlungen des IX. Parteitages der Sozialistischen Ein-heitspartei Deutschlands 18. bis 22. Mai 1976 im Palast der Republik in Berlin, 2 vols (1976) (Berlin, DDR).

Radde, J. (1976): *Die aussenpolitische Führungselite der DDR* (Cologne).

Radde, J. (1977): *Der diplomatische Dienst der DDR: Namen und Daten* (Cologne).

Richert, E. (1963): *Macht ohne Mandat*, 2nd edn (Opladen).

Rush, M. (1974): *How Communist States Change their Rules* (Ithaca and London).

Schenk, F. (1962): *Im Vorzimmer der Diktatur* (Cologne).

Scheurig, B. (1969): *Free Germany* (Middletown, CO).

Schiller, K. J. (1976): *Die Sorben in der antifascistisch-demokratischen Umwälzung 1945–1949* (Bauzen).

Schlenk, H. (1970): *Der Binnenhandel der DDR* (Cologne).

Schneider, E. (1975): *Die DDR Geschichte, Politik, Wirtschaft, Gesellschaft* (Stuttgart).

Schoenhals, K. (1974): 'The "Free Germany" Movement and its Impact upon the German Democratic Republic', *East Central Europe*, vol. I, no. 2.

Schubbe, E. (ed) (1972): *Dokumente zur Kunst-, Literatur- und Kultur-politik der SED (1949–1969)* (Stuttgart).

Schultz, J. (1956): *Der Funktionär in der Einheitspartei: Kaderpolitik und Bürokratisierung in der SED* (Stuttgart and Düsseldorf).

Schwarzenbach, R. (1976): *Die Kaderpolitik der SED in der Staatsver-waltung* (Cologne).

Schweizer, C. C. (1976): *Die deutsche Nation Aussagen von Bismarck bis Honecker Dokumentation* (Cologne).

Sikora, F. (1977): *Sozialistische Solidarität und nationale Interessen: Polen, Tschechoslowakei, DDR* (Cologne).

Slusser, R. (ed) (1953): *Soviet Economic Policy in Postwar Germany. A Collection of Papers by former Soviet Officials* (New York).

Sontheimer, K. and W. Bleek (1973): *Die DDR: Politik, Gesellschaft, Wirtschaft* (Hamburg).

Staritz, D. (1976): *Sozialismus in einem halben Land: Zur Programmatik und Politik der KPD/SED in der Phase der antifascistisch-demokratischen Umwälzung in der DDR* (Berlin).

Statistisches Jahrbuch der DDR (Berlin, DDR), various years.

Stern, C. (1957): *Porträt einer bolschewistischen Partei* (Cologne).

Stern, C. (1963): *Ulbricht: Eine politische Biographie* (Cologne and Berlin).

Stern, C. (1966): 'East Germany' in W. E. Griffith (ed), *Communism in Europe* (London).

Streisand, J. (1979): *Deutsche Geschichte in einem Band Ein Überblick*, 4th edn (Berlin, DDR).

Studiengruppe Militärpolitik, (1976): *Die Nationale Volksarmee Ein Anti-Weissbuch zum Militär in der DDR* (Hamburg).

Thomas, S. (1964): *Entscheidung in Berlin: Zur Entstehungsgeschichte der SED in der deutschen Hauptstadt 1945–46* (Berlin, DDR).

Trittel, G. J. (1975): *Die Bodenreform in der britischen Zone 1945–1949* (Stuttgart).

Ulbricht, W. (1953–71): *Zur Geschichte der deutschen Arbeiterbewegung*, 10 vols (Berlin, DDR).

Ulbricht, W. (1966a): *Die nationale Mission der DDR und das geistige Schaffen in unserem Staat* (Berlin, DDR).

Ulbricht, W. (1966b): *Probleme des Perspektivplans bis 1970* (Berlin, DDR).

Ulbricht, W. (1966c): *Whither Germany? Speeches and Essays on the National Question* (Dresden).

Ulbricht, W. (1966d): *Zum neuen ökonomischen System der Planung und Leitung* (Berlin, DDR).

US Congress Senate Committee on Foreign Relations (1961): *Documents on Germany 1944–1961* (Washington, DC).

Vogelsang, T. (1973): *Das geteilte Deutschland* (Munich).

Wallace, I. (ed) (1981): *The GDR under Honecker 1971–1981* (Dundee).

Weber, H. (1963): *Der deutsche Kommunismus Dokumente* (Cologne and Berlin).

Weber, H. (1968): *Von der SBZ zur DDR 1945–1968* (Hanover).

Weber, H. (1969): *Die Wandlung des deutschen Kommunismus Die Stalinisierung der KPD in der Weimarer Republik*, 2 vols (Frankfurt-am-Main).

Weber, H. (1971): *Die Sozialistische Einheitspartei Deutschlands 1946–1971* (Hanover).

Weber, H. (1974): *Die SED nach Ulbricht* (Cologne).

Weber, H. (1976a): *DDR; Grundriss der Geschichte 1945–1976* (Hanover).

Weber, H. (1976b): *SED: Chronik einer Partei 1971–1976* (Cologne).

Weber, H. (1980): *Kleine Geschichte der DDR* (Cologne).

Weber, H. and F. Oldenburg (1971): *25 Jahre SED Chronik einer Partei* (Cologne).

Wettig, G. (1976): *Die Sowjetunion, die DDR und die Deutschland–Frage 1965–1976: Einvernehmen und Konflikt im sozialistischen Lager* (Stuttgart).

Windsor, P. (1971): *Germany and the Management of Detente* (New York).

Winkler, H. A. (ed) (1979): *Politische Weichenstellungen im Nachkriegsdeutschland 1945–1953* (Göttingen).

Wolff, W. (1975): *An der Seite der Roten Armee: Zum Wirken des Nationalkomitees 'Freies Deutschland' an der sowjetisch-deutschen Front*, 2nd edn (Berlin, DDR).

Zauberman, A. (1964): *Industrial Progress in Poland, Czechoslovakia and East Germany 1937–1962* (London).

Zimmerman, H. (1978): 'The GDR in the 1970s', *Problems of Communism*, no. 2.

20 Jahre Sozialistische Einheitspartei Deutschlands Beiträge (1966) (Berlin, DDR).

20 Jahre SED – 20 Jahre schöpferischer Marxismus (1967) (Berlin, DDR).

Index

Abortion, 180
Abrasimov, P., 143—4
Abusch, Alexander, 40, 58, 94, 145
Acheson, Dean, 60
Ackermann, Anton, 10, 14, 28—9, 51, 70, 195, 197, 216
Adenauer, Konrad, 60—3, 204, 207, 215, 221, 223, 227
Afghanistan, 150, 190, 193, 264
Africa, 191—2, 224, 233
Agriculture, 22—6, 42, 54—6, 67—73, 76—8, 98, 101, 104, 165—6, 171—8, 193, 215, 217, 219—23, 228—9, 240, 256
Aircraft industry, 111
Albania, 79, 205
Allied Control Council, 9—10, 19, 34, 60, 199, 201, 243
Apel, Erich, 122, 131
Apetz, Bruno, 96
Arab-Israeli War (1973), 149
Arzinger, Rudolf, 232
Association for Mutual Peasant Aid (VdgB), 24, 30—2, 34, 49, 200, 203
Attlee, Clement, 17—18, 196
Auschwitz, 96
Austria, 27, 73, 252, 258
Axen, Hermann, 130, 256

Baender, Paul, 82
Bahr, Egon, 138, 248
Bahro, Rudolf, 168—9, 256, 258, 260
Barlach, Ernst, 58
Bartsch, Karl-Heinz, 131

Basic Treaty (FRG—GDR), 149, 162, 189, 244, 248—9
Bauer, Leo, 51
Baumann, Edith, 106
Bebel, August, 107
Becher, Johannes R., 58
Becker, Jurek, 147, 186
Behrens, Fritz, 85—6
Belgium, 61
Beling, Walter, 29
Bengsch, Cardinal, 261
Benjamin, Hilde, 68, 106
Bentzien, Hans, 122, 234
Beria, L., 64, 70
Berlin Agreement, 139—40, 143, 149, 162, 187, 247
Berlin Blockade, 35, 59, 202, 204
Berlin Wall, 3, 5, 67—8, 103—4, 134, 145, 226
Berlinguer, E., 190
Bevin, Ernest, 17, 60
Biermann, Wolf, 122, 146, 149, 185, 234, 255
Bitterfeld conference, 95, 146, 222, 224, 231
Bloch, Ernst, 40, 83
Bobrowski, Johannes, 147
Bogdanov, A. A., 154—5
Böhme, Hans-Joachim, 262
Bölling, Klaus, 262, 264
Bolz, Lothar, 36, 50, 203, 222
Brandt, Heinz, 86
Brandt, Willy, 136, 138—9, 236, 241—3
Braun, Volker, 146, 148, 185
Bräutigam, Alois, 261

Bräutigam, Hans Otto, 264
Brecht, Bertolt, 40—1, 58, 146, 257
Bredel, Willi, 80, 227
Brezhnev, Leonid I., 122, 139, 151,
    189—90, 232, 234, 251, 253,
    260
  doctrine, 138, 167
Brundert, Willi, 206
Buchenwald, 3, 96
Bukharin, N. I., 79, 155
Bulganin, Marshal, 75, 97
Bulgaria, 44, 137, 205, 214,
    238—40, 256
Bundestag (FRG), 134—5, 139,
    204, 211, 213—14, 236
Bureaucratic centralism, 50
Burghardt, Max, 219, 248
Byrnes, James F., 17

Carrillo, S., 190
Casablanca conference, 9
Ceausescu, N., 190, 256
Central Commission for State
    Control, 47
Chile, 245, 249
China, People's Republic of, 74, 79,
    102, 205
Christian Democratic Party (CDU),
    16, 20—1, 23—5, 29—32,
    36—7, 44—5, 48—50, 52—3,
    72, 91, 99, 118, 160—1,
    197—8, 200—1, 203, 210,
    219
  founded, 16, 196
Christians, 5, 59
Chuikov, Marshal Vasily, 12, 45
Churchill, Winston, 10, 17—18, 73,
    196
Claudius, Eduard, 94
Clausewitz, 4
Cold War, 32—5, 54
Collectivisation, 42, 56, 67, 71, 98,
    101, 125, 223
Comecon, 54, 76, 89—90, 203, 207
Cominform, 34, 39, 53, 202
Comintern, 7
Communist Party of Germany
    (KPD), 2, 12—13, 15, 20—1,
    23—5, 36—7, 40, 51, 195,
    197—8, 212

  fused with SPD, 26—9
  refounded, 14
Communist Party of the Soviet
    Union (CPSU), 26, 39, 43,
    50—2, 71, 187
  Twentieth congress, 3, 78—82, 94,
    216
  Twenty second congress, 125—6
  Twenty fourth congress, 153,
    245
  Twenty fifth congress, 165
  Twenty sixth congress, 262
Conference of Foreign Ministers
    (France, Great Britain,
    United States and Soviet
    Union), 33—4, 36, 198—9,
    201, 204, 212, 214—15
Constitution, 37, 142—3, 164, 199,
    203—4, 239
Council of Europe, 61
Council of State, 112, 124, 143,
    151, 233, 235, 237, 239, 242,
    249, 254
Cuba, 133, 228, 261
Culture, 40—1, 57—9, 94—6,
    145—8, 155, 184—7, 222,
    224, 248, 250, 258, 263
Cybernetics, 126
Czechoslovakia, 18, 74, 84, 108,
    110, 120, 124, 137—8, 205,
    237, 239—40, 246—7,
    256—7
  intervention, 138

Dahlem, Franz, 14, 29, 51, 69, 216
Dahrendorf, Gustav, 15
Democratic centralism, 157, 159
Democratic Peasants Party of
    Germany (DBD), 44—5, 48,
    52, 72, 91, 99, 118, 202, 263
  founded, 36, 202
Democratic Women's Association
    of Germany (DFD), 38, 53,
    105, 118, 162, 199, 209, 231
Dertinger, Georg, 53, 210, 213
Dessau, Paul, 58
Dialectical materialism, 83
Dickel, Major General Friedrich,
    118
Dictatorship of the proletariat, 14

Dieckmann, Johannes, 45, 53, 99, 230, 241
Djilas, Milovan, 7
Dohlus, Horst, 130, 152, 166
Dönitz, Grand Admiral, 6, 195
Dubček, Alexander, 137—8, 240
Dulles, John Foster, 97

Ebert, Friedrich, 51, 71, 97, 203, 260
Economic System of Socialism (ESS), 103, 123—5, 154
Eden, Anthony, 73—4
Education, 18, 24, 57, 92—4, 105, 120, 162—3, 172, 182—3, 197, 216, 220, 229, 233, 259
Egypt, 133
Ehlers, Hermann, 209
Eisenhower, General/President Dwight D., 9, 75
Elections, 29—32, 260
Ende, Lex, 51
Engels, Friedrich, 3, 53, 79, 83
Erhard, Ludwig, 135, 230—1
Ermisch, Luise, 106
Ethiopia, 192, 261
European Advisory Commission (EAC), 9—10
European Defence Community (EDC), 61—2
Evtushenko, E., 119

Fascism, 1, 147
Fechner, Max, 15, 29, 45, 68, 82, 211
Felfe, Werner, 157—8, 166, 262
Feuchtwanger, Lion, 41
Field, Noel H., 52
Fischer, Ernst, 146
Fischer, Hans-Joachim, 259
Fischer, Oskar, 257
Fischer, Otto, 252
Florin, Peter, 263
Forck, Gottfried, 263
France, 18—19, 47, 61—2, 196
  and Germany, 33—4, 36, 198—9, 201, 204, 206—7, 209, 212, 214—15, 220, 222
Franke, Egon, 253

Frederick the Great, 4
Free Democratic Party (FDP in FRG), 217
Free German Trades Union Association (FDGB), 13, 16, 18, 34, 37, 44, 46, 49, 53, 63, 70, 100, 118, 161—2, 164, 197—8, 202—3, 212, 216, 254, 263
Free German Youth Movement (FDJ), 17, 37, 44, 49, 53—4, 57, 70—1, 91—2, 118—19, 123, 157, 161—4, 167, 185, 198—9, 204, 206, 217, 222, 229—30, 238, 249—50, 259
Friedrich, Walter, 250
Friedrich, Werner, 209, 259
Friedrichs, Rudolf, 20

Gaus, Günther, 250, 262
Gerlach, Manfred, 53, 99
German Economic Commission (DWK), 33—4, 38—9
German Gymnastics and Sports Federation (DTSB), 92, 218
German road to socialism, 28, 34
German Society for Sport and Technology (DGST), 209
German-Soviet Non-Aggression Pact (1939), 7
Gierek, E., 256
Gniffke, Erich, 29
Goethe, Johann W., 4, 59, 185
Golderbaum, Ernst, 202, 263
Goldhammer, Bruno, 51
Göring, Bernhard, 197
Götting, Gerald, 53, 99, 241, 246
Great Britain, 47
  and Cold War, 32—4
  and GDR, 248, 254, 262
  and Germany, 17—20, 29, 60—2, 73—6, 97—8, 139—40, 195—6, 200—2, 204, 206—7, 209, 212, 214—15, 220, 222
  and Soviet Union, 7, 17—18, 97, 230
Gromyko, Andrei A., 60, 138, 258

Grotewohl, Otto, 23, 29, 45, 51,
    62, 65, 71, 99, 118, 131, 150,
    198, 207, 211, 216, 221, 227,
    232
    becomes Prime Minister, 45, 205
Grüneberg, Gerhard, 130—1
Guinea, 191
Guinea Bissau, 192
Gysi, Klaus, 234

Hacks, Peter, 148
Hager, Kurt, 86, 130, 154, 248
Hahn, Erich, 242
Halbritter, Walter, 131, 157
Hamann, Karl, 82, 213
Handke, Georg, 45
Harich, Wolfgang, 83—4, 217, 232
Havemann, Professor Robert,
    121—2, 137, 169, 186, 231,
    235, 260, 263
Heine, Heinrich, 59
Heinemann, Gustav, 242
Helsinki Final Act, 137, 149, 189,
    249
Hennecke, Adolf, 38
Hermes, Andreas, 23, 197
Hermlin, Stefan, 40
Herrmann, Joachim, 158, 166, 234,
    261
Herrnstadt, Rudolf, 51, 64, 69,
    211—12
Herter, Christian, 97
Hertwig Hans-Joachim, 157
Herwegen, Leo, 82, 206
Heuss, Theodor, 204, 208
Heym, Stefan, 40, 94, 122, 146,
    185—6, 234, 260
Hickmann, Hugo, 45
Hitler, Adolf, 6, 80
Höcker, Wilhelm, 20
Hoffmann, General Heinz, 157—8,
    170
Hoffmann, Heinz-Joachim, 263
Homann, Heinrich, 99
Honecker, Erich, 51, 71, 99, 121—2,
    129—30, 149—94, 196, 198,
    219, 245—6, 252, 254—9,
    261—4
    and Brezhnev, 253

    and culture, 146—7, 184—7
    and ideology, 153—5
    and social policy, 178—84
    and the economy, 171—8
    becomes First Secretary, 130,
        143—5, 150—2, 245
Honecker, Margot, 118, 132, 162,
    259
Hübener, Friedrich, 20
Huchel, Peter, 146
Hungary, 18, 27—8, 44, 67, 79, 83,
    85—6, 137, 205, 238—40,
    258
Husak, Gustav, 256

India, 259, 262—3
Industry, 24—6, 38, 54—6, 63—6,
    76—8, 88—90, 100, 102, 104,
    107—16, 125, 155—6, 165—6,
    171—8, 193, 217—18, 222,
    225—9, 231, 233, 240, 244,
    246
    Economic System of Socialism
        (ESS), 123—5
    New Course, 64, 67—73, 95,
        210—11
    New Economic System of
        Planning and Management,
        107—16, 122, 140, 147,
        229, 231
    Scientific-technical revolution,
        125—7
International Olympic Committee,
    120, 214, 234
Iraq, 241
Ireland, Republic of, 262
Italy, 61

Jahn, Günther, 238
Japan, 7, 111, 122, 257
Jarowinsky, Werner, 130
Jaruzelski, General Wojciech, 263
Jendretzky, Hans, 51, 70, 197, 216
John Paul II, Pope, 261
Joyce, James, 58

Kafka, Franz, 58, 146
Kaiser, Jakob, 23, 32, 36, 62,
    197—8, 201

Kampuchea, 261
Kant, Hermann, 147, 186, 258
Karlovy Vary, 137—8, 140, 237,
    240
Karmal, Babrak, 264
Karsten, August, 29
Kastner, Hermann, 45
Kaunda, President Kenneth, 192
Kennedy, President John F., 101—2
Kern, Käthe, 29
Kessler, Colonel General Heinz, 259
Khrushchev, Nikita S., 3, 72, 75, 81,
    85—7, 89—90, 97, 101, 104,
    113, 126, 140—1, 214,
    220—1, 229, 232
Kiesinger, Kurt-Georg, 237—9
Kirsch, Sarah, 146
Kissinger, Henry, 139
Klaus, Georg, 126, 154
Kleiber, Günther, 131
Kohl, Michael, 244, 248, 250, 263
Kohlmey, Günther, 85
Königsberg, 18
Korea, 44, 61, 73, 205, 257
Kosygin, Aleksei N., 151, 232
Kreikemeyer, Willi, 51—2
Kreisky, Bruno, 258
Krenz, Egon, 166
Krolikowski, Werner, 104, 131,
    151—2
Kulturbund, 49, 53, 199, 219, 224,
    238, 248, 256
Külz, Wilhelm, 24, 32, 36, 198, 207
Künert, G., 186
Kunze, Reiner, 255

Lamberz, Werner, 130, 132, 136,
    152, 192, 256—8
Lange, Ingeborg, 158
Lattre de Tassigny, General, 9
Law *see* Volkskammer
Lehmann, Helmut, 29
Lemmer, Ernst, 23, 36, 197, 201
Lenin, Vladimir I., 3, 37, 50, 53, 79,
    83—4, 104, 106, 154
Leonhard, Wolfgang, 11
Leuschner, Bruno, 71, 90, 131
Liberal Democratic Party of
    Germany (LDPD), 16, 20—1,

24—5, 29—32, 37, 44—5,
    48—50, 52—3, 72, 91, 99,
    118, 160—1, 196, 198, 200,
    210, 217, 219, 255, 263
Liberman, Evsei, 108—9
Libya, 256—7
Liebknecht, Karl, 107
Lieutenant, Arthur, 36
Lippmann, Heinz, 71
Lobedanz, Reinhold, 45
Loch, Hans, 50, 53
Löhr, Jonny, 45
van Loyen, Peter, 260
Ludz, Peter Christian, 176
Lukács, György, 94
Luther, Martin, 4
Luxembourg, 61

Mach, Ernst, 154
Machel, President Samora, 192
Macmillan, Harold, 101
Malenkov, Georgy M., 64, 75
Mann, Heinrich, 41
Marchais, Georges, 190
Marchwitza, Hans, 215
Marshall Plan, 33, 61, 200
Marx, Karl, 3, 53, 79, 83—4, 210,
    239
Marxism—Leninism, 51, 53, 57, 79,
    104, 132, 141, 152—7, 160,
    169, 186, 251
Matern, Hermann, 45, 51, 71, 240
Mecklenburg, Ernst, 263
Meier, Otto, 29
Meisner, Joachim, 261
Merker, Paul, 29, 51
Mielke, Colonel General Erich, 131,
    152, 166, 170
Mikoyan, Anastas I., 13, 195
Militarism, 9
Mittag, Günter, 90, 116, 130—2,
    140, 151, 157
Moldt, Ewald, 258
Molotov, V. M., 17, 64, 73—4
Mongolia, 193, 206, 240, 255
Montgomery, Field Marshal, 9
Moog, Leonhard, 36
Moscow Treaty (1970), 138
Mottek, Heinz, 250

Mozambique, 192
Mückenberger, Erich, 51, 72
Müller, Gerhard, 261
Müller, Heiner, 148
Müller, Margarete, 106

National Committee for a Free
   Germany (NKFD), 11
National Defence Council, 99
National Democratic Party of
   Germany (NDPD), 36—7,
   44—5, 48—50, 72, 91, 99,
   118, 161, 202—4
   founded, 36
National Economic Council,
   112—14, 116, 234
National People's Army (NVA),
   74—6, 102, 117, 164—5, 216,
   224, 228, 240, 262
   see also People's Police in
   Barracks (KVP)
National service, 116—17
National socialism, 9
   NSDAP, 18, 24
Naumann, Konrad, 157—8, 166
Netherlands, 61
Neumann, Alfred, 72
Neutsch, Erik, 147
New Economic System of Planning
   and Management of the
   Economy, 107—16, 122, 140,
   147, 229, 231
   price reform, 114
Noll, Dieter, 96
Nomenklatura, 3, 131, 160
Norden, Albert, 130, 236
North Atlantic Treaty Organisation
   (NATO), 60, 87, 204, 213,
   243
Novotny, Antonin, 137
Nuremberg trials, 18, 197
Nuschke, Otto, 45, 50, 53, 201,
   203, 262, 264
Oelssner, Fred, 45, 51, 71, 85—6,
   90, 219
Ollenhauer, Walter, 221
Ott, Harry, 263

Paff, Werner, 242

Palestine Liberation Organisation,
   261
Paul, Rudolf, 20
People's Police in Barracks (KVP),
   21, 47, 61, 65, 74, 209
   see also National People's Army
   (NVA)
Philippines, 257
Pieck, Wilhelm, 14—15, 27, 29, 36,
   45, 51, 71, 99, 150, 198, 201,
   205, 208, 224
Planning, 63, 90, 175, 227, 231,
   240
   Five Year Plan: first, 43, 50, 54,
   76; second, 80; 1976—80,
   165—6, 253; Half year plan
   (1948), 38; Seven Year
   Plan, 89—90, 224; Two
   year plan (1949—50), 50,
   202
Plenzdorf, Ulrich, 185
Podgorny, Nikolai V., 151
Poland, 1, 9, 18, 28, 33, 52, 74, 79,
   83, 85—6, 137, 144, 150,
   169, 178, 184, 190—1, 193,
   205, 213, 218, 237, 239—40,
   244, 246, 256, 263
   and Solidarity, 190—1
Potsdam Agreement, 17—20, 62
Potsdam Conference, 17, 196
Proust, Marcel, 58
Puja, Frigyes, 258

Rapacki, Adam, 87, 218
Rau, Heinrich, 38, 45, 50—1, 71,
   90, 201
Reingruber, Hans, 45, 49
Reinhold, Otto, 72, 193
Religion, 169—70, 210, 242, 249,
   251, 258, 261—3
Reparations, 19, 25—6, 50
Rietz, Hans, 99
Romania, 136—7, 205, 234, 237,
   247, 256
Roosevelt, President Franklin D.,
   8—10, 33
Ruling class, 5
Rumpf, Willy, 90

Schaffran, Gerhard, 261–2
Scheel, Walter, 249, 259
Schirdewan, Karl, 71, 80, 85–6,
    151–2, 219
Schmidt, Elli, 29, 51, 70, 216
Schmidt, Helmut, 191, 252, 261,
    263
Scholz, Paul, 90
Schön, Otto, 100
Schönherr, Albrecht, 263
Schreiber, Walter, 23, 197
Schumacher, Kurt, 26, 61
Schuman, Robert, 60
Schumann, Horst, 91, 119, 122–3,
    157, 222
Schürer, Gerhard, 158
Schütz, Klaus, 245
Scientific-technical revolution,
    125–7, 155
Seghers, Anna, 41, 186, 225, 241,
    250, 258
Selbmann, Fritz, 45, 85–6, 90
Semenov, Vladimir, 210
Sholokhov, Mikhail, 58
Sindermann, Horst, 131, 245, 249,
    254
Sobottka, Gustav, 10, 14, 195
Social Democratic Party of Germany
    (SPD in GDR), 13, 15, 24,
    26–9, 39, 196–8
    fused with KPD, 26–9
Social Democratic Party of Germany
    (SPD in FRG), 61, 135–6,
    212, 216, 221–2, 226–7,
    235–6
Social policy, 165–6, 178–84,
    247, 249, 252, 254, 257
Social structure, 76–8, 173
Socialist Unity Party of Germany
    (SED)
    becomes party of new type,
        39–40, 202
    Central Committee (CC), 29, 38,
        68–70, 83, 86, 93, 95, 98,
        100, 102, 107–9, 115,
        122, 129–31, 134, 141,
        143–4, 150, 152, 157,
        166, 168, 170, 204, 206,
        208, 210–12, 214,

        216–29, 231–5, 240,
        244–5, 247, 249, 259
    Central Party Control
        Commission, 39–40, 203,
    Central Secretariat, 29, 40, 198,
        200, 204
    Conference: first, 40, 203; third,
        80–1, 216
    Congress: second, 34; third, 50,
        206; fourth, 71, 212; fifth,
        86–9, 91–3, 220; sixth,
        108, 129, 228; seventh,
        123, 131, 153; eighth, 129,
        131, 152, 155, 188, 245;
        ninth, 165–7, 254, 262;
        tenth, 170–1
    democratic centralism, 50
    elections, 30–2
    founded, 26–9, 198
    Politburo, 40, 51, 64–5, 70–3,
        105, 109, 112, 119, 125,
        130–1, 150, 158, 166,
        168, 170, 210, 225,
        229–31, 240, 246,
        249–53, 256, 262
    programme, 50, 167–70, 228
    purge, 70
    Secretariat, 40, 130–1, 158,
        168
    social composition of, 128–30,
        158–9, 170–1
    statute, 50, 167–70, 253
Society for German-Soviet
    Friendship, 53
Society for Sport and Technology
    (GST), 91, 163, 216, 224
Sokolovsky, Marshal Vasily, 12
Sorbs, 130, 263
South West Africa People's
    Organisation (SWAPO),
    257
Soviet Limited Company (SAG),
    24–6, 38, 56, 69, 212
Soviet Military Administration in
    Germany (SMAD), 12–13,
    17, 20–1, 23–5, 27, 32, 34,
    36, 38, 40, 195–8, 200–1,
    206–7, 215
    dissolved, 45, 205

Soviet Union
  and Cold War, 32—4
  and Germany, 8—10, 13, 19, 29,
    42, 44, 59—64, 73—6,
    96—102, 139—40, 195,
    200—2, 204, 212—15,
    220—2, 225
  and United States, 12, 19, 101,
    230
Spain, 252
Spellman, Cardinal, 8
Stalin, J. V., 7, 12, 17—18, 26, 43,
  53, 63—4, 73, 78—81, 104,
  154—5, 195—6, 210
Stalinism, 42—66, 103, 121
State Planning Commission, 38,
  110, 112—13, 124, 158, 227
Steinbeck, Max, 243
Steinhoff, Karl, 20, 45
Stoph, Willi, 71, 74, 138, 151, 157,
  228, 232, 238, 243, 245—6,
  249, 254, 258
Strittmacher, Erwin, 147, 215
Switzerland, 248

Tanzania, 233
Tehran conference, 9
Ten commandments of socialist
  morality, 88
Third World, 191—3
Tisch, Harry, 131, 152, 162, 252
Tito, Josip Broz, 7, 51, 190, 232, 261
Tolstoy, Leo, 59
Trade unions *see* Free German
  Trade Unions Association
  (FDGB)
Treaty of Paris, 61
Trotsky, Leo, 79
Truman, President Harry S., 10,
  17—18, 33, 196
  doctrine, 33
Tyulpanov, Colonel S. I., 36

Uhse, Bodo, 40, 206
Ulbricht, Walter, 10—11, 15, 17,
  29, 34, 42, 45, 50, 64, 67,
  69, 71—2, 74, 79, 82, 126,
  130—1, 137—8, 153, 155,
  187, 195, 206, 211, 215—16,
  221, 223—4, 229—33, 236,
  238—42, 244, 246—7
  and Brezhnev, 122, 141
  and culture, 58, 95, 146
  and de-Stalinisation, 67, 79—82,
    85, 104—5, 226
  and Marx, 140—3
  and NES, 108, 115
  and Berlin Wall, 97—102
  becomes C in C armed forces, 99
  defeats critics, 83—92
  dies, 143, 249
  elected Secretary-General, 50
  personality cult, 107
  removed as First Secretary, 139,
    143—5, 149—50, 245
United Nations, 8, 62, 149, 187,
  224, 235, 248—9, 260
United States
  and Cold War, 32—4
  and GDR, 251, 260
  and Germany, 7—8, 29, 60—2,
    73—6, 97—8, 139—40,
    195—6, 200—2, 204,
    206—7, 209, 212, 214—15,
    220, 222
  and Soviet Union, 12, 19, 97,
    101, 230
Uprising of 17 June 1953, 2, 63—6,
  68—9, 211
Uschkamp, Irma, 132

Vatican, 249
Verner, Paul, 52, 100, 130, 136
Verner, Admiral Waldemar, 259
Vietnam, 192—3, 213, 257
Vieweg, Kurt, 85—6
Volkskammer, 45—6, 49, 62, 72,
  81, 84, 92, 99—100, 116—18,
  120—1, 135, 142—3, 151,
  163—4, 189, 205—9, 213—14,
  216—17, 219, 221—3, 225—7,
  231—4, 236—9, 241—2,
  244—5, 248, 250—2, 254,
  256, 259—61, 263
Vyshinsky, Andrei, 60

Walde, Werner, 166
Wandel, Paul, 45, 86, 137

Warnke, Herbert, 72, 162, 252
Warsaw Pact, 74—6, 102, 214, 225, 236—7
Wehner, Herbert, 236
Wehrmacht, 6—7, 195, 197
Weidig, Rudi, 241—2
Weimar, 16
  republic, 16
Weinert, Erich, 40
Weiterer, Maria, 51
Wilson, President Woodrow, 8
Winzer, Otto, 134, 239, 247, 249
Wittkowski, Margarete, 106, 132—3
Wolf, Christa, 96, 147—8, 185
Wollweber, Erich, 85—6, 219
Women, 105—6, 132—3, 227, 231, 241
Works' Councils (Betriebsräte), 37

Yalta conference, 9
Yemen, 261
Young Pioneers, 53
Youth *see* Free German Youth Movement (FDJ)
Yugoslavia, 110, 133, 137, 202, 218, 236
  Communist Party of, 39

Zaisser, Wilhelm, 51, 64, 69
Zambia, 192
Zentrum Party, 13, 16
Zhukov, Marshal Georgy, 9, 12, 16, 20
Ziller, Gerhart, 85—6
Zinoviev, Gregory, 79
Zweig, Arnold, 40, 58, 206